Fame Games

The Production of Celebrity
in Australia

The areas of publicity, public relations and promotions have
been considered to be on the periphery of the media. Yet this
revealing new book demonstrates that they form a fundamental
component of the media industries, with the decline of hard
news being accompanied by the rise of gossip and celebrity.
In addition to making a substantial contribution to our
understanding of the cultural function of celebrity, *Fame Games*
outlines how the promotion industry has developed and how
celebrity is produced, promoted and traded within the
Australian media. While their analysis will inform academic
debates on media practice internationally, the authors have
taken the unique step of investigating the workings of the
Australian promotion industry from within. Interviews with over
twenty publicists, promoters, agents, managers and magazine
editors have provided a wealth of information about the
processes through which celebrity in Australia is produced.

All three authors work at the University of Queensland.
Graeme Turner is director of the Centre for Critical and
Cultural Studies and has published many influential books in
media and cultural studies, including *British Cultural Studies:
An Introduction* (1996) and (with Stuart Cunningham) *The
Media in Australia: Industries, Texts, Audiences* (1997), the
standard media studies text in Australia. **Frances Bonner**,
Department of English, is a co-editor of *Imagining Women:
Cultural Representations and Gender* (1992). **P. David Marshall**,
Department of English, is the author of *Celebrity and Power:
Fame in Contemporary Culture* (1997) and *Modes for Cultural
Analysis: Media in Cultural Studies* (in press).

Fame Games

The Production of Celebrity in Australia

Graeme Turner
University of Queensland

Frances Bonner
University of Queensland

P. David Marshall
University of Queensland

CAMBRIDGE
UNIVERSITY PRESS

PUBLISHED BY THE PRESS SYNDICATE OF THE UNIVERSITY OF CAMBRIDGE
The Pitt Building, Trumpington Street, Cambridge, United Kingdom

CAMBRIDGE UNIVERSITY PRESS
The Edinburgh Building, Cambridge CB2 2RU, UK
40 West 20th Street, New York, NY 10011–4211, USA
10 Stamford Road, Oakleigh, VIC 3166, Australia
Ruiz de Alarcón 13, 28014 Madrid, Spain
Dock House, The Waterfront, Cape Town 8001, South Africa

http://www.cambridge.org

© Graeme Turner, Frances Bonner and P. David Marshall 2000

First published 2000

Printed in Australia by Brown Prior Anderson

Typeface Adobe New Aster 9/12 pt.   *System* QuarkXPress® [BC]

A catalogue record for this book is available from the British Library

National Library of Australia Cataloguing in Publication data
Turner, Graeme.
Fame games: the production of celebrity in Australia.
Includes index.
ISBN 0 521 79147 2
ISBN 0 521 79486 2 (pbk.)
1. Mass media – Australia. 2. Public relations – Australia.
3. Fame. I. Bonner, Frances. II. Marshall, P. David.
III. Title.
302.230994

ISBN 0 521 79147 2 hardback
ISBN 0 521 79486 2 paperback

Contents

Tables and Illustrations

Tables

Illustrations

Interviewees

BUNTY AVIESON editor, *New Idea*

WINSTON BROADBENT director, Saxton Speakers Bureau
and Management Group

GEORGIE BROWN Georgie Brown Publicity

JUNE CANN June Cann Management

LOUISE CARROLL Louise Carroll Publicity

ANDREW FREEMAN publicity, Random House Australia

REA FRANCIS freelance public relations consultant

VICCY HARPER director, Hilary Linstead and Associates

BARBARA LEANE theatrical agent

SUZIE MacLEOD publicity manager, Village Roadshow Film Distributors

TRACEY MAIR Tracey Mair Publicity

HARRY M. MILLER Harry M. Miller and Co. Management

MARK MORRISSEY Morrissey Management

JANE NICOLLS deputy editor, *Who Weekly*

KERRY O'BRIEN Kerry O'Brien Publicity

KEVIN PALMER Kevin Palmer Management

PETER RIX Peter Rix Management

GARY STEWART Melbourne Artists Management

LESNA THOMAS corporate relations, Southern Star

SUE-ELLEN TOPFER editor-in-chief, *TV Hits*, *Smash Hits*

HEIDI VIRTUE publicist, Nine Network

BRIAN WALSH director of programming, promotions and publicity, Foxtel,
and managing director, The Promotions Dept. Pty Ltd

ANTHONY WILLIAMS   Anthony Williams Management
REBECCA WILLIAMSON   June Cann Management

Throughout the book, where there is no bibliographic reference supplied for a quotation from these practitioners, the extract has been drawn directly from the transcripts of the interviews. The interviews were conducted by David Marshall in Sydney and Melbourne in June, July and October 1997.

Acknowledgements

This book could not have been written without the assistance of the many people in the publicity and media industries who agreed to be interviewed and quoted. For their patience and generosity, as well as for the quality of the insights they provided into the playing of the fame games, we would like to thank Bunty Avieson, Winston Broadbent, Georgie Brown, June Cann, Louise Carroll, Andrew Freeman, Rea Francis, Viccy Harper, Barbara Leane, Suzie MacLeod, Tracey Mair, Harry M. Miller, Mark Morrissey, Jane Nicolls, Kerry O'Brien, Kevin Palmer, Peter Rix, Gary Stewart, Lesna Thomas, Sue-Ellen Topfer, Heidi Virtue, Brian Walsh, Anthony Williams and Rebecca Williamson.

For assistance in working out how to assemble the information collected in this book, as well as advice on how we should go about dealing with this topic in the first place, we owe thanks to a number of colleagues: they include Barbara-Ann Butler, John Hartley, Annette Henderson, Catharine Lumby, Louise McBryde, Susan McKay, Meaghan Morris, Tony Stevenson, Angela Tuohy, McKenzie Wark and Clara Zawawi. We would also like to thank our research assistants, Rebecca Farley, Megan Sandaver and Simone Murray, for their contributions to the project, and Ruth Delaforce, Susan Lochran and Cathrine Liebich, who transcribed the interview material. Phillipa McGuinness at Cambridge University Press has had a guiding interest in this book for some years, and we are grateful to her for seeing it through (almost) to the end.

Permissions for the reproduction of illustrations were kindly granted by Australian Consolidated Press, *Girlfriend*, *TV Hits*, Pacific Publications,

New Idea, Louise McBryde and Jon Reid. We gratefully acknowledge their cooperation and assistance.

For permission to quote from Don Walker's 'Ita', we acknowledge the assistance of Rondor Music (Australia) Pty Ltd; and we also acknowledge the kind permission of Exile Publishing Ltd. for permission to quote lyrics from 'New Biography' by Van Morrison.

Finally, the research that went into this book would have been impossible without the support of the Australian Research Council, which funded the project between 1997 and 1999.

Chapter 1

Celebrity and the Media

It's the fame game
The name game
It's such a crying shame
Just tell me what's to blame?
Van Morrison, 'New Biography', Back on Top

This book examines a major shift in how the Australian media now operates. The activities of the publicity and promotions industries have been comprehensively incorporated into all aspects of media production: the celebrity story on the news, the preview of the hot new film on *60 Minutes*, the exclusive deals between people in the news and the media outlets who buy the rights to their stories, the advertorials in lifestyle and children's programs, the devotion of whole magazines to circulating 'a little gossip', the alleged agreements on positive media treatment for the Sydney Olympic bid committee. The steady progress of this trend has not gone unnoticed. Those committed to the function of the 'fourth estate' – the media's role as democratic watchdog – have expressed alarm at what appears to be a retreat from the fundamental responsibility of the press to inform and a corresponding increase in the proportion of stories aimed merely at diverting or entertaining their consumers. Whether that is the appropriate way to understand it or not – and we will deal directly with that issue in this book – it is clear that the media's function and its mode of operation have undergone a major redefinition.

It is important to recognise that this is not simply a cyclical shift in patterns of media consumption, a change in fashion affecting what media

1

audiences want to read in the newspapers or hear on the radio or watch on television. It is also a change in the system of production: this means that we may need to reassess our assumptions about how stories get into the media, and about how those stories which *do* 'get a run' are represented by the media.

A fundamental factor in this redefinition has been the importance of stories about celebrities – and, increasingly, about Australian celebrities. In Australia, celebrity stories dominate the women's mass-market magazines, they constitute a significant proportion of the content of television news, current affairs and magazine programs, and the rate of their appearance in newspapers has increased dramatically over the last twenty years. There is now an Australian celebrity industry. Where once our celebrity material was overwhelmingly dependent upon Hollywood, or perhaps British entertainment industry organisations like J. C. Williamson's or Rank, now we have our own publicity and promotional industry which supplies media outlets with their staple diet of stories on Australian celebrities, day in and day out. It is time we understood more about this publicity industry: how it works, in whose interests, and what its development might mean for the social function of the media in Australia. That is the objective of this book.

Flashpoints, the everyday, and 'junk journalism'

> We used to have great access to great events and report them with Lippmannesque certitude. Now our goal is to tell stories that connect with the way we live. We want to know about the debates happening around the dinner table rather than the Senate committee tables.
> *Walter Isaacson,* Time

It would be hard to exaggerate the pervasiveness of celebrity in the contemporary media. It has been growing for years, and every year brings another reminder of the emotional power of people's connections to figures they know only through their representations in the media. While the generation now in their forties or fifties may be somewhat bemused by the media frenzy around the deaths of Michael Hutchence or Kurt Cobain, they are just as likely to have strong personal memories of the deaths of Buddy Holly or Marilyn Monroe or Elvis Presley or Janis Joplin or John Lennon. It has been clear for many years that our everyday lives can be indelibly marked by celebrity events – deaths, births, marriages, disasters, accidents. The power of a globalised media to saturate all media forms and outlets with the top international story, and the relatively recent but now fundamental importance of the everyday celebrity story for contemporary media producers and consumers, have dramatically enhanced that emotional potential in recent years.

Increasingly, we encounter 'flashpoints' in contemporary culture, where a particular celebrity completely dominates media coverage, producing an excessively focused global public. The death of the Princess of Wales in 1997 was such a flashpoint: the story's exorbitant visibility broke out of all the available classifications. It was simply uncontainable as news, as obituary, as identity politics, as entertainment, as myth or narrative, or as gossip. It dominated the 'quality' newspapers as well as the mass-market magazines and tabloids. Through all these avenues, the images which had created Diana's highly public life – the cover girl, the tabloid telephoto revelations, the official royal video footage, the romances – were replayed and reinterpreted. While many still argue about what it all 'meant', it is undeniable that the live broadcast of the funeral through television networks around the world generated an extraordinary international outpouring of emotion. For a short time, the shrine of flowers at the Kensington Palace gates became as recognisable an international marker of location for television reporters as the White House or 10 Downing Street.

Its almost perfectly symmetrical US counterpart came in 1999: the death of the favourite son of an American 'royal' family, John F. Kennedy Jr, in an airplane crash. Again, coverage on the cable news networks went wall-to-wall; newspapers within the United States and the rest of the world focused with an extraordinary concentration on the assassinated president's only son. In an echo effect of JFK's death over thirty-five years before, the Kennedy family's significance to American public life was retold through a tragic narrative of service and shocking death that was played out in editorials, in a massive number of magazine features and probably most immediately in the television coverage of the four-day search for the plane and the bodies in the waters off Martha's Vineyard. The image of 'John-John' as a 3-year-old saluting at his father's grave was repeated in print and on television in order to reinforce the sentimental significance of his death. Combined with the representation of his wife, Caroline Bessette (also killed in the crash), as, the *Australian* intoned, the 'modern day Garbo',[1] the tragedy was further connected to a thwarted mythic fantasy: the accession of American political royalty to a future presidential throne. Understandable within the United States, one might think, but even in Australia the emotional register of the newspaper and television coverage eschewed any pretence at objectivity in favour of a frank sentimentality.

Most analysts of these flashpoint events would describe them as extraordinary and it would be difficult to disagree. That is their point. It is their disproportionate nature that makes them so important: the scale of their visibility, their overwhelmingly excessive demonstration of the power of the relationship between mass-mediated celebrities and the consumers of popular culture. They are also unusual in that, while they were of international interest because they concerned a public persona which had been built through years of careful media management, they were themselves unpredictable, eruptive events which suddenly broke free of this form of management to become 'real' or uncontrolled events – for many, genuinely moving events – within our everyday lives. In such flashpoints, the potential of the modern audience's relationship with a person they know solely through their media representations, but who nevertheless plays a part in their lives, is made vividly, if bewilderingly, apparent.

Of course, most of the time, the celebrity participates in our everyday lives in much more mundane ways than this. Furthermore, and under ordinary circumstances, our access to information about celebrities is strategically regulated in the service of interests which are those of the agent, the promoter, the publicist, the media outlet or the celebrity themselves, rather than those of the consumer. Some examples of the publicity surrounding local celebrities make this clear. In late 1998, Mimi Macpherson, sister of supermodel Elle Macpherson but best known for running a whale-watching business in southern Queensland, appears wearing lingerie in a group cover image for the first issue of the Australian version of British men's magazine *FHM*. This image appears months after her first hosting job on Australian television has ended. In August 1999, the final Stanley Kubrick film, *Eyes Wide Shut*, starring Tom Cruise and Nicole Kidman, is released in Australia. During the period preceding its opening, Cruise is photographed watching the South Sydney rugby league team and is the subject of numerous gossip items (dropping into the Balmain pub for a spot of pool with the boys); Kidman appears on more than nine magazine covers, from *Vogue* to *New Idea*, as well as in countless features in newspapers and on television; and the two of them wind up on the cover of *Time* magazine (the film was a Time–Warner production). She laments publicly that 'I'm even sick of seeing me' staring back at her throughout the promotional tour of Australia.

This form of media visibility is in a sense the reverse of the flashpoint, although its cumulative effect is what gives the flashpoints their potential and cultural power. It is a form that is anything but unpredictable and eruptive; it is the product of an incredible amount of energy and resources, all devoted to making such stories appear – in the right place, at the right time, and preferably without costing a cent. How, and in whose interests, such stories appear does vary. The Mimi Macpherson story is the product of a system of publicity that is focused on the professional interests of the personality rather than those of an organisation, such as the network screening Mimi's television series. The *Eyes Wide Shut* stories, in comparison, are evidence of the deployment of an established celebrity in the service of a specific product – the film – and thus in the interests of the producers and distributors rather than, at least in the first instance, those of the stars themselves. Enabling each of these examples, though, is an industrial structure: a professional articulation between the news and entertainment media and the sources of publicity and promotion.

How does the production of celebrity work in Australia? How are celebrity stories generated and placed? What is the function of the agents and managers who orchestrate the kinds of images and stories that *are* placed? What is involved in deciding which personality ultimately makes the cover of *Women's Weekly* or appears exclusively on *60 Minutes* or *A Current Affair*? The answers to these questions reveal a complex and important support industry, filled with media buyers, editors, writers, agents, publicists, managers and promoters who produce the blend of national and international celebrity stories that has become familiar to us all. Through the operations of the 'fame games' in Australia, this cadre of largely unseen workers – in actual fact, an industry within an industry – determines an increasing proportion of our media content.

There are standard points of view within the academy and among media commentators (although there is very little research and almost no information) on the developments examined in this book. The approach taken here can be distinguished both from the conventional lament for the decline of journalism and from usual assumptions about the function of celebrity journalism for its consumers and producers. Our view is that there is a common element which links the flashpoint moments with an industry that supports itself by producing celebrity for everyday consumption. That element is the appeal of the celebrity for media audiences.

The promotion of celebrity has been widely represented – even within the media which depends upon it – as the epitome of the trivialisation of the media, of the duping of contemporary consumers into pathetic relationships with fantasy figures peddled to them through the tabloid press. It has become commonplace for criticism of the news media to deplore the amount and intensity of attention given to the personal lives of celebrities. Bob Franklin's *Newszak and News Media*, for instance, laments the triumph of 'the trivial over the weighty', as the 'intimate relationships of celebrities from soap operas, the world of sport or the royal family are judged more "newsworthy" than the reporting of significant issues and events of international consequence'.[2] Coverage of celebrities within news and current affairs is widely cited as evidence of a decline in 'hard' news values, the ascendancy of infotainment, and the decline of the press as an independent source of information.

Some of these criticisms express taste preferences which are generally hostile to popular cultural forms, or gender biases which regard the masculine staples of institutional and political news as the most fundamentally important components of the news agenda. Others, however, have significant ethical concerns. Julianne Schultz's *Reviving the Fourth Estate* reports findings which indicate that a large number of journalists remain committed to the ideals of 'watchdog journalism', to the media as a fundamental support for the democratic state. Among the factors that journalists perceive as significant threats to these ideals, however, are the rise of what Sylvia Lawson calls 'junk journalism' ('screaming headlines, titillation and pseudo-crises'); the melting of journalists' ethical standards under the heat of competition, and the consequent decline in public respect for the profession (the evidence here includes the popular assumption of the paparazzi's complicity in Diana's death); and the capturing of the industry by promotions and public relations (the role of 'news management').[3]

Although some of this comment is just as applicable to other commercial spheres (it could be said of business journalism, in general), all of these factors are implicated in the rise of celebrity journalism. The importance of the industry which produces celebrity is directly addressed by Schultz's claim that many journalists have found themselves 'unwitting agents for the distribution of commercially prepared information', while others do little more than simply 'recycle press releases'. Changes within the media industries over a number of years have made certain sectors – the mass-market women's magazines, for instance – structurally dependent on what Schultz calls 'information management',[4] or what is often (but, as we shall see in Chapter 2, imprecisely) referred to as 'public relations'. Clara Zawawi, too, has published research which tracks the take-up rate of press releases through the media and finds that their success rate is sufficiently high to challenge our assumptions about the role of journalism, rather than that of publicity or public relations, in generating and selecting media content.[5]

These are legitimate considerations, which will be directly addressed in the following chapters. However, there are countervailing views which are especially pertinent to the cultural role played by celebrities in this changing media environment. Catharine Lumby, McKenzie Wark, David Marshall and John Hartley all suggest that there is more to this trend than simply an opportunistic, ethically relaxed response to an increased intensity in competition. Rather, they see it as evidence of a change in the function of the media generally, as it moves away from a primary role of providing information to that of more directly and fundamentally participating in the cultural construction of social identity. Hartley, in particular, has proposed that the popular media has created a 'postmodern public sphere' which challenges traditional definitions of what constitutes useful or appropriate knowledge about public affairs. In their place are new 'ways of forming the public, and of communicating and sustaining what it means to be the public'.[6] The source of these new kinds of knowledges is not the experts or the social elites, but the popular media.

This leads us, briefly, into a slightly specialised group of debates. Hartley's critique of a 'traditional public sphere' – where public debate is dominated by social, cultural or institutional elites – is a response to Jurgen Habermas' account of the structure of public debate in England during a golden period in the eighteenth century.[7] Centred around a culturally homogeneous group of Enlightenment intellectuals committed to the process of rational debate, their ideas circulating among a limited but influential public, Habermas' ideal public sphere offers us a snapshot of what can happen when cultural leadership is comfortably vested in an educated and privileged elite. Hartley argues that Habermas' advocacy of this ideal, beguiling as it is, radically overplays the extent to which the Enlightenment public sphere was in fact 'achieved as an institutional and socially pervasive reality'.[8] Others, too, have noted its exclusive social structure and coterie status within a society where literacy was not universal and where women were not admitted to public debate.[9]

Most damaging, for Hartley, the elitist idealism which underpins nostalgia for this eighteenth century version of the public sphere is particularly disabling for understanding the popular cultural forms of today. It has proven, he says, 'to be an impediment to understanding the role that the popular media do play in producing and distributing knowledge'.[10] To misunderstand the role of the popular media is to ignore the fact that the 'major contemporary political issues' of today (environmental, ethnic, sexual and youth movements, for instance) all arose outside the traditional public sphere. Instead of being generated through intellectual, social or political elites, they were 'informed, shaped, developed and contested within the privatised public sphere of suburban media consumerism'.[11]

There are others who also defend the contribution of the suburban media consumer. Drawing on feminist cultural studies approaches, Lumby contests the view that we are witnessing the breakdown of serious debate in the media and culture because of, for instance, the contemporary 'cult of celebrity' identified with the mass or tabloid media.[12] Instead, we are witnessing a redefinition of what counts as interesting to media consumers, which reclaims the importance of the domestic, the feminine, the private and the personal. As a result,

> [the] past few decades have seen an overwhelming democratisation of the media – a diversification not only of voices, but of ways of speaking about personal, social and political life ... Contrary to the common view that the global mass media has suppressed political speech and replaced it with commercially viable drivel, I argue that the contemporary media sphere constitutes a highly diverse and inclusive forum in which a host of important social issues once deemed apolitical, trivial or personal are now being aired.[13]

Using Ruth Barcan's essay from the *Planet Diana* collection,[14] Lumby argues that an event such as Diana's death and the 'global mourning' it occasioned demonstrates that there has been a significant change in the structure of the popular 'media sphere'. The whole point of Diana's appeal is that it was 'grounded in the way her image transgressed the split between the public and the private, the highbrow and the lowbrow, the quality press and the tabloid weeklies'.[15] The global character of the mass media event, and the apparent 'reality' of so many people's response to the death of a woman they had never met, suggested that other structures were losing their definition as well:

> Rather than seeing the massive response to Diana's death as an extension of 'real life' or local emotions to a figure known only via the global media, we can also see it is as a sign of a subtle but important reversal of the relationship between these two zones [the global and the local]. In a world where our sense of reality is constantly filtered and informed by the media, media celebrities come to seem literally larger than life. As one man said in a radio talkback session, 'I didn't cry this much when my wife died'. His remark illustrates a strange possibility: that the vast media coverage of Diana rendered her more real to many people than real life itself.[16]

More than those who tend to write off such details merely as symptoms of media consumers' stupidity, Lumby's work asks us to take fresh angles of approach to the significance of celebrity gossip, public confessionals and the emergence of media populism – 'life in a tabloid world', as she calls it – that at least poses the possibility that the media is serving a different function for us now than it did twenty years ago. The connection between celebrities and the personal identities of consumers is one of the provocations that she offers for considering such a possibility.

If such readings of the contemporary function of the media are at all suggestive – and we think they are – then it becomes extremely important to closely consider what kinds of cultural functions media representations of celebrities might be serving.

The meaning and significance of celebrity

> All around me were women who seemed to be wanting gossip;
> they wanted to know more about Elvis, and his first grandchild,
> and Elizabeth Taylor, and Hazel Hawke, weddings on *A Country
> Practice* ... nothing nasty; not the horror stuff.
> *Nene King*, Woman's Day

The concept of celebrity is a little slippery, partly because its constitutive discourses have leaked into such a wide range of media formats and practices (not to mention everyday life: the best soccer player in the local under-10s is widely referred to as 'a legend', while his 10-year-old sister wins a shopping centre competition for a Spice Girl look-alike by lip-synching to 'Do You Wanna Be My Lover'). Today, we hardly notice the high degree of personalisation that is used routinely within media reports as a means of producing drama. Further, given that news necessarily individuates its subjects, foregrounding the major players in all kinds of stories (perfectly ordinary businessmen, for instance, become 'corporate raiders' whose dealings are injected with personality), it can be difficult to satisfactorily determine what is a celebrity story and what is not. There is a syllogistic logic lurking behind discussions of celebrity: celebrities are people the public is interested in; if the public is interested in this person, they are a celebrity; therefore, anyone the public is interested in is a celebrity. Alberoni's well-known account of 'stars' reads a little like that when he claims that they are especially remarkable, not because they possess a particular level of economic, political or religious power but because 'their doings and ways of life arouse considerable interest'.[17] While they enjoy some of the social privileges of an elite, however, Alberoni argues that they are, institutionally, a 'powerless elite'. Celebrities, to some extent then, are the objects of an interest over which they have no control.

Control, of course, is exactly what the celebrity industry aims to achieve. And it is possible to see the discourses of celebrity – the visual, verbal and rhetorical means of signifying celebrity in the media – as accessing power, not surrendering it. John Langer has implied precisely that by pointing out that even those who *do* possess institutional power can – and do – choose to represent themselves through the modes used to represent celebrities. Politicians are surrounded by party press officers, or 'spin doctors', intent on massaging the political message reaching the electorate. At the same time, the press officers are concerned with constructing the politician's personal image. Especially where it concerns the representation of political leaders, the construction of the political image – as distinct from the marketing of political policies – is indistinguishable from the marketing of the latest film or CD. The promotion of former premier Jeff Kennett, through the jeff.com celebrity website during the 1999 Victorian election, is a precise demonstration of this point. As his fate in that election also demonstrates, however, the deployment of practices used within the celebrity industry, while thoroughly integrated into the contemporary performance of politics, does not necessarily guarantee success in terms of either votes or consumption. Federal politicians Amanda Vanstone and Natasha Stott Despoja have both promoted themselves through, for instance, appearances on *Good News Week*, but only Stott Despoja is a celebrity.

Newsagency windows advertising magazines, using posters of their covers dominated by famous faces

That said, it is not easy to be confident about such statements. In practice, the distinction between celebrity and other kinds of social or political elite status is becoming less clear as the signs of celebrity drive out less powerful alternatives. According to Langer, today virtually any kind of construction of an elite proposes the individuals concerned 'as especially remarkable simply by featuring them in terms of their "doings and ways of life" – that is, through an individuated account of their personal lives as a means of acknowledging or proposing their importance'.[18] This has the important implication of suggesting, as does David Marshall in *Celebrity and Power*,[19] that celebrity is not a property of specific individuals. Rather, it is constituted discursively, by the way in which the individual is represented. Through what Langer, after Monaco, calls a 'calculus of celebrityhood', celebrity is constructed rather than immanent:

> A calculus of celebrity is relatively flexible and can be opera-
> tionalised 'down' as well as 'up', in the direction of those who have
> neither power in an institutional sense nor any kind of elite
> standing as celebrities but who, through specific personal
> achievements – their doings, rather than their ways of life – gain
> an appearance in the news and concomitantly considerable albeit
> fleeting public attention.[20]

This 'calculus' of discourses, then, passes through the living, breathing individual as if they were a temporary host to the desires of the audience, and those of the cultural industries whose interests are served by the celebrity's promotion.

It is important to understand this dual aspect of the production of a public personality. For example, the figure we recognise as Ray Martin presents this complex twinning of audience desires and commercial interests. As a television host, Martin is, for a large portion of the public, a reliable figure who presents a concerned and informed voice which speaks for some of the needs and desires of his audience when he interviews John Howard or Tom Cruise. Here, the celebrity stands in place of the audience and their cultural power is related to their ability to successfully occupy that role. But, for many years, Martin was also the principal public face of the Nine Network. Like network news anchors in the United States, he perfectly represented the 'ultimate integrity of the network' as his institutional identity merged with the constructed personality.[21] The celebrity is therefore a combination of the commercial interests of a cultural industry – in Martin's case, a television network – and the shifting desires of an audience. The celebrity's personality must negotiate between these differing, sometimes competing, conceptions of a public. Serving different political ends for each component of this relationship – as a means of reaching a fragmenting mass market (for the production industry), and as a means of comprehending a fragmented and confusing culture (for the audience) – the celebrity is at their most active and significant when they mark a point of convergence or, as Marshall puts it, when they can provide 'a bridge of meaning between the powerless and the powerful'.[22]

Among the defining attributes of the signifying system which produces celebrity is the dissolving of the boundary between public and private lives. By this, we mean that a key marker of celebrity treatment is evident when someone who has been newsworthy due to, for instance, the part they play in the public domain – they may be contestants in a legal case, say, or victims of a natural disaster – also attracts interest to their private lives. What the discourses of celebrity characteristically do is go beyond the primary public activities into the personal and private in order to elaborate on what Dyer has called 'the authentic self' of the individual.[23] On the one hand, the celebrity might represent the ultimate in unauthenticity through the perceived artificiality of their personality, their reputation or even their bodies (think of, for instance, Pamela Anderson), but, on the other hand, audience interest is nevertheless aroused by the possibility of penetrating that construction and gaining access to some essential knowledge about that celebrity.

While the effect of such media treatment (rumours, gossip, paparazzi shots) may be unpleasant and destructive in many instances, it also carries some benefits for its objects. Far from enrolling them in Alberoni's 'powerless elite', the achievement of celebrityhood is a means of signifying and establishing success in a wide variety of domains: business, sport, entertainment, the arts, and so on. While the individuals concerned may sacrifice their privacy to this achievement, celebrity status 'confers on the person a certain discursive power within the society ... the celebrity is a voice above others, a voice that is channelled into the media system as being legitimately significant'.[24] Such people are a natural topic for news. What Langer calls their 'very-being-as-they-are' becomes a readily available source of occurrences that require only the slightest 'twitch' (the excitation of mild surprise, as in the headline, 'Melanie Griffith's cosmetic surgery shock') to generate news stories.[25]

The effect is, of course, to turn celebrities into commodities, products to be marketed in their own right or to be used to market other commodities. The celebrity's ultimate power is to sell the commodity that is themselves. This fact has been thoroughly integrated into contemporary popular culture and the marketing of the celebrity-as-commodity has been deployed as a major strategy in the commercial construction of social identity. Within a highly fragmented but increasingly globalised mass market, the use of celebrities has become a very efficient method of organising cultural significance around products, services and commercially available identities.

Their combination of commercial and cultural function remains, though, highly contradictory. Celebrities are brand names as well as cultural icons or identities; they operate as marketing tools as well as sites where the agency of the audience is clearly evident; and they represent the achievement of individualism – the triumph of the human and the familiar – as well as its commodification and commercialisation. Like all commodities, however, their trade needs to be organised and controlled and, as a result, the production and commercialisation of celebrities has become an industry too. Typically, the celebrity industry is structured around the need to acknowledge conflicting objectives: the commercial objective of maximising the income generated by the celebrity-commodity, and the celebrity's personal objective of constructing a viable career through the astute distribution and regulation of the sales of their self-as-commodity.

Marketing this self-as-commodity is not a simple matter, of course. The nature of public interest in the celebrity is itself highly contradictory. As signs of the potential for ordinary people to transcend their condition, celebrities are inspirational; as signs of the unauthenticity and superficiality of success, they are consoling. The legitimacy of celebrity is always radically provisional. While celebrityhood can represent success and achievement in the social world, it can also be ridiculed and derided 'because it represents the centre of false value. The success expressed in celebrity is seen as … success without the requisite association with work.'[26] Indeed, this is fundamental to the desirability of celebrity status. Even when they are engaged in activities that are patently 'work', such as promoting their new record, film or stage production, the actual representation of celebrities' behaviour will often deliberately elide any contextualisation that might foreground what they are doing as promotion. So, a celebrity will 'meet with reporters' in a leisure location, like a golf course or a resort.[27]

According to Ian Connell, there is a heavy weighting of scepticism in the public consumption of celebrities. For him, the display of celebrities through the popular media satisfies the 'oppositional resentment' of the popular audience. On the one hand, the success of celebrities who claim no special entitlement to their privileged position can appear to be especially valorised for maintaining their intrinsic 'ordinariness' and disavowing their elite status. On the other hand, the success of such celebrities 'encourages and nourishes scepticism about the legitimacy of the … personalities to act as they do'.[28] Connell argues that the thirst for stories about celebrities is fuelled by a vision of them as 'members of a privileged caste' against which the typically cheeky and iconoclastic stories of the tabloid press mount a 'populist challenge'.[29]

Contradictory and tainted with unauthenticity as they may be, it seems clear that celebrities perform a significant social function for media consumers. Langer argues that examination of the discourses used to represent celebrity can teach us a great deal about how 'values and attitudes are assembled and disseminated at particular historical conjunctures'. Echoing Dyer's argument that the 'star' represents 'the type of the individual' within their culture, Langer suggests that the 'celebrity can operate as a site from which key ideological themes can be reiterated and played out'.[30] Marshall, too, sees the celebrity as tightly articulated with the value systems of democratic capitalism, 'wedding consumer culture with democratic aspirations' while participating in the 'active construction of identity in the social world'.[31]

Constructing identity seems to be getting a little more complex and a lot more public than it used to be, requiring as it does the negotiation of key aspects of Hartley's postmodern public sphere: the dissolution of the boundaries between the public and the private, and the elevation of the personal, in media discourse. McKenzie Wark has long argued that we inhabit a world structured by unstable categories and fluid identities, for which the media is an indispensable navigational tool. As his second book argued, there is nothing surprising about the notion that the Australia we inhabit is a 'virtual republic', created by collective acts of imagination and facilitated by the communication technologies which enable us to share words, images and sounds across the nation.[32] In *Celebrities, Culture and Cyberspace*, Wark, like Marshall, argues that the representations of celebrities operate as a kind of bridge between the private world and public debate. For him, too, celebrities become crucial elements in the formation of individual and collective identity:

> Australians have many different ways of thinking and feeling, but nevertheless share a cyberspace within which cultural differences are not only negotiated and adjudicated, but creatively combined. The most visible signs of this process are celebrities. They embody not just the particular cultures from which they come, they embody also something beyond. We may not like the same celebrities, we may not like any of them at all, but it is the existence of a population of celebrities, about whom to disagree, that makes it possible to constitute a sense of belonging. Through celebrating (or deriding) celebrities, it is possible to belong to something beyond the particular culture with which each of us might identify.[33]

A key factor (although not only in cyberspace) is simply 'talk', and there is a rich literature on the social function of gossip as one of the means through which we construct, modify and negotiate our individual and collective identities.[34] Robin Dunbar claims, hyperbolically, that 'language evolved to allow us to gossip',[35] while others have argued that gossip operates as a form of social bonding, that it helps to negotiate norms for social behaviour, and that it plays an important role in providing information and social knowledge. As a consequence of their familiarisation through the media, it seems that the celebrity is (virtually) added to our social circle, and gossip about the celebrity serves similar functions to that about other (non-virtual) members of the social group. The connection between the production of celebrity and the construction of community, then, may be far more direct than is customarily accepted.

In a useful example from an earlier phase of celebrity production, Jackie Stacey's *Star Gazing* provides detailed evidence of the cultural roles played by Hollywood stars of the 1940s and 1950s for women in postwar Britain.[36] The women upon whose experiences she draws speak of the importance of their interest in stars such as Rita Hayworth, Lauren Bacall and Doris Day in constructing their identities, in exploring the pleasures of consumption, and in dealing with the pressures of a particularly austere everyday life. The rise of the gossip magazine in recent years must tap directly into this kind of potential too.

It is the celebrity's complex entanglement with, and contribution to the augmentation of, the discursive or meaning-making structures of their society that dominates most contemporary academic accounts of the cultural function of celebrity. Crudely, it is argued that the mass media celebrity is folded into our ways of making sense of our world.[37] A clue to how that might work within a world where traditional structures are shifting, and where the pace of change and the notification of that change have accelerated dramatically, can be found in Colin Sparks' discussion of the British tabloid press. Sparks acknowledges the importance accorded to individual experience within the contemporary press, even as a means for understanding large, complicated and structural social change. As he says, this is a problem for contemporary culture, that the focusing on 'the experiences of the individual as the direct and unmediated key to the understanding of the social totality' has become a common, deeply embedded feature of social-democratic popular journalism.[38] Indeed, it may well be that the more dramatic, rapid and disruptive the rhythm of social change, the greater the recourse to the personal, the domestic, the melodramatic and the sensational as a means of explanation. Gripsrud's analysis of the uses of melodrama in popular journalism comes to that conclusion, quoting Elsaesser's observation that 'popular culture has resolutely refused to understand social change in other than private contexts and emotional terms'.[39] The role of the celebrity may well be to deal with the gap between the social and the private, between stability and change. While it is probably just as well something is serving this purpose, one has to admit that the commodification of the celebrity would not have been an ideal first choice. Nevertheless, the fact that such arguments are made indicates the importance of understanding these issues better than we do now.

Whatever the explanatory power of these arguments, they have the virtue of approaching the media shifts we have been describing in something like their own terms, rather than seeing them as a subsection of arguments about media ethics or media fashion. The clear indication of the work on celebrity today is to regard the interest in celebrities as another symptom of the media's gradual disarticulation from a model of media practice that foregrounds the dissemination of information, and its increasing alignment with a model that more directly participates in the process of disseminating, interrogating and constructing identities.

Celebrity coverage: Media survey results

What precisely is the extent of the media's interest in celebrity? Has it grown in recent years? Has there been an increase in the number of Australian celebrities dealt with in the media? Our view, supported by empirical evidence, is that this media category is significant and increasing. The evidence comes from a content analysis of selected programs and publications across three media forms: television, newspapers and magazines.

Our survey counted the number of stories dealing with celebrities carried by the target media outlets. In most cases, these stories dealt with high-profile individuals whose celebrity was well known and whose role as a public figure was almost routinely embellished or backgrounded by the stories concerned. In other cases, it involved acknowledging that a certain transformation had occurred: where a person whose particular public office or business activity made them newsworthy was also treated in such a way as to focus on their private life. Our noting of such stories has implicitly refused to distinguish in terms of the magnitude of the celebrity of an individual at this stage, and so our survey does capture stories that produce celebrity-like features on previously unknown personalities as well as regular reports on the private and public movements of well-known people. As noted earlier, celebrity is a product of the manner of representation. Occasionally, we had to make difficult judgements. The task of distinguishing between a celebrity story and a review of a film, stage performance or recording proved to be too complicated in some cases to perform consistently, so our sample did not include any of these forms.

The principal survey was conducted over two weeks in each of February and July of 1997. The monthly magazines (*Dolly, Cleo* and *Australian Women's Weekly*) were collected later to comprise a comparable number of issues. Four newspapers were monitored: *Sydney Morning Herald, Australian, Courier-Mail* and *Herald-Sun*. We counted the number of stories which dealt with celebrities in each of these papers on each day. The selection of sample magazines was made before the recent development of middle-market men's publications such as *Ralph* and *Max* and hence it is skewed towards women's magazines, the major commercial group then as now. Ten magazines were monitored: *Dolly, Cleo, New Idea, Woman's Day, Australian Women's Weekly, TV Week, Who Weekly, New Weekly, Time Australia* and *Bulletin*. We counted the number of celebrity stories in each of these publications and the number of pages they occupied, and calculated the proportion of stories as a percentage of total magazine content.[40]

With television, the evening news bulletins on all free-to-air channels were monitored as well as the current affairs programs *Extra, A Current Affair, Today Tonight, 7.30 Report, Sunday, Insight* and *60 Minutes*. The third program format was the daytime talk and variety show represented by *Today, Midday Show* (now defunct), and *Good Morning Australia*. Again, results were expressed as percentages of the total program content.

What did we find? The total number of stories dealing with celebrity over this period through these media outlets was 3141 (Table 1). The majority were about international celebrities (1717), but a significant proportion concerned Australian celebrities (813). The combination of Australian celebrities with those who have both international and national affiliations (Mel Gibson, for example) accounted for 1275 stories altogether, and this means that more than two-thirds of the total had Australian connections of one kind or another. By far the most popular source of celebrities, unsurprisingly, was the

Table 1 Celebrity stories in various media, February and July 1997 (total numbers)

	February	*July*	*Total*
Television			
Daytime shows	164	153	317
Current affairs	34	38	72
News	143	137	280
Total	**341**	**328**	**669**
Newspapers			
Herald-Sun	325	362	687
Courier-Mail	204	256	460
Australian	134	175	309
SMH	184	193	377
Total	**847**	**986**	**1833**
Magazines			
Entertainment	142	157	299
Women's	125	156	281
News	30	29	59
Total	**297**	**342**	**639**
Total media	**1485**	**1656**	**3141**

Note: SMH = Sydney Morning Herald

Table 2   Origin of celebrities in surveyed media

	Number
Geography	
Local	90
National	813
International	1717
National–international	462
Multiple	58
Field of original activity	
Entertainment	1730
Sport	488
Politics	266
Relationship (to a celebrity)	140
Serious arts	105
Ordinary citizens	93
Royalty	90
Business	69
Law	64
Journalism	47
Science/technology	28
Health/medicine	16
Various	4

entertainment industry (1730 stories), with sport a distant second (488). Most surprising was the low score for royalty (90 stories), wedged on the league table between 'ordinary citizens' (93) and business (69) (Table 2).

The treatment of celebrity in the daily metropolitan press is highly variable but seems to reflect news values in much the way one would expect from other news categories. The results do suggest some specific determinants are in operation, though: we can detect the influence of such things as the weekly entertainment supplements or high-profile news events involving celebrities or individuals who become celebrities (such as the death of Versace or the rescue of Stuart Diver). The key factor to note is the difference between the numbers generated by the two relatively 'mass-market' papers, the *Courier-Mail* (a total of 460 stories) and the *Herald-Sun* (a total of 687), taking a much greater interest in celebrity stories than the more upmarket *Australian* (309) or *Sydney Morning Herald* (377). Story counts per day in the February sample ranged from a high of 42 for the *Herald-Sun* to a low of 4 for the *Australian* (Table 3).

To place these figures in a comparative context, a sample Monday edition of the *Sydney Morning Herald* from 1977 revealed only 6 celebrity items (none of them Australian). The Monday editions in our February 1997 survey scored 12 and 19. Similarly, in a Saturday edition from 1977, the story count was 6

Table 3 Celebrity stories in selected newspapers, 10–23 February and 14–27 July 1997 (daily numbers)

February	Mon 10	Tue 11	Wed 12	Thu 13	Fri 14	Sat 15	Sun 16	Mon 17	Tue 18	Wed 19	Thu 20	Fri 21	Sat 22	Sun 23
SMH	12	12	15	12	20	16	..	19	9	14	16	6	33	..
Courier-Mail	8	16	11	29	9	21	M	10	7	8	28	8	11	38
Australian	5	14	12	10	5	18	..	4	17	6	11	9	23	..
Herald-Sun	12	21	34	42	20	15	19	21	20	25	25	13	22	36

July	Mon 14	Tue 15	Wed 16	Thu 17	Fri 18	Sat 19	Sun 20	Mon 21	Tue 22	Wed 23	Thu 24	Fri 25	Sat 26	Sun 27
SMH	10	9	14	17	20	33	..	18	10	7	9	19	27	..
Courier-Mail	7	13	15	29	10	14	43	10	9	13	28	8	14	43
Australian	7	15	18	12	6	22	..	9	23	11	9	21	22	..
Herald-Sun	13	18	36	31	M	36	31	16	19	34	32	18	43	35

Notes: SMH = Sydney Morning Herald; M = missing; . . = not applicable

(one of them Australian), as against the February 1997 scores of 16 and 33. This reflects a dramatic increase in the number of stories devoted to celebrities in the daily press, as well as significant growth in the proportion of stories devoted to Australian celebrities.

The magazine sample substantiated the commonly held view that celebrity stories have become a highly significant component of the successful women's magazine in the Australian market. With the curious exception of *Cleo*, which printed the smallest percentage of celebrity stories of the whole sample (possibly displaced by its focus on sex), the selected magazines devoted between 25% and 32% of their content to this material. *New Idea*, arguably the most 'tabloid' of the women's magazines, scored the highest average (32%), although *Woman's Day* had the highest percentage of celebrity stories in a single issue (38%) (Table 4).

Comparison with sample issues of the *Australian Women's Weekly* from 1977 reveals a dramatic change in the amount of celebrity material, and in the number of Australian celebrities dealt with in its pages, over the twenty-year period. Whereas the 1997 survey had celebrity stories in this magazine accounting for an average of 26% of the total content, the 1977 issues averaged only 6.8%. The number of pages devoted to celebrities was 48 and 68.7 in 1997, and 11 and 9.33 in 1977. Of the celebrities dealt with in the 1977 issues, only two were Australian.

Predictably, celebrity stories are fundamental to the entertainment magazines, averaging 46% of their content. They are most suited to that part of celebrity coverage that displays the 'authentic' person who exists behind the performance, and the least influenced by conventional news values. Less predictable was the high proportion of news magazine content devoted to celebrity; at almost double the percentage of television news, the average score of 18% suggests that celebrity has become a substantial item within magazines normally assumed to be among the more committed defenders of hard news values. While their figures fluctuate dramatically from issue to issue (from 4% to 34% for *Time Australia*), this is clearly a product of their news values; their content is highly 'event-driven', and in the period surveyed celebrity news events included the murder of Versace and the O. J. Simpson verdict. Nevertheless, the news magazines produced a higher proportion of celebrity stories than expected. The only other notable feature in relation to magazines is simply the volume of material pumped out by the entertainment publications, with *Who* publishing 40% celebrity content per issue and *New Weekly*, 53%. The supply required to satisfy that level of demand is something that will concern us in later chapters.

Television news is increasingly regarded as being in the thrall of info-tainment and this is substantiated by the proportion of celebrity stories in news bulletins, averaging 9% (Table 5).[41] This is a substantial proportion of program content and there is evidence to suggest that it constitutes a

Table 4 Celebrity stories in selected magazines, 1997 (number and percentage of total content)

	Issue	Total pages (N)	Cele-brity pages (N)	Cele-brity stories (N)	Cele-brity pages (%)	Sample average (%)
Women's						
AWW	Mar.	258	48.0	20	22	
	Sep.	308	68.7	32	29	**26**
Dolly	Apr.	132	38.3	16	29	
	Sep.	132	27.1	19	21	**25**
Cleo	Mar.	156	16.0	12	10	
	Aug.	160	19.0	15	12	**11**
New Idea	15 Feb.	96	28.8	19	30	
	22 Feb.	96	35.8	22	37	
	19 July	96	28.4	20	30	
	26 July	96	30.4	21	32	**32**
Woman's Day	17 Feb.	104	24.5	19	24	
	24 Feb.	104	27.7	20	27	
	21 July	104	39.7	21	38	
	28 July	104	27.9	26	27	**29**
Entertainment						
TV Week	15 Feb.	80	37.4	32	47	
	22 Feb.	80	34.2	32	43	
	18 July	80	46.7	27	58	
	26 July	80	31.0	28	39	**47**
Who Weekly	17 Feb.	104	40.6	24	39	
	24 Feb.	98	41.3	19	42	
	21 July	100	39.4	16	39	
	28 July	100	39.2	18	39	**40**
New Weekly	24 Feb.	92	54.8	35	60	
	21 July	92	45.7	38	50	
	28 July	92	45.2	30	49	**53**
News						
Time	17 Feb.	84	28.7	14	34	
	24 Feb.	88	3.1	3	4	
	21 July	72	22.4	5	31	
	28 July	124	2.7	10	2	**18**
Bulletin	18 Feb.	84	18.5	8	22	
	25 Feb.	84	11.0	5	13	
	22 July	84	12.5	6	15	
	29 July	84	18.0	8	21	**18**

Note: AWW = *Australian Women's Weekly*

Table 5   Celebrity stories in television news bulletins, 10–23 February and 14–27 July 1997 (%)

Television station	Celebrity content average (%)	
	February	July
7	8.0	8.2
9	9.0	11.1
10	12.9	9.7
SBS	14.3	9.3
ABC	8.5	6.9

dramatic increase. A series of content analyses of news bulletins conducted in 1978, 1980, 1983 and 1986, all produced very similar figures for celebrity or 'famous persons' stories in the news (interestingly, even the word 'celebrity' is not used in most of these analyses, presumably because it was simply not seen as an important content category at the time). Their percentage share of the bulletins ranged from 3.2% to 4.2%.[42] As was the case with our sample survey of the press in 1977, Henningham found that the overwhelming majority of Famous People in his 1986 study were 'foreigners'; Australian celebrities made up only 0.6% of the total sample.[43]

In television current affairs, the results reveal wide variations between the programs, with average proportions of celebrity stories ranging from a low of 2.1% (*Extra*, February) and 1.9% (*7.30 Report*, July), to a high of 30.5% (*60 Minutes*, February) and 56.5% (*60 Minutes*, July) (Table 6). Apart from *60 Minutes'* high scores in both survey periods, which demonstrates the importance of celebrity stories to its format, there is little consistency in these results and no evidence upon which to base an argument that current affairs in general, or a specific program in particular, is dependent upon celebrity stories. Certainly, it is hard to argue that the proportion of current affairs television devoted to celebrities has increased dramatically over recent years. Bell, Boehringer and Crofts provide figures for *Willesee at 7* from 1980 which have the program scoring a massive 58.9% celebrity content at its peak. Consumer stories and celebrity interviews were then the primary genres of the program, so the current form of *A Current Affair* probably provides a more varied and traditional coverage of hard news than its forerunner.

Bell and others also provide some figures for *60 Minutes* which suggest, however, that it has increased its use of celebrity stories since then. Over the four weeks surveyed in 1980, the program scored 25.8% celebrity content,[44] about half its peak in the 1997 survey. Interestingly, it dealt with roughly three times as many foreign celebrities as locals, suggesting that the increase in local celebrities noted more generally may be one of the factors responsible for the increased proportion of celebrity stories in the current sample.

Table 6 Celebrity stories in television current affairs programs, 10–23 February and 14–27 July 1997 (%)

Television program	Celebrity content average (%)	
	February	July
Extra	2.1	7.2
A Current Affair	17.8	4.6
Today Tonight	18.4	8.8
7.30 Report	15.1	1.9
Sunday	13.0	36.0
Insight	34.0	M
60 Minutes	30.5	56.5

Note: M = missing

Finally, daytime television. As with the magazines, it was no surprise to find how heavily dependent these programs are upon celebrity material; they are the preferred site for celebrity exposure outside prime time. All recorded consistent scores over the two survey periods: *Today* scoring 17.9% and 14.9%; *Midday*, 40.8% and 43.6%; and *Good Morning Australia*, 30.9% and 26.7%. Rather than reflecting the news values operating at the time, this is indicative of producers' decisions about program format: the precise mix of news, personalities, performances and consumer information that they regard as appropriate for their audience.[45]

Filling the gap in media research

The results of our research provide clear evidence that a massive production process has developed in Australia, since the mid-1980s, around the trade in celebrity stories. This implies that a fundamental reshaping of production practices for major sectors of the media industry must have occurred over this period. Not only does our survey point to the overall presence and significance of celebrity reportage in Australian media, there is related evidence that, increasingly, Australian personalities are being developed through a system of celebrity promotion and production. Where once Australian celebrities were virtually non-existent, now they are the subject of between a quarter and a third of all celebrity stories in the media forms we examined. What we have labelled as the Australian celebrity production industry is almost completely uncharted territory for media and cultural studies, and we need to know more about its operation and its practices.

Our starting-point has been to find out what is involved in producing celebrity. We have focused on those largely unseen workers who set up media events or influence casting decisions in a particular television series or organise publicity tours for visiting international stars promoting their latest product. The activity of these workers occurs behind the scenes, even though the outcomes are highly visible; they are the key sources for so much of the content of Australian magazines, newspapers, and television and radio programs. They may manage the talent or they may simply work to get photographs of that talent into the entertainment sections of newspapers. They may provide press releases or electronic press kits; they may contact magazine editors to ensure that the coverage of a particular opening is both targeted widely and in distinctly niche-marketed media forms. Or they may actively control media access to information about their clients or organisation and so shield their celebrity from media attention.

The problem we faced in researching the emergence of these new professional or industrial practices is that very little has been written about these jobs, the history of their emergence or the industrial conditions which made them necessary – precisely how their functions have been integrated into the production schedules of the contemporary media. This celebrity industry has developed over the last twenty to thirty years, maturing into a set of well-developed professional and production practices in Australia across the last fifteen years, but it has been virtually unexamined by anyone outside it.

To retrieve the major elements of an unwritten industrial history, we interviewed key practitioners as well as seeking information in the popular, business and trade press, in industry training manuals and textbooks, and from professional bodies such as the Public Relations Institute of Australia. Comparing the products of these inquiries with our own knowledge of Australian media histories, we have pieced together the patterns that have developed around the practices of promotion, publicity, public relations, talent management and personal representation. What emerges is very different from, say, the North American celebrity industry, with its proliferating specialisms and clear job delineations; the industry in Australia is vigorously hybridised, with the demarcation between tasks and responsibilities often provisional and ad hoc. Profiling its structure is much more difficult, therefore. As one would expect from an industry that has developed through small agencies and industry networks, rather than through large studios or production houses, its shape has evolved progressively in ways that reflect the varying contexts of operation.

For our survey of Australian industry practices, we conducted a series of interviews with agents who are responsible for representing a range of personalities, from presenters to actors (their clients have included Judy Davis, John Wood, Jason Donovan, Rachel Griffiths and Steve Bastoni). Within this group were Barbara Leane, Gary Stewart and June Cann, who each have had a lifetime of experience as an agent and could provide a sense of the twenty-year transformations identified from our other research sources. Other agents, such as Anthony Williams, Rebecca Williamson and Kevin Palmer, were invaluable in describing current practices and their central role in moving talent into streams of stardom, as well as the differential principles which apply to various domains – from the theatre to television or film, for instance.

We also interviewed a number of managers whose duties went beyond representation or booking agentry into the shaping and development of careers. Harry M. Miller, a major figure in Australian entertainment and an equally formidable presence in celebrity management, explained how he controlled the production of a celebrity while creating value and leverage for his clients. Mark Morrissey and Viccy Harper, whose two firms combined the dual roles of manager and agent, were extremely helpful in describing important transitions in the film, television and theatrical parts of the industry as well as in identifying the flexibility of job classification in the production of Australian personalities. Peter Rix, a key figure in Australian popular music for many years and personal manager of musicians such as Marcia Hines, recounted the distinctive patterns of management that have evolved from within the local music industry. Winston Broadbent, of Saxton Speakers Bureau, provided insights into the cultural economies of the more exclusive corporate event circuit which promotes celebrity speakers for conferences and conventions.

The professional linchpin of the celebrity production industry – the publicist – has its origins in press agentry and public relations. Publicists such as Kerry O'Brien in Melbourne, and Georgie Brown and Louise Carroll in Sydney, richly detailed their involvement in events and the promotion of stars related to particular cultural products (feature films, concert tours, television programs). Rea Francis provided an insight into the objectives of the public relations style of managed media events, as well as the importance of promotion to the emergence of the Australian film industry. Tracey Mair's involvement in recent film and television production, particularly with the ABC, allowed us to distinguish and develop an understanding of further subcategories within the profession, such as the unit publicist. (Then) Nine Network publicist Heidi Virtue supplied invaluable background about the corporate synergies between television, magazines and newspapers as celebrity stories connected to network personalities were developed and placed. Similarly, Lesna Thomas, Suzie MacLeod and Andrew Freeman outlined the forms of personality or product promotion and publicity generated from media and entertainment corporations, such as the television production company Southern Star, the film distribution and exhibition company Village Roadshow, and the multinational publishers Random House. Foxtel director Brian Walsh has been a major figure during many of the key transformations that the celebrity industry has generated in Australian popular culture. He was able to provide a detailed history of program

promotions and personality publicity related to network television, particularly in relation to the marketing of rugby league and the establishment of the
teen market for *Neighbours*.

Finally, from our analysis of celebrity story production across media forms
(and especially since the demise of television's *Midday*), it was evident that
the mass-market women's magazines, the gossip magazines and the teen
magazines had developed into the most significant locations for the presentation of celebrity content in the Australian media. In order to examine the
selection and placement of celebrity stories in these magazines, we interviewed three editors: Bunty Avieson at *New Idea* (formerly of *Woman's Day*),
Jane Nicolls at *Who Weekly* and Sue-Ellen Topfer at *TV Hits* and *Smash Hits*.

It is worth emphasising that this approach represents something of an
innovation in media studies. There have been no studies of the Australian
media industries that in any way resemble what follows. Indeed, there has
been very little study at all of media professional practices. There have been
some sociological studies of media workplaces: Philip Schlesinger undertook
participant observation of production processes in news in the United
Kingdom, for instance, and John Henningham's work performs a similar
service for television news in Australia.[46] Todd Gitlin's landmark book on US
television production, *Inside Prime Time*, is also based on a combination of
interview and observation as a way of cracking the codes which underpin
professional practice in television production and programming.[47] Largely,
though, these works set out to understand the value systems or ethical frame-
works which guide practice in these sectors and are implicitly descriptive in
their interest. Our interest certainly includes the need to describe an area of
activity about which most of us know very little. And the value systems which
underpin professional practice do concern us, from time to time, as well. But
this is not our only interest.

Our premise has been that the role of the publicity or promotional
industries has become far more fundamental to the operation of the media
than most observers have so far accepted – and, therefore, that conventional
assumptions about the function of the media (for instance, the relevance of
the watchdog role) need to be revised. Without any published research to provide us with evidence to support this premise, we have attempted to closely
analyse a particular sphere of cultural production – from the outside, through
conventional methods of research and inquiry, but also and more importantly
from the inside, through seeking information from those who actually produce this form of culture. What emerges is a little like what is called 'thick
description' in ethnographic studies, although what we have done is not
ethnography and our conclusions are not descriptive. It is, however, an
attempt to learn about *what the industry itself thinks of as its professional
practice*, as a first step to evaluating important and far-reaching shifts in the
structure and operation of certain areas of the Australian media and their

interrelations with the various sectors of the entertainment industry. Consequently, we have learnt a lot, in new ways, through the participation of industry practitioners and we are grateful to them for the honesty and lucidity with which they discussed their work.

Of course, this analysis of cultural production could not have been generated without a contextualised reading of media texts, media forms and media histories; this is what has identified the objective of the study. Further, we would see the results of our work contributing to the growing body of material in media studies which assesses changes in audience reception and consumption of media forms, and to the developing arguments about how media forms – and celebrities, in particular – are heavily implicated in contemporary constructions of social identity.

This book acknowledges the importance of what the industry practitioners told us by foregrounding their information as primary source material in most chapters. To begin with, however, in Chapter 2 we try to piece together a history of the Australian celebrity industry from independent published sources, a history which places the industry's origins in the development of public relations as well as in the growth of particular sectors of the entertainment industry: popular music, film and television. Two trends became increasingly visible during the 1980s: an expansion of the promotional industries as a whole, and a corresponding expansion of the presence of Australian celebrities in the media. Considering how this may affect news media practice, the chapter reviews the available research on the growing dependence of journalists on publicists.

Chapter 3 looks at what the celebrity industry actually does. Drawing on the interviews in detail, it outlines the contemporary practices of the industry's professionals. Much of this is new; publicity practitioners are rarely asked to talk about their work or the principles which guide it. Along with identifying the hybrid functions that practitioners serve while promoting personalities, the chapter examines the daily dealings of the celebrity industry and the structural alignment between these professionals and the business of entertainment and news production.

Chapter 4 approaches the media as a problem to be managed, regulated and controlled. Media exposure, even for the publicity industry which depends upon it, has its dangers. On the positive side, the industry's exercise of media management is a means of building a professional career for its clients. Reflecting ethical concerns from liberal critics outside the media and professionals within it, the chapter focuses on the power of the media to create celebrity in unpredictable and personally damaging ways, the predatory manner in which this power can be exercised, and how this is managed by the industry.

Chapter 5 presents a detailed study of the use of celebrities in the mass-market women's magazines: the historical growth of the importance of the celebrity to these magazines; the varying social, cultural and entertainment functions they serve for their audiences; and the body of academic (feminist and otherwise) and industry criticism that has accompanied their rise to prominence in recent years. It is in this chapter that we most directly consider the cultural function of celebrity gossip and examine conventional assumptions about this genre of media performance. Concluding the chapter is a related account of the training ground for the mass-market readership – the teen magazines.

Chapter 6 identifies the insights derived from the study in order to discuss the significance of the production of the Australian celebrity for Australian contemporary culture. Here we make an argument about the cultural function of the promotion industries and the audience interest in their products. We consider the cultural politics of the industrial structure we have described, as well as a range of ethical and political issues to do with the responsibilities and function of a democratic media.

Chapter 2
The Rise of Promotional Culture

Public relations, I mean, it's sort of the generic term, but I don't know if it describes the industry any more.
Brian Walsh

It has become commonplace today for discussions of contemporary culture to emphasise the cultural and economic centrality of various forms of publicity: advertising, promotion, marketing, and public relations. Within the academic literature, Andrew Wernick's phrase – 'promotional culture' – provides a handy means of referencing the full range of activities performed by what John Hartley has sardonically called 'the smiling professions'.[1] While the terms 'promotions' and 'promotion' have specific meanings for the industry, 'promotional culture' is a useful phrase for our, more academic, purposes to describe the cultural and industrial shifts in which we are interested.

A more widely understood but, lately, less strictly accurate label for a similar range of activities, still conventionally used in most public and media commentary, is that of 'public relations'. Bob Franklin, in his 1997 critique of contemporary journalism in Britain, refers to the growth of 'public relations', including 'government, party and industry-group press offices, agency and in-house corporate communications, and ... the public relations staff which even charities and voluntary organizations now employ'. Like many media commentators, within the academy and elsewhere, he criticises the degree to which the practice of journalism is being contaminated from outside. The 'fourth estate' is in danger of being overwhelmed by the 'fifth estate', the growing number of 'PR merchants and spin doctors' influencing the news agenda.[2] The target of this critique is not only the increasing size of this so-called fifth estate; it is also their effect on media content. Jeremy Tunstall suggested back in 1971 that public relations had displaced journalism.[3] In his account of the contemporary situation, Franklin cites the editor of the British magazine *PR Week* who estimates that over 50% of the content of every section (except sport) of every broadsheet newspaper would be PR-generated.[4]

Public relations has become a convenient catch-all term in most circumstances when publicity and promotion are discussed outside the media industries. There may have been a time when it was the appropriate description for what was still a new and developing industry sector, but it is no longer an accurate label. Its use obscures important differences between the various activities customarily assumed to fall under its ambit, as well as the various purposes behind these activities. We need to sort these differences out a little before going any further, by relaying what appears to be the industry's consensus on what constitutes those activities properly identified with public relations, with publicity or with promotion.

The term 'public relations', it has to be said, can carry some negative connotations within the industry as well as outside. Among publicists, it seems to be considered rather dated. Foxtel's Brian Walsh, who does not identify what he does as public relations, is dismissive: 'Public relations, I've always thought, were people who [organised] a smart cocktail party and [had] a hyphenated surname'. Freelance public relations consultant Rea Francis *does* identify with the term, albeit a little reluctantly. While she is not keen to be described as a publicist – 'I don't actually like the term publicist, I never have' – she is also uneasy about some of the connotations associated with public relations: 'There was time when public relations had a nasty smell about it, there were so many bad practitioners', and this obviously contributed to a sleazy reputation.

Francis' interview provides some hints as to the likely provocation for Walsh's unflattering description. The account of her career is dominated by references to the successful promotional event (more than just smart cocktail parties, it should be said), but she has a very particular attitude to these events. Walsh, as a publicist, conceives of the smart cocktail party as designed to generate free space in the news media. Francis, as a public relations consultant, is much more concerned with the 'success' of the actual event for those she invites to attend. While there may be publicly visible coverage in newspapers or magazines, the most important outcomes do not involve the general public at all, at least at the time. For those concerned, the event is an experience as well as a promotional opportunity – and a particular kind of experience, at that. Francis' conversation is littered with accounts of encounters with famous names at mythic places – parties at Cannes, connections in Los Angeles – and her engaged descriptions of a world of showbiz high society seem to offer the consumption of gratuitous glamour as an end in itself. Certainly, and this is where the purpose of public relations contrasts with that of publicity, the end product is not likely to be measured in column inches; rather, it is more likely to be a relationship – with a sponsor or a lobbyist or an organisation. The smart cocktail party is a site where the networking part of business can be conducted and, in the cases Francis cites, in an atmosphere rendered glamorous by the deployment of celebrity.

There is also an organisational aspect to the kind of public relations that Lesna Thomas provides for Southern Star: 'A great deal of my work … is public relations in the sense that so much of [it] is probably 40–50% … corporate … I get shareholders ringing, public image … queries and stuff like that'. Freelance publicist Tracey Mair sees her role as 'positioning an organisation, and that can be as much about deflecting publicity as it is about generating positive information for that client'.

The time frame for public relations, in comparison with that for promotions or publicity, is distinctive too. Because so much of it is about the progressive process of 'branding' (Winston Broadbent, from Saxton Speakers Bureau, makes this point), its strategies are customarily aimed at what Louise Carroll described as 'long-term credibility building for companies'. Some of this long-term work does involve celebrities and publicity, of course. Harry M. Miller and other celebrity managers have been very successful in securing positions for their clients as spokespersons for corporations (Deborah Hutton and Peter Brock, for instance, as the faces of Holden). Nevertheless, it is clear from the responses in our interviews that a great deal of what we talk about in this book – the production and marketing of celebrity – is not public relations as most practitioners understand it.

Promotions, it seems agreed, is very different from public relations. Within the industry, 'promotions' is a highly specific term which refers to 'special events and the merchandising that goes on around them' (publicist Georgie Brown) or, as Suzie MacLeod from Roadshow puts it, 'promotions is giveaways, ticket giveaways'. It might involve arranging for radio stations to give free air time to concerts or films by setting up competitions in return for tickets, or contacting community groups as potential audiences for a film. For the television industry, the term refers specifically to the on-air advertising of particular programs. The use of celebrities – for personal appearances, for endorsements, and so on – is reasonably well integrated into this part of the industry but is not an essential or indispensable component.

Of the three terms we canvassed, 'publicity' is the one which most generically describes the central processes through which celebrity is manufactured and traded in the Australian media today. Publicity is bluntly described by Kerry O'Brien as getting 'free editorial or free coverage on television, radio, the papers and magazines'. Publicity is designed to turn advertising into news. Its value is that you gain media space without paying for it and that its positioning as news rather than advertising gives it greater credibility.

Celebrities are essential to this process – they are what the publicist has to offer the news outlet.

Discussing a change in social reporting and in the composition of 'high society' since the 1980s, the *Australian*'s George Epaminondas notes the rise of what he terms 'quasi-public events', like celebrity parties and movie premieres, and how an invitation to such an event is 'leveraged and exploited in the service of a movie or a designer or a magazine'. He quotes Simon Lock of the Spin agency, observing: 'Parties happen to communicate a brand, a new product, a new vision'.[5] Peter Metzer, the agent who organised the launch of the Australian version of *marie claire* and the twenty-fifth anniversary of *Cleo*, noted that the success of an event is 'judged on … how many clippings, how much television, how much publicity there was out of it'.[6] The way such coverage is gained is overwhelmingly through the presence of a celebrity: the *Cleo* party was heavily reported on the basis of the presence of Guy Pearce and Russell Crowe, themselves both engaged in promoting *LA Confidential*. Similarly, O'Brien talked of the relative ease with which she gained front-page coverage of a Planet Hollywood opening: the presence of Bruce Willis and Sylvester Stallone ensured the attendance of entertainment photographers and the event became news.

As these examples indicate, publicity's pervasiveness is normally, necessarily, obscured by its absorption into other forms of communication. However variously they were described through their organisational roles, the vast majority of those we talked to were involved in generating publicity of some kind or another. So, if we were to choose which was the more comprehensive term to describe what people in this industry do, 'publicist' would ultimately be our choice. That said, Walsh also made the point that there are good reasons why it is difficult (and probably undesirable) to maintain a clear distinction between public relations, promotions and publicity. For a start, the roles that practitioners are required to play within the industry have changed significantly over the period of its expansion:

> BRIAN WALSH: I think 20 years ago, yeah, sure, you could call yourself a public relations consultant and your job was to, you know, give strategic advice to companies on how they should position themselves in the marketplace. You could have been a promotions manager and organised consumer competitions through radio and newspapers. You could have been a publicist who escorted, you know, a rock star around Australia and do press conferences at airport arrivals. Those have all gone, it's all changed.

The discrete labels, and the demarcation between the various services performed, no longer apply:

BRIAN WALSH: I think publicity has changed enormously in the last 15 years and I think that the job now is a marriage of all those three things … You have to be able to devise a good promotion. You have got to be able to sell the promotion end. You have got to leverage the promotion with editorial space. You have got to be able to write a press release … You have got to know what a good headline is … what is going to sell, a good photo idea, and you have to know how to organise a good event and a good party, and get good coverage, and it's a combination of all these things that makes you successful in the game today.

This point of view is substantiated by Thomas when she describes her role:

LESNA THOMAS: I look after the corporate imaging. Now that can be anything from the sign out the front to our letterhead through to all the media, all the work that I'll be doing with analysts who are watching our company and advising people about investing in our company and then the next layer right down to promoting our programs, helping to sell our programs worldwide.

The importance of their capacity to work across such a range of activities is underscored when you look at the kinds of backgrounds from which our interviewees, all successful practitioners, have come. None of them has worked solely within one sector of the industry. Kerry O'Brien started out as a receptionist and went on to organising promotions (such as fashion parades and concerts), before working as a publicist. Andrew Freeman started out in a public relations firm doing corporate work, before moving to publicity at Random House. Brian Walsh started out promoting surf films with David Elphick but much later set up the public relations division of BSkyB in London, and likewise for Star in Hong Kong, and then handled promotion and publicity for (among others) the Nine Network's *Wide World of Sports* and rugby league, before directing programming, publicity and promotion at Foxtel.

Our discussion of the growth in promotional culture in Australia will reflect this hybridisation of the various activities within the industry (Chapter 3 will deal with this in detail). From time to time, our focus will shift between promotions and publicity, and the kind of media management most properly associated with public relations. This latter term is the one most commonly linked, for good or ill, to the changes in media content which first provoked our interest. More importantly, the history of these changes in Australia has to begin with a brief account of the growth of public relations within the private sector and within government since the beginning of the 1980s.

Public relations in Australia

> Public relations is the deliberate, planned and sustained effort to
> establish and maintain mutual understanding between an organi-
> zation and its publics.
> *Public Relations Institute of Australia*

Although the context in which we have placed public relations for this project
emphasises its involvement in promotion and publicity (and, indeed, most
sources agree this would constitute approximately 60% of the work now
carried on under the label of public relations),[7] public relations, in its purest
and most self-conscious form, has much loftier aspirations than this would
suggest. It thinks of itself as a socially important profession. One of the
founding fathers of public relations in the United States, Ivy Lee, remarked
in 1991 that he felt public relations should be taken 'seriously, like law or
architecture'.[8] Textbooks for those studying public relations in tertiary institutions make clear connections between public relations and democratic
principles, such as freedom of information: Quarles and Rowlings claim, for
instance, that the 'health and size of the public relations profession in any
country is in direct proportion to the freedom of information in the society'.[9]
Their argument is that, where information is not freely available, it is usually
controlled by a central government – so it is, more or less, propaganda. The
standards claimed for professional practice in such textbooks are high.
Quarles and Rowlings argue that public relations must always be honest if it
is to be respected: 'Any freedom carries responsibility, and public relations'
responsibility is that of always being based on truth'.[10] Not the popular
perception, perhaps, but certainly a principle consistently articulated by
those who speak on behalf of the profession.

   Modern public relations began in the United States around the turn of the
twentieth century. Helen Wilson suggests that it developed out of a nineteenth
century system of press agentry for entertainers, before being taken up as a
means of protecting early modern capitalists from the interests of the press.[11]
Apparently, the term was first used by the US National Association of
Railroads in 1897, with the first consultancy formed in the United States in
1906.[12] Tymson and Sherman name George Fitzpatrick as the first Australian
practitioner and wryly draw attention to the candour employed in his 1930s
telephone book entry which lists him as a 'registered practitioner in public
persuasion, propaganda, publicity'.[13] Others claim that the beginnings of
public relations in Australia were linked to General Douglas MacArthur's
visit in 1942.[14] Surprisingly, given its interest in managing the public image
of organisations, the profession of public relations has not provided us
with substantial published accounts of its own history in Australia. Indeed,
accessing any form of detailed published information about the industry

is difficult, even though it has had a professional association (the Public Relations Institute of Australia) since 1960.

Oddly enough, the PRIA has not developed in the way many other industry associations (perhaps directly assisted by their public relations officers) have done: as lobby groups aimed at managing the public perception of the profession and the regulatory climate within which it operates. Instead, the PRIA's attentions have been directed inwards, anxiously examining its status as a profession. This was a dominant concern during the 1980s. The most common element in the textbooks and other published accounts of public relations in Australia is a list of the accredited tertiary courses in the field (the first, in 1970, was the Mitchell College of Advanced Education, now Charles Sturt University, Bathurst). Ironically, this exemplifies the PRIA's own argument that organisations need outside bodies to handle the production of their public 'face'. Also important in the PRIA's conversation with itself has been its advocacy for the professional status of public relations in business: the degree of seriousness with which public relations expertise is regarded in the boardroom, for example. When Tony Stevenson completed his review of the profession in 1990, a review which was funded by the PRIA but never published in full, he reported 'perceptions that it did include strategic planning, lobbying and marketing support, but on a limited basis, and that it was integral to management where used on that level, but not regarded widely as a decision-making function'.[15] The concern underlying this observation is relatively typical of those central to the PRIA's interests. Given that one definition of public relations is the 'management of communication between an organization and its publics',[16] it is not surprising that the PRIA and its members felt that business should take their advice seriously as fundamental components of operational planning and development.

Nevertheless, a consequence of this particular focus is that it is very difficult for an outsider to establish authoritative figures for the size of the industry, the scale of its growth since the end of World War II, the major activities of its participants, and so on. Notwithstanding the lack of such evidence, it seems to be agreed that there have been at least two major growth periods. During the late 1950s and early 1960s, largely as a result of the success of the Eric White agency which dominated public relations in Australia for many years, revenue from the industry is reported to have grown tenfold.[17] After 1964, the same report claims, it went into a five-year decline before recovering ground in the late 1970s.

The period which concerns us most in this book, however, is the mid-1980s, when the increase in public relations, publicity and promotion agencies, and in the visibility of Australian celebrities, seem to have been substantial – and, we would argue, interrelated. Again, hard data on such a shift in the scale, volume or profitability of the industry is impossible to find. Total billings, campaign budgets, net income figures, and so on are usually regarded as commercially sensitive, so most published figures are estimates – and can be widely divergent. *B&T* (the broadcasting and television magazine) provides some form of evidence of the growth in the size of the industry in its annual listing of agencies and consultancies. The number listed in 1976, Australia-wide, is 58. By 1984 this has risen to 225, and in 1986 it peaks at 270, remaining above 200 from then on. Wilson claims that spending on public relations services Australia-wide in 1985–86 grew by 15%, while Tymson and Sherman report a 25% increase in turnover for 'several major public relations consultancies' in 1988, and this is repeated in 1989.[18] Rod Tiffen doesn't provide us with authoritative sources either, but his 'rough estimate' is that 'the numbers employed in the mid-1980s were at least ten times greater than those employed in the mid-1960s'.[19] Some sense of the dollars involved is given by noting that International Public Relations, the largest Australian firm at the time, billed $5 million in 1986, and by Tymson and Sherman's undated claim that the top eight firms in Australia earn something like $32 million a year between them.[20] While none of this provides the detail one would like, it does indicate a major expansion of the industry during the mid-1980s.

Barbara-Ann Butler explores another angle on this expansion in her examination of the development of the use of public relations by government in the early 1990s.[21] Her account is a history of the relationship between government and the media, not private industry and the media. Among the elements she focuses on is the growth of media and information units in government, units which are precisely about 'managing the relationship between an organization and its publics' through media advisers, press officers, and the like. Since 1972, federal governments have recruited communications professionals with the expertise to supply the news media with ready-made news – and the number of these professionals employed has increased dramatically. For example, when Whitlam was in power, the total number of government media advisers or press secretaries was 128; 20 of them were on his personal staff. When Fraser replaced Whitlam, he set up the Government Information Unit to coordinate the publicising of federal government policy, centralising control over all government public relations activities in order to 'set the news agenda on a regional or national scale'. Fraser's personal staff of media advisers numbered 22, and he had control over another 20 in the information unit. A decade later, the increase in media advisers was substantial. The Hawke government employed a total of 224, and by the time Keating was in control in 1991 the number had risen to 299. The amount spent by the federal government on public relations – and it hardly needs pointing out that the primary objective of this expenditure is more likely to be political than administrative – is both enormous and impossible to nail down. In Queensland, though, it has been estimated that, in the financial year 1991–92, the government spent $36.6 million on public relations. At the time, it employed 200 ministerial media advisers; the Opposition had 20.[22]

PUBLIC RELATIONS AND THE NEWS

While the PRIA might describe the growth of public relations through the development of tertiary training programs for the profession, others might look at the influence of public relations on news. (Usually, in this context, public relations is thought of in its broadest sense, including all kinds of press releases from government and industry.) There are structural changes which have enhanced the potential for such an influence. The establishment through AAP (Australian Associated Press) of the Medianet service (first set up as PR Wire in 1982) structurally merges public relations media releases and news releases, effectively turning advertising into news.[23] Journalists almost routinely deny that this sort of influence is either strong or growing. However, those outside journalism have long claimed that public relations has increasingly infiltrated the processes of news gathering, perfecting the strategy of selling its products as news. Tiffen notes the contradiction between these two points of view but suggests that there may be some truth on both sides. While only a small proportion of public relations material makes it into the news (the journo's view), a large proportion of news is the product of public relations efforts (the public relations' view).[24]

Such studies of the relationship between public relations and the news concentrate on politics or business; in the area of entertainment news, it seems pretty hard to deny the importance of information fed to journalists through publicists or other industry avenues. Tracey Mair says that, while 'generally journalists don't like to acknowledge their dependence on publicists … those people who work in entertainment are absolutely dependent on us because we're the ones that give them access'. Lesna Thomas is 'amazed' at the amount of information she has to 'hand-feed' to journalists: 'I mean, when I was a working journalist, I would hardly have had contact with the PR. I would go to the chief executive myself.' Most of the publicists we talked to acknowledged that newspapers now have fewer staff and resources, despite operating within an increasingly competitive environment. Most recognised that these factors increased journalists' dependence upon the publicist. As a result, certain areas were utterly dependent on the material fed to them. Nine Network publicist Heidi Virtue, for instance, said that most stories in the television listings are 'true fact but [written] by publicists'.

Less widely acknowledged is the influence of public relations–sourced information in areas, such as the business press, which are not so obviously publicity-dependent. In Britain, in 1996, Sarah Whitebloom, a city reporter for the *Guardian*, provoked hostile responses from within journalism when she broke ranks to criticise the cosy relationship between financial journalists and their sources:

> A glance at almost any day's financial pages betrays the great fiction that this is news. The remarkable similarity of the stories in all the papers is no coincidence. There are the carefully managed, set piece events such as the launching of a new product concerning a company's latest brilliant initiative, and whether it be a takeover bid or a city scandal, there is a PR man at the end of the line pumping out his client's specific version of the truth.[25]

This sort of accusation can be aimed at the Australian business press, too. Tiffen's *News and Power* singled out business journalists as the least independent of their sources, estimating that 60–90% of their stories were drawn directly (and, implicitly, unchanged) from business sources.[26] Graeme Turner's discussion of the business press in the 1980s, in *Making It National*, argues that the sycophantic relation which builds up between business journalists and their sources contributed to the complicity of the business press in what he calls 'larrikin capitalism', the risk-taking entrepreneurialism which produced the excesses of that decade.[27]

Whitebloom's accusations were taken up by Radio National's *Media Report* (15 August 1996), which asked if there were similarly cosy arrangements between public relations and the media in Australia. The answer seemed to be, overall, yes, although with significant differences of opinion. Richard Jabara, from IMD Pacific Communications, compared the public perception of journalists as 'out there in trenchcoats, running up and down Collins Street getting their stories' with what he saw as the reality: 'They're getting their stories from us' (that is, public relations). He regarded that as an acceptable situation as long as each party dealt honestly with the other. The public relations firm's role in this context was not so much to give the content of the message its spin (although it certainly was that as well), as to provide expert advice about the best possible outlet for the story:

> I will certainly advise a client, 'Look, that's a current affairs story, that's a BRW story, no, forget the ABC, they're not interested in that. I think the way we'll do it is, we'll go to Tony Barber' ... So there's all these different angles. And basically, from our perspective, I have a motto to say never tell a lie, [but] it's how you tell the truth. And you're not lying, you're telling the truth, it's just the spin.

Jabara's account was challenged by another contributor to the program, Arnis Verbikis, a lecturer in media law, who retained a commitment to the importance of journalism's independence, to the fourth-estate watchdog role. From Verbikis' perspective, the idea of 'spin' invoked too cynical a view of public relations. Instead, public relations consultants 'ought to be placed in the same perspective as, say, lawyers in terms of advocacy'. The role of public relations was 'to present the client's message in the best possible way, without lying, without breaching the law, or without doing something that is ... morally unacceptable'. Public relations 'ought to be perceived as ... advocacy'.

This is not the commonly held view of the role of public relations. As Rea Francis points out, though, some of the negative connotations associated with public relations over the years have started to migrate towards another term: 'spin-doctoring'. 'Spin doctor' has achieved widespread media currency and is usually held to be a sign of, in particular, the control of political debate by public relations experts employed by government or political organisations. While political parties defend their use of such personnel to get their point of view across, many journalists are deeply suspicious of this practice and resent the way in which their access to what should be public information is controlled and orchestrated by private employees. The nature of the contribution made by the spin doctor is described by BBC journalist Nicholas Jones in a conversation with Radio National's Robert Bolton on *Media Report* in September 1998:

> We've had occasions when Mr Blair has given a speech and said that, for example, he is going to rewrite the Labour Party's constitution because he wants it to be more modern. We then hear subsequently that the spin on that ... in fact means that the Labour Party here in Britain dropped ... its commitment to the nationalisation of public services. Now Mr Blair didn't say it in his own words, but the spin was what we got from the spin doctors. That is what the words [meant]. So you can see how important it is, if you're a political journalist, and that's why we're vulnerable and possibly can be manipulated, because we are taking from the spin doctors their interpretation of the speech or the event or the decision that's just been taken.[28]

Australian contributors to the program, however, argued that this level of control was not replicated in Australia. Graham Morris, former chief of staff to Prime Minister John Howard, argued that Australian journalists are not that easily fooled: 'Australian journalists are more aggressive, more cynical than any journalist around the world, and they will not accept a sort of a line which doesn't pass the crap test'. In response to the popular perception of spin doctors as Machiavellian figures manipulating politicians and exerting personal influence on political agendas (a perception, it has to be said, that the media has an interest in popularising), Morris was dismissive: 'That is a perception ... promoted by people who like seeing their name in the paper, and like being seen as manipulative clever dicks after the event. Like after an election, when they're claiming credit for something ... it was probably the leader or the ministers or the combination that won the election, not the clever, self-appointed, so-called spin doctor.' As to the possibility of spin doctors hijacking the political agenda and taking it in a direction of their own choosing, Morris said that such a person 'would last about two weeks' in any Australian political organisation.[29] Comforting as such a confident statement may be, David Oldfield's evident influence within Pauline Hanson's One Nation Party should encourage us to take it with a grain of salt.

More convincing than seductive demonologies about spin doctors, than assurances that Australian politics is robust enough to resist such forms of manipulation or than those disingenuous defences of spin which describe it as nothing more than effectively managing the communication process is the kind of account Margaret Simons presented in this edition of *Media Report*, which emphasises the cultural and professional connections between the various players in the process, connections which inevitably foster close working relationships and common ethical orientations:

> Australia is probably the only western democracy where you get all the political minders, the staffers and the journalists, and the politicians all resident in the same building for large parts of the year ... So what this means, of course, is that the political minders and the journalists are drinking coffee in the same coffee shop, they're eating meals in the same canteen a lot of the time ... On top of that, of course, you've got the fact that most of the media minders, who are employed by politicians, are themselves former journalists, and many of the press gallery journalists have also in their time worked for politicians ... Now while I think on a day to day level they operate [with] ... a reasonable amount of independence from each other, it's not surprising that they come to share a certain world view.[30]

That does not mean that they are incapable of critically or sceptically evaluating information they receive from each other. But there are conditions which can discourage that scepticism. Simons continues: 'The agreement on what is important, what is credible, what is worthy of front page news, or what is worthy of detailed analysis, that's the level on which you get the unexamined agreements between political staffers and journalists, and, indeed, politicians'.

The level of interdependence that Simons describes between politicians, political staffers, media advisers and journalists does raise concern outside of these professions. Butler suggests that the introduction of public relations methods to restrict media access to sensitive information during World War II 'permanently altered the relationship between the federal government and the media'.[31] She expresses anxiety about the blurring of the distinctions between journalists and public relations practitioners in the management of federal and state politics, noting the increasing trade in personnel between the two professions – the number of journalists who become media advisers for government, for instance. Changes in their professional environment – the reduction in staff numbers, the withdrawal of research time and facilities, the commercial pressures exerted through management, and so on – are frequently cited by journalists and by those working in the promotions industries as factors which increase the news media's dependence on commercial sources for information. The relationship between television news and public relations, particularly during elections, is singled out for strong criticism in Butler's research. She locates the source of the problem in structural changes within the television industry itself which have created conditions receptive to the commercialisation of news values:

> It is not unreasonable to question whether the independence of television news journalists may have been compromised by changes that have taken place in the television industry in the past two decades. These changes include concentration of media ownership of television stations, falling profitability, cutbacks in newsroom staff and newsgathering resources, the introduction of centralised newsgathering routines and an increase in the amount of material being syndicated within networks.[32]

At this point it is worth consulting the empirical evidence for the kind of influence we have been discussing by reviewing research which has investigated the proportion of news stories which can be sourced to press releases, promotional handouts, publicity and public relations. According to the journalist, academic and, more recently, head of the ABC's Corporate Relations, Julianne Schultz, much journalism does 'simply recycle' press releases. Further developing her 1990 study, which examined accuracy and corroboration,[33] her most recent book contains claims that even many 'apparently comprehensive reports accept the line and language of the spin doctors with little real attempt to provide context, background, analysis or insight'.[34] In the 1996 *Media Report* quoted above, Verbikis referred to the research of a colleague, Jim McNamara, who found that approximately 80% of the stories in 'your daily paper' emanated from 'public relations firms or media releases issued by public relations firms or a PR individual'.[35] Also, Jabara mentioned a study of the *Washington Post* which put the figure at around 70%. There is no shortage of relevant studies, and they all come up with similar results.

One of the larger studies was financed by the Queensland government in 1993. The Electoral and Administrative Review Commission (EARC) produced conclusive evidence that newspaper, radio and television journalists in Queensland reproduced the content of official news releases virtually unchanged and apparently without clear evidence of verification or corroboration. Among the research strategies pursued in generating this report was the tracing of 279 media releases from government ministers. Newspapers took up 200 of these releases and 140 of them were reproduced virtually verbatim. The take-up in television was less, influenced of course by the fact that television uses fewer stories anyway. The key factor, however, was the lack of corroboration: 60% of the items used were not verified.[36]

The most interesting Australian study so far is by Clara Zawawi, who sets out to test the kinds of estimates provided by the industry and others we have quoted above.[37] Her methodology is different from that employed in the EARC and other similar surveys, as she does more than trace known press releases through to their destination. She demonstrates how it is possible to detect what she calls 'public relations activity' in the text of news stories, whether they acknowledge an institutional or official source or not. Using a wider range of items than previous research has considered, Zawawi analysed stories where the source was unclear or unacknowledged for evidence of public relations activity and followed up a sample of those that did show such textual signs. This whole sample turned out to have originated as press releases. She then analysed a large sample of news and business stories from an issue each of the *Gold Coast Bulletin*, the *Sydney Morning Herald* and the *Australian*. The results are telling:

> The evidence indicates that Schultz's PR consultant's boast is correct and that PR practitioners do originate more than half of the content of newspapers. In terms of percentages, if 2 June 1993 was a typical day, apparent levels of public relations influence would seem to be, in news and business combined, some 64 per cent in *The Australian*, 53 per cent in *The Gold Coast Bulletin*, and 65 per cent in *The Sydney Morning Herald*.
>
> If the data are broken down into a division between news and business stories, it would seem that public relations activities have greater influence in the area of business news, with percentages of 93 per cent in *The Australian*, 90 per cent in *The Gold Coast Bulletin*, and 84 per cent in *The Sydney Morning Herald*.[38]

Zawawi concludes that perhaps researchers working on journalism should 'adopt a model that removes the journalist from the centre of the news process in the print media and give more emphasis to the role of the public relations practitioner'. Her point, though, is different from Franklin's. Far from critiquing 'media or journalistic integrity', she suggests that the media surveyed were 'fairly scrupulous about signposting their externally received material'. She is at pains to point out that what she is investigating has more to do with changes in work practices, resource allocation and management directions than with the revision of ethical standards. More importantly, though, her research points to broader issues about the way the media operates today and the pressing need to update and revise our understandings of how 'information is conveyed to the general public'.[39]

So what has all this to do with the production of celebrity industry in Australia? At the simplest level, it can be established that the interest in celebrity evident in our media survey (see Chapter 1) has been accompanied by an expansion in the size and influence of those sectors of the media industries required to feed and satisfy that interest – public relations, promotion and publicity. It can also be argued that this expansion has in turn accompanied and enabled the recent development of a local industry marketing Australian celebrities.

Promotion, publicity and the celebrity

> We didn't have a celebrity industry when I started this game.
> *Rea Francis*

> If there wasn't a star system in Australia, I wouldn't be able to ring up a restaurant and get a table that was booked for you.
> *Harry M. Miller*

Our research has shown that celebrity stories are a significant component of the Australian media diet and that publication of them has increased dramatically since the mid-1980s. The publicists and agents we talked to certainly held this view. Mark Morrissey made the point that there has been an increase both in supply and in demand: 'There are many more opportunities and there is a lot more product. And we're doing a lot more. There are more overseas contracts signed and developed. There is a lot more tabloid coverage since the 1980s.' The view is also supported by Rea Francis, who worked for the Australian Film Commission in the mid-1970s when there was only 'Jack [Thompson] and Bryan [Brown] and a couple of other blokes [who] were figures from early television days [who moved] into film'. In order to develop an Australian film culture, she had to find ways to address the absence of any kind of star system here by generating stories that would gradually raise the profiles of individuals within the film industry. With a movie audience used to choosing its films from the available menu of Hollywood stars and genres, Australian film was starting from the rear of the field in attempting to build a profile for its products and performers.

The broader cultural context, still affected at the time by the residue of the 'cultural cringe', did not help. In most sectors of the media during the 1950s and 1960s, Australianness was a positive disadvantage for the aspiring performer. This only slowly broke down during the 1970s. Morrissey recalls of the 1960s – and many others would share this recollection – that there was a prejudice against Australian accents in the media and the performing arts. In the theatre, it was conventionally assumed that actors required English accents. On radio, on-air accents ranged from the BBC-like pronunciations of the ABC announcers to the Americanised intonations affected by the first generation of popular music disc jockeys (Bob Rogers, Ward Austin, even John Laws), but there were very few ordinary Australian voices. On television, the first newsreader for TCN9 in Sydney was Chuck Faulkner, his American accent bringing authority and modernity to the evening news, while ABC-TV opted for the tradition and stability implied by the Home Counties inflections of its announcers (Michael Charlton, Tanya Halesworth).

By the early 1980s, however, there are signs of a shift towards the commercial production of an Australian celebrity: an increase in the 'demand for information on the popularity of media, social and sports personalities', possibly in 'response to the need to increase advertising impact in today's tight economic conditions'.[40] This refers to what was still a relatively novel advertising strategy – using local celebrities to endorse products. Another report challenges this use of 'personalities' in advertising and their association with specific brands. Under a *B&T* headline which asks whether talent is getting too 'grasping', Pat Rogers doubts the viability of an industry built around celebrity endorsement and wonders whether there is a supply of 'big enough Australian personalities who aren't already over-exposed'.[41]

Notwithstanding these reservations, the prevalence of this form of advertising does seem to have grown over the 1980s. The combination of an economic recession and the beginnings of a local celebrity market offered advertisers a new means of positioning their products. The tactic had success. The same issue of *B&T* has a short case study of the revival of *TV Week*.[42] At the time, the magazine was facing stiff competition from *Australian Women's Weekly* and *Woman's Day*, both of which had published their own zip-out TV guide as a free supplement to their magazine, with resulting increases in sales. *TV Week* ran an advertising campaign which made heavy use of radio jingles, varied to match the music format of the stations concerned, which were delivered by high-profile radio personalities. This tactic prefigured the importance of celebrity to *TV Week*'s continuing survival, and circulation increased from 635,000 to more than 700,000 over the life of the campaign.

The 1980s also saw an increase in advertising which foregrounded the representation of company CEOs in order to, in effect, construct a degree of celebrity around them. In a highly tautological strategy, such entrepreneurs as Bob Ansett, of Budget Car Rentals, used their own advertising campaigns to turn themselves into public figures; then, demonstrating the value of celebrity in reinforcing market appeal, these CEOs traded the celebrity-commodity their own ads had created by endorsing their own companies.

Harry M. Miller had provided celebrity management well before the 1980s, although only on a relatively small scale for real high-flyers like Graham Kennedy, but this was to expand into a major activity over the course of that decade. A further indicator of the growing marketability of the local celebrity in the early 1980s is the arrival of one of those most closely identified with celebrity management over the 1990s: Max Markson. His agency, Markson Sparks!, was established in 1982 and eventually developed along the lines of the hybrid manager/impresario role pioneered by Miller. However, where Miller had built his reputation by mounting large theatrical productions like *Hair* and *Jesus Christ Superstar*, Markson began by organising publicity stunts such as pavlova-diving, dwarf-throwing, and the infamous bellyflop diving contest at Pier One in Sydney Harbour where the wharf collapsed and nine people were hospitalised. According to Mike Safe, in these early days Markson became known as 'PR's equivalent to the used car salesman'.[43] By 1986, Markson had branched out into sports management, starting with the Mean Machine, the gold medal–winning freestyle relay team from the Moscow Olympics. By 1988, he was concentrating on celebrities, albeit mainly sportspersons such as Jane Flemming and Greg Matthews. In 1994, he attracted notoriety when he and Flemming launched the 'Golden Girls' calendar, which translated the fashion for male pin-up calendars featuring footballers or firemen into a fashion for female celebs exploiting outlets other than the traditional men's magazine for stylish, arty, or 'tasteful', nude photo shoots.

By the end of the 1980s, the celebrity industry had established itself. The trade in celebrities is the topic of a Lenore Nicklin article in the *Bulletin* in 1989. According to her, the opportunities available had grown to the point where, as Rogers had predicted, they outstripped the supply of local celebrities: 'Newspaper and magazine editors and television producers are facing a serious personality shortage. The readers are there, the advertisers are there, but it's the people to write about and point cameras at – that are the problem. There are not enough personalities – let alone full blown celebrities – to go around.'[44] Our interviews with industry personnel suggest that the expansion of consumer interest that Nicklin's article reflects has been even greater during the second half of the 1990s. Sue-Ellen Topfer, once editor of the teen magazine *Dolly*, has noticed an exponential change: 'In my days at *Dolly* [1993] ... out of 124 pages we would run four pages of celebrities. Now *Dolly* is almost 60% [celebrities].' Mair suggests that the expansion of interest reflects a change in the way the culture views celebrities:

TRACEY MAIR: As American stars, in particular television stars, have become more and more famous as individuals rather than as actors, or for their programs, [this] culture has seeped into Australia. [This has been] particularly generated by the women's magazines ... [It] was necessary for women's magazines to develop home-grown stars to talk about because they can't rely entirely on everything from the US.

Mair says that the trend has now spread beyond the women's magazines as television networks 'are much more inclined to put their people out there in the firing line', and as we see related changes in newspaper content, such as the introduction of 'lifestyle' sections: 'Both the Sundays in Sydney have launched colour magazines as well. They've got to fill the pages, and there's really been no diminution in the public's desire to read about the lives of celebrities.' As a result, there are more celebrities and agents in the market and the beginnings of a star system in both television and film.

The disadvantages of using celebrity endorsement have become apparent, too. At the beginning of 1999, cricketer Ricky Ponting became newsworthy because of his drunken behaviour in a Sydney nightclub. His contract to promote Nestlé's Milo was put at risk and discussion in the industry about the dangers of endorsements ensued, with much reference to O. J. Simpson's contract with Hertz. Harry M. Miller was quoted as advocating intensive research about the private lives of potential endorsers: 'When Maggie Tabberer joined Black and Decker the company did all the work before she joined'.[45]

What are the factors which have contributed to this change in the importance of celebrity in popular culture? Of course, these shifts – the drift towards celebrity and lifestyle journalism – are not confined to Australia. They are symptoms of a change in the function of journalism across the western media.[46] Further, the increasing importance of the media within western democratic societies, both as an industry and as the location for the performance of a public consciousness,[47] is also implicated here. While it might be tempting to see this as a dramatically new phenomenon in Australia, and while it might be tempting to regard the appeal of celebrity journalism as a relatively sudden eruption influenced by the local effects of media globalisation, the development of this interest and the industry which supplies it has been more gradual and progressive than such an analysis would imply. One can see early evidence of the use of scandal in the case of Lola Montez, performing in vaudeville halls on the Victorian goldfields in the nineteenth century and publicly threatening to whip the editor of the (Ballarat) *Courier* who had made disparaging remarks about her. One could also note J. C. Williamson's importation of international theatre performers (often offered to the Australian public as 'stars' solely on the basis of their overseas origins) during the middle of this century.

What are most significant for our purposes here, however, are the changes in the scale, focus and intensity of publicity that commenced in Australia with the introduction of television in 1956 and built up gradually over the 1960s and 1970s. During this period, Australian celebrities certainly existed but they were fewer in number and lower in profile. The systems which placed them at the centre of public attention were less formal, less industrially structured, less dominated by the interests of the media and entertainment industries, and much, much smaller. For instance, a category of Australian celebrity which has now virtually disappeared (indeed, the organisation which produced it is winding up in 2000), but which was prominent in the 1950s and 1960s, was composed of the winners of the annual Miss Australia Quest. Most baby boomers would be able to recall the name of at least one winner of this competition during their childhood or teenage years but probably not since then. The name most likely to be recalled is that of Tania Verstak, a first-generation Russian migrant whose parents were refugees from Communist China, who became a highly visible Miss Australia (and, subsequently, Miss International) in 1961 and an important influence on the acceptance of what was then described as the 'New Australian'. Even for a Miss Australia, Verstak's celebrity was exceptional for the time, and the level of media attention she attracted almost unprecedented.

1956 is a year which always figures in discussions of Australia's embrace of an internationalising modernity. It was the year television arrived, the year of the Melbourne Olympics, the year teenagers rioted in cinemas while watching their first rock'n'roll band on the screen (Bill Haley and the Comets) in *Blackboard Jungle*, and so on. An account of the modern development of the Australian celebrity could probably begin around this time, too, with the sudden invention of the teenager in the mid-1950s – as a marketing category, as a target audience, as a social problem, and as the key consumer of stories about the stars of television, the music industry, and the movies. The *Australian Women's Weekly* introduced its teenagers' supplement in 1954, 'anticipating the full-blooded market trend by at least a year'.[48] It was turned into a liftout magazine called 'Teenagers' Weekly' in 1959, responding to what had become a clearly defined market for coverage of teen fashion, music and television. It entered an environment in which the first Australian rock'n'rollers were earning public recognition; where the high-profile Sydney promoter Lee Gordon was booking American rock'n'roll performers into Australian stadiums; where the local surf club dance was drawing turnaway crowds of teenagers; where radio formats were now dominated by the 'Top 40' and presented by disc jockeys with names like Ward 'Pally' Austin and Mad Mel who completely identified with their teenage audience's interest in rock'n'roll; where fashions could now be bought in the shades of Sinatra Red, [Guy] Mitchell Blue and Presley Purple; where *Bandstand* and *6 O'Clock Rock* were creating a television audience for local pop musicians; where 'juvenile delinquency' and teenage fashion were provoking regular moral panics; and where *77 Sunset Strip*'s Edd 'Kookie' Byrnes' identifying mannerism of continually combing his hair was copied by teenage boys all around the country. This is the period in which Australia embraced American popular culture with enthusiasm and then set about finding ways to indigenise it. It is hard to imagine more fertile soil for the kinds of developments we are tracing here.

The main cultural shifts with the potential to produce celebrities during the 1960s related to the production of local television drama. Crawfords Productions' police series *Homicide*, which started in 1964, was the first local drama to outrate American imports and, on the strength of this success, the company produced two other top-rating crime shows, *Division 4* and *Matlock Police*. Although the lead actors in these programs were highly popular, there was no industrial system in place to support their promotion. Crawfords was purely a Melbourne production house (rather than an operation like a Hollywood studio) and there was no national television network to coordinate and benefit from publicity for the programs. The same could be said to apply to undoubtedly the most prominent and talented television star of the period: *In Melbourne Tonight*'s Graham Kennedy. Far from achieving a national profile as a result of the work of publicists, Kennedy's national fame owed much to his intermittent and enthusiastically reported encounters with the regulatory body, the Australian Broadcasting Control Board, over alleged obscenity.

It is possible to nominate other figures from successful local television programs who were highly visible for periods of time through the 1960s and 1970s: the stars from the successful soap *Number 96*, for instance, especially Abigail. However, as we move forward into the 1970s and 1980s, it is possible to specify a number of key structural and systemic developments which seem to have especially influenced the production of the Australian celebrity: the revival of the film industry required the marketing of Australian films to the home audience and overseas; the development of a successful recording industry for Australian pop and rock music was built on the marketing of specific artists and the development of their public image; and the youth audience for locally produced television soap opera provided a clear marketing opportunity for television networks aiming to cement their programs into Australian audiences' daily routines.

When the federal government began to invest in the revival of the film industry at the end of the 1960s and expanded its level of support throughout the 1970s, there was initially no audience for Australian film. There had been occasional locally produced films, or co-productions set in Australia, which had attracted large audiences over the previous decade (the *Smiley* films, for instance), but there was no existing framework of stars and genres which would help the new industry reach its audiences in a businesslike manner. Furthermore, while the number of local films increased throughout the first half of the 1970s, they were usually produced by one-off companies with little capacity for long-term marketing support and certainly no capacity for what would now be called industry development. It fell to the new institutions, such as the Australian Film Commission and the various state film commissions, to market the local product, to nurture the profiles of local actors and to generate audience interest in Australian cinema. This occurred at a time when those professions dealing with publicity in Australia were in their infancy; where they existed they were connected to the theatre or to television. The development of the film industry expanded the opportunities available for this kind of work.

A number of the publicists we talked to had worked with the Australian Film Commission or on specific film projects during this period. Most significant in this regard was Rea Francis, who was the public relations and marketing officer for the commission from 1976 to 1981. This was something of a golden period, during which the success of director Peter Weir and actors Jack Thompson and Judy Davis attracted local and international attention. But this level of attention did not happen by itself. Francis recalls that her job was to 'put Australia on the map internationally' by lobbying to get local films into competition at the Cannes Film Festival. To capitalise on the glamour associated with the festival, an event that was in any case a key marketing avenue for Australian films, she would take a contingent of the Australian press to Cannes with her. There they would see Australian stars responding to the international media attention it was her job to create. Francis' role, throughout the festival, was multifaceted. She would adopt the party/event-oriented mode of promotion customary there to attract buyers and to give Australian films a high profile (a combination of publicity and public relations). Through the cultivation of government representatives visiting the festival, she fed what she called the 'Australian political ego' by using the glamour and status of Cannes to demonstrate the effectiveness of government investment in film as an export and nation-building enterprise (in this capacity, operating pretty much as a lobbyist). And she also used the spectacular display of celebrity at the festival as a source of publicity for audiences back home, 'feeding public interest in Australian personalities'. It was a continual and complex process which 'built up the star system here'. A Cannes appearance provided the overseas validation of local celebrity in a way that has continued to be important not only in the continued use of the festival in particular (central in the public careers of Jane Campion and Toni Collette, for example), but also in the way in which success in an overseas forum can readily be translated into local celebrity.

Agent Gary Stewart's view is sympathetic to this account, although it shows a greater complexity in the way 'overseas' was mobilised. He presented a picture of the 1970s, in particular, as a period when the combination of the revival of the film industry and the 'TV–Make It Australian' campaign (which

contested the domination of local television by imported programs) generated real momentum in support of the development of the local film and
television production industry. As a result, the work was there for his actors,
the work they won was highly publicised, and the Australian audiences'
interest in Australian material was established and reinforced. For his own
part, Stewart says, 'I managed to get the actors and get them into films and
the series and away we went'.

While several of the publicists we spoke to agreed that the development of
the local film industry contributed to the growth in publicity over the 1970s
and 1980s, and that the local production industry operated as a training
ground for many people who would end up working as publicists or public
relations consultants in other sectors of the media and entertainment
industries, there are limits, even now, to how wholeheartedly the Australian
film industry uses the full range of publicity outlets available to it. Tracey
Mair chooses to work for 'quality' production outlets such as the ABC or
Southern Star, rather than commercial television, because she 'cares about
film and quality production'. For her, the kind of celebrity promotion the
commercials use to support their projects often 'trivialises': 'I resent the fact
that so often the interest is in somebody's personal life and not the work
they do'. So, while she has 'worked very hard at making Australian films
interesting to the media', and feels that she has been able to build up 'a touch
of respect' there, she is very wary about exploiting such avenues of publicity
as the women's magazines. As such, she is representative of the dominant
culture within Australian film which remains uncomfortable with celebrity or
star-based publicity and which wants to foreground 'the project' as an artistic,
rather than merely a commercial, activity.

One result of this is that most Australian film is regarded as 'arthouse' and
is released in the smaller (and less profitable) independent cinemas. The
difficulty of doing otherwise is detailed by Mary Anne Reid in her examination of the campaign to get *Strictly Ballroom* into mainstream cinemas, a
campaign that hinged on its successful reception at Cannes.[49] In this respect,
the film industry differs from the television industry:

> BRIAN WALSH: The film industry in this country ... has been very
> much based on its work and its creative base. It has never really
> fallen into the Hollywood sausage factory [model], in terms of
> PR and publicity. That is why I think the industry is so well
> regarded around the world. That the people who make films in
> this country are passionate film-makers and are not driven
> necessarily by Hollywood success, but by film success. [Although]
> the directors, producers and stars are ... hotly sought after ...
> these films are created within a culture that is very proud of its
> individual approach to film-making. That's very different to the

television industry in Australia which … primarily went [through] that period of soap success and created stars overnight. Jason and Kylie were always going to be much more popular in this country to the press than, say, Sam Neill or Judy Davis. And that's simply because the machine driving television in Australia is a very different machine to that driving the film industry.

As we will see, many publicists may have trained in the film industry but the greater opportunities for employment have led them to the television industry.

It is in television that the most substantial investment in celebrity-driven publicity has occurred. Early fan magazines imported from the United States were dominated by American television stars, as were the Australian TV guide magazines such as *TV Week* and the now-defunct *TV Times*. Teenage audiences, in particular (as noted earlier, a market which was influenced in Australia by the close temporal conjunction of the arrival of both television and rock'n'roll),[50] have been interested in television stars. So, it is probably not too surprising that some of our interviewees nominated the promotion of *Neighbours* to teen audiences in the mid-1980s as representing a defining moment in the marketing of Australian celebrities. As Stewart said, 'The networks with *Neighbours* went into overdrive, in the end you were beaten to death. They were on Cornflakes packets and all kinds of things.'

The key strategy, and the one which seems to have been most successful in establishing the young soap stars as celebrities, was the shopping centre appearance:

> GARY STEWART: The networks were kind of promoting the series by taking them [soap stars] up into shopping centres on weekends and signing autographs and being seen. I mean, young kids took off on it really. It was a series they identified with, the same age group, they were getting thousands of people into shopping centres to look at the local talent.

Stewart, who was Jason Donovan's agent over this period (1986–87), dealt with much of this directly: making the booking, invoicing the shopping centre, organising security, booking the limo, and so on. The fee appears to have been around $5000–$7000 a time, enough to make it worthwhile (it had to be fitted into the performer's shooting schedule and was often interstate).

The real driving force behind this strategy, though, was Brian Walsh, the Ten Network publicist at the time:

> BRIAN WALSH: We did shopping mall appearances every Thursday night and every Saturday. We must have had about six or eight

Neighbours promotions running in other newspapers, radio, across television, just to get the awareness factor up. And ... I knew that the show had potential because when we did the shopping mall appearances there were literally hundreds and hundreds of young kids that would come along to get a glimpse of the stars. The ensemble cast consisted of ... eight, nine young people and six or seven older actors but I could see the real groundswell was coming around the young actors and, in particular, Kylie Minogue, who played a character called Charlene (who was a bit of a tomboy character in the show), and Jason [Donovan]. who was a young, blond, good-looking kid.

For Kylie and Jason, these appearances made them into genuine stars, known as much for their celebrity as for what they did as performers. For most of the large number of young soap stars who have succeeded them, however, their celebrity has been much more categorically linked to their appearances on the soap. As we will see in Chapter 4, the celebrity produced by such strategies as the shopping mall tours has its downside when media interest is suddenly withdrawn.

Once it demonstrated that Australians would come out to see their own stars in the flesh, the shopping mall appearance was widely used to promote other kinds of entertainers and personalities, such as high-profile sporting figures. Popular music stars also employed this tactic. Working to an audience too young to go to the pubs, and lacking the credibility to make it in these core venues in any case, pop acts faced some difficulty in building up a grassroots audience through live performances. Rock manager Peter Rix recalls taking his band, Hush, to a range of under-18 venues – from the local civic centre to Sydney's Hordern Pavilion – in the attempt to find their youthful audience. To music promoters during the mid-1980s, the shopping malls presented an ideal location. Up until then, Rix points out, the only musical performances in malls were by 'Kamahl, at the Raindrop Fountain in Roselands singing versions of his Mother's Day album'. That changed when the industry noted the methods used to promote American singer Debbie Gibson:

PETER RIX: She would go and play these big American shopping malls and ten thousand people would come along and half of them would go and buy the album afterwards ... Then some record companies worked out that you didn't need to have major radio airplay. If you had somebody out there who did five shopping centres a week in various parts of America, you could chart the record.

It is a tactic that is still around, and most recently employed by the American group, Hanson. Inevitably, in Australia, there was a convergence in the kind of star and product promoted in the shopping centres. It did not take long for the record companies to become interested in cashing in on those television soap stars who had already become shopping centre celebrities.

This was not the first instance of such a close relationship between teen-agers, television and popular music. In Australia, the local production of rock'n'roll occurred on television well before it ever made it to vinyl. The first phase of development of the local music industry in the 1950s occurred through television music shows: ABC-TV's *6 O'Clock Rock*, starring pioneer-ing Australian rocker Johnny O'Keefe, and Nine's much more wholesome *Bandstand*, hosted by Brian Henderson.[51] Teenage rock audiences were addressed through the 1960s and 1970s by *GTK*, *Sounds* and *Countdown*, before being thoroughly indulged by the multiple MTV look-alikes which dominated youth television programming in the 1980s. Almost from its inception in Australia, television had used popular music as a means of attracting a teenage audience. Teenagers constituted a highly desirable market demographic (until recently, the most desirable, but now they have been overtaken by the high-spending 'young adults'). They were a high-consuming fraction of society and thus a target for advertisers. Unfortunately, television is the one medium of which teenagers consume progressively less from the age of 14 onwards (they increase their consumption of film, and radio remains roughly static).

The desirability of winning back this audience is reflected in the television industry's interest in youth music forms, but this interest began to slowly shift away from music and towards the teenage soaps during the late 1980s (assisted by the pay-for-play dispute which eventually wiped out most of the music video shows). The cultural associations which had already connected youth audiences with television and with popular music – both of them definitively suburban cultural forms – developed another set of suburban connections, as the teenage soap fans followed their stars into the shopping mall. Building on this complex of relationships and modifying them for the late 1980s, then, the Australian recording company Mushroom saw enough market potential to put their rock credibility on the line when they produced Kylie Minogue's first single, 'Locomotion'. While their credibility did suffer for a time, no one doubted the commercial astuteness of the move. Many other soap stars were to attempt to achieve the same kind of success and for a few, most recently Natalie Imbruglia, it paid off.

This was not the only, nor even the most effective, means of establishing oneself within the popular music industry at the time. The role of radio airplay and, increasingly, exposure on *Countdown* or one of the many music video programs which went to air during the mid-1980s exercised a dominant influence on record sales. Further, the shopping mall strategy was employed most often for pop artists promoting singles, rather than for album-oriented or rock acts. (Over this period, there was a relatively clear division between the pop and rock sectors of the industry and musical credibility really only attached to the rock end. In this, Australia was not alone. Simon Frith, among others, has written at length about the fundamental political contradiction between television and rock.)[52]

Although long-term success in the music industry was not particularly likely to spring from these beginnings, as a means of generating a profile as a celebrity it worked very well. The perceived tension between being known for one's work and being known for one's private life continues in this arena too. But it is important to remember that this was occurring at a time when the Australian rock and pop music industry, overall, was thriving and highly visible: it was enjoying enormous international success through such bands as INXS, Midnight Oil and AC/DC, while Australian artists were dominating the sales charts at home; it had developed a strong local touring circuit which enabled Australian acts, from Cold Chisel to John Farnham, to sell out the big concert halls; and the pub rock scene was operating as a first-rate training ground and marketing structure. As with the film industry, the music industry in the 1980s provided early opportunities for people who now work in publicity across the various media forms. Louise Carroll, for instance, started out marketing Australian music in the early 1980s, when 'we had 20 good strong Australian artists who could fill a Festival Hall', before moving into publicity and corporate public relations.

This account of the rise of Australian celebrity would not necessarily be unanimously endorsed by those working within the media and publicity industries. Some argue persuasively that, notwithstanding the growth in the volume of publicity for Australian stars, there is still an overwhelming preference for overseas celebrities. Topfer suggested that the lure of America still dominated our teenagers' imaginations:

> SUE-ELLEN TOPFER: Australian teenagers are more American driven … It's always this image that you live in Hollywood and, you know, it's so cool … We love to support our Australian talent, we all want Australian talent to do well but most Australian teenagers are like, 'Well, I can do that, I can be on *Neighbours* but, oh my God, imagine if I was on *90210!*'

Suzie MacLeod has spent a lot of her time looking after Hollywood stars doing promotional tours. In comparison, it can be 'quite hard to sell Australian stars because … we are so in awe of American and Hollywood stars … we can't actually believe that we're capable of having somebody that big'. Publishers can also find it easier to arrange media interviews with overseas writers:

> ANDREW FREEMAN: Australian authors are much more difficult to get publicity for. People in the media will talk to an overseas novelist because they are an overseas novelist, or because they've got a name that people will know even if they haven't read any of their books, they can talk about something with them. Quite often they'll talk about American politics.

As that example suggests, the Australian celebrity remains definitively domestic while they continue to live in Australia.

While the international star jetting in for a whirlwind round of interviews and personal appearances is accorded automatic celebrity status here, signs of interest from the outside world themselves still provide the material for publicity. Recent newspaper articles about the previously unknown Sydney author, Suneeta da Costa Peres, hinged entirely on the sale of her first novel to an American publisher. Notwithstanding the advantages of an overseas profile, however, our research establishes that, where once the Australian celebrity was virtually an empty category, they are now among the most visible signs of individuality and success in Australian popular culture. They are also signs of the success of publicity and, as such, have contributed to the extension of promotional culture from the entertainment industry into other sections of society.

Spreading the word: The normalisation of publicity

> I think a publicist has to work damn hard for their money because there [are] so many [kinds] of people using publicity.
> *Louise Carroll*

There is no shortage of evidence of the importance of publicity across the media and entertainment industries, not only in ensuring that individuals or projects reach their audiences but also in deciding which individuals or projects to take on in the first place. Literary agent Anthony Williams says that the first question a commercial publisher asks about a prospective author is: 'Is he or she promotable?'. 'By that they mean, how are they going to go on the talk show guest circuit, *Midday*', and so on. These days, Williams says wryly, 'they've got to be able to tap dance as well as write'. This correctly implies that there is now far less choice about whether or not an artist involves themselves in publicity. That has not always been the case. Theatrical agent Barbara Leane recalls actors such as Judy Davis refusing point-blank for many years to do publicity ('I will not speak to the press, they are charlatans, they are terrible people', says Leane, imitating Davis), before suddenly agreeing to 'do the odd one'. That choice is probably less available now. Doing publicity for their projects is commonly regarded as an actor's responsibility and is usually stipulated and enforced within their employment contract.

The enfolding of publicity within news has also become normalised. This has not only occurred in the manner suggested earlier – through a submersion of the publicity process in order to make the item saleable as news in the first place – but also through a restructuring of news values to include the unashamed exploitation of public interest in celebrities. Bunty Avieson, who as editor of *New Idea* is in a good position to comment on this, cited the example of Kylie Minogue's 1998 MTV award making the evening television news: 'The national 6 o'clock news is running footage of Kylie winning an award. [This is] a big change from 10 years ago.' The change in the visibility and the perceived importance of such stories has been assisted by a broad acceptance of the need to directly address a market that had previously been left to the mass-market women's magazines. As Avieson says, because these magazines have been so 'phenomenally successful, they're all having a go at it'. As a result, the field is becoming increasingly congested. There is intense competition from all sides – between outlets for stories, and between publicists for access.

While in some areas, Freeman argues, the avenues for product-based publicity may have begun to close up, celebrity remains a highly tradable commodity. Evidencing the increase in the general level of publicity are those spin-off industries which feed off the public profile developed by individuals through their performances in another arena of activity. Where celebrities once earned their living doing the things for which they were celebrated, today this earning power may be dwarfed by that of their endorsing a product or service.[53] In the case of high-profile athletes in so-called amateur sport, such as Susie O'Neill or Kieren Perkins, this is their primary method of providing for their financial security after their sporting careers conclude. Another avenue is the speaking engagement. Winston Broadbent reports 70–80 requests a week for celebrity speakers for conferences, conventions, and the like. His organisation is now the sixth largest of its kind in the world and his speakers demand single-appearance fees of thousands of dollars. And it has been reported that certain celebrities charge a fee for their attendance at parties or promotional events. According to a *Courier-Mail* story, 'rent-a-celebs' are paid hundreds or even thousands of dollars simply to turn up at a function for an hour by promoters desperate to attract media coverage.[54] None of our interviewees mentioned this practice.

There are many other kinds of commercial ventures which ride on the back of an achieved celebrity. A great deal of the work of publishing, for example, involves generating commercial projects and this can include 'making writers out of celebrities', as in the case of Cheryl Kernot's biography:

> ANDREW FREEMAN: That's taking a personality and making a book out of it ... Quite often our publishing department will go to somebody who's high profile and say, 'Do you want to write a book, doesn't necessarily have to be a biography, or it can be thoughts on something?'. Quite often [we] go to a radio personality and say, 'People might want to know your thoughts on things'.

There are some constraints, though, on this practice that are peculiar to the publishing industry, because 'not only do you try to make your authors celebrities, you try and make them ... experts. Because writing is seen as a very substantial activity, and writers on subjects are always seen to be more worth talking to.' That factor does circumscribe decisions about which celebrities are going to be promotable as writers.

There is an incremental expansion under way whereby the processes of publicity which have developed primarily around the entertainment and media industries have come to permeate other areas of endeavour. There are now small private schools with publicity officers, for example. The increasingly widespread sense that publicity is required for all kinds of different activities, not just show business, multiplies the number of people competing for column inches, for spots on the television shows, for a market. On some occasions, it can get completely out of hand: Louise Carroll remarked, for instance, that at one Michael Jackson press conference she attended there were more publicists than media. The spread of publicity and celebrity management has had particularly dramatic effects on professional sport. We could talk about this at the level of the individual: the importance of a personal manager for Shane Warne or a network publicist for Sam Newman or Paul Vautin. However, there are more expansive examples of the integration between promotional culture and sport.

Brian Walsh was the man responsible for successfully re-branding the sport of rugby league as suitable for family consumption. He planned the Tina Turner promotions of the late 1980s – the promotions which made rugby league look attractive enough for Rupert Murdoch to attempt to buy the game. Walsh took on the task of promoting the NSW Rugby League in 1987, at a time when the sport was going through a bad period. It wasn't attracting crowds, and the level of violence evident on the field (and fundamental to the game) made a lot of parents reluctant to let their children play it. The NSW

Rugby League wanted a change of image. Walsh's positioning strategy was, at first, similar to the methods he used with the soap stars: he created celebrity around a particular personality chosen to represent the game. His 'role model' was Wayne Pearce, a footballer 'who was articulate, presentable, would be attractive to women, all those things'. He started up football clinics that Pearce would take to schools, shopping malls, and so on.

Next was a more traditional marketing move: finding a piece of music for the television ads which would appeal to a broader demographic than was currently being reached. Tina Turner's 'What You Get Is What You See' was used for the 1988 campaign and was so successful that the NSW Rugby League brought Turner out to Australia to participate in the following year's promotion effort, to record the commercials (around the new song, 'Simply the Best'), and then to perform at the Grand Final. Turner, and all she represented, became identified with the game. When Pearce retired from football, he was replaced by Andrew Ettingshausen as the 'face of rugby league'. He was 'young, great looking, articulate, clean image' and, together with Turner, he helped rugby league to substantially reposition itself, leaving behind 'all those negative things' and becoming 'absolutely the hot ticket'. The 'Simply the Best' campaign was outstandingly successful in its exploitation of Turner's celebrity and in its capacity to enhance the celebrity of a large number of photogenic elite players from the rugby league.

The interesting thing about this campaign is that the existing fan-base of the sport was not its primary target. Instead, it addressed a mass audience in order to represent rugby league as spectacular entertainment for the whole family. Importantly, this was also carried over into the presentation of the game, with dancing girls and high-profile music acts at half-time and massive fireworks at the kickoff. 'We brought Hollywood to the football stadiums', says Walsh, unapologetic about this orientation:

> BRIAN WALSH: Some people have been critical of some of my work in sport [but] purists will always follow the game and they will always go there ... [My aim was] to get the broader mass attracted to the game ... I didn't even go near the sports pages. I mean, I rarely spoke to a journalist writing about the game for the game's sake. My objective was to get the sport up the front of the paper, not down the back of the paper. I wanted to get people who are commuting to work on trains and buses and stuff, who read the first ten pages of the paper, to turn onto an identity or a property that I was marketing, and not for the people who were looking for the score to go to the back of the paper. And that's where Tina Turner took us; she took us into a whole new area of selling sport in Australia, and that was my objective.

The point of this is that rugby league changed its social meaning for large numbers of Australians because of a promotional strategy which produced and manipulated celebrity as its primary marketing tactic. The procedures followed by Walsh do not fall neatly into the categories of public relations, publicity or promotion but the campaign required the performance of a range of activities which could be filed under any or all of these categories.

Chapter 3

Producing Celebrity

This chapter has a classificatory objective: to sort out the various activities performed by publicists, agents, managers, and others. Importantly, it hopes to make these activities more visible. Unlike the celebrities they help to produce, those who work in publicity, promotion or management remain relatively private figures. They calculate their professional achievements through the exposure of their clients. How many column inches received in newspaper coverage, which television program appeared in, which magazine did a cover story, or what kind of contract negotiated – these are among the registers of success. Included within this calculation of success, however, is the invisibility of the work required to achieve it. People in this industry work long and hard, but a great deal of effort goes into masking that fact: into blurring the divisions between work and leisure while generating publicity, and between the constructed and the spontaneous in the outcomes. As a result, finding out what work is actually done constitutes an important part of the project of this book.

In a mature manufacturing industry, the delineation of jobs is relatively clear. Even in film production, through a combination of necessary skill development and union regulations, the categories of gaffers and script supervisors, best boys and editors are all well defined in larger productions. However, in the industry that produces Australian celebrities, job categories are in much greater flux. There are distinct names for some categories – agents, managers, publicists – but, on the ground, there is often considerable hybridity and no unequivocally clear system of nomenclature for describing what people actually do.

Unlike Hollywood, where the scale of the industry has necessitated the proliferation of the categories of support required to manage the professional and public careers of the major stars, the Australian industry simply cannot support a great deal of differentiation. Jobs merge into each other and career trajectories take individuals from one sector of the promotions industry to another: Suzie MacLeod of Village Roadshow was in promotions before she moved into publicity; Tracey Mair, who now works mainly as a unit publicist, originally worked for women's magazines as a writer/editor; Georgie Brown has migrated from publicity at television networks to freelance publicity, management and public relations. Several, like Southern Star's Lesna Thomas, have moved from journalism into public (in this case, 'corporate') relations.

What follows has been drawn from our interviews with practitioners, most of whom learnt their craft through on-the-job training. They have been grouped into the categories they use to describe their principal activities. Our objective is not to nail down the categories or to prescribe a more consistent system of nomenclature. Rather, and at the most basic level, we are simply interested in using what our interviewees have told us as a means of describing in some detail the kind of work which goes on endlessly, frenetically, within an industry which depends on masking its processes in order to enhance the magical plausibility of its results.

The agent

> It's very full on and it's very exciting; and some days it can be very frustrating and other days it can be exhilarating. Most days are fantastic.
> *Viccy Harper*

MAKING CONNECTIONS

The oldest and most traditional job in this industry is the agent. There can be any number of adjectives qualifying specific areas of interest – one can be a talent agent, a sports agent, a theatrical agent – but the key task of the agent is to book talent. For this service, the agent receives what has become an international standard: 10% of the talent's fee. The role of Australian agents resembles that of their British and American counterparts and some of the agencies are global in their reach, although the vast majority are very small operations with limited international connections. The William Morris Agency, which began in the early twentieth century in New York and became a major Hollywood entertainment agency, has a small office in Sydney run by Anthony Williams. Trained in the William Morris style, Williams probably typifies the most 'classical' version of an agent in Australia. The traditional name for the craft comes from the pre-film era – Williams is a theatrical agent. In that tradition, the agent, in an unobtrusive dark-suited, white shirt and tie uniform, is an unseen figure who performs the task of getting employer and employee together:

> ANTHONY WILLIAMS: [Theatrical] agent is a slight misnomer – it's what it is known as generally; but we represent actors, writers, directors in film, television, radio and we also represent book writers – fiction, biography, autobiography. And we're basically an employment agency. We find people whom we think that we can represent and sell. And we charge a commission on what we get for them.

Barbara Leane, who has run her own agency in Sydney for twenty years, is a slightly more visible figure in the entertainment scene than the traditional agent. She explains that a new wave of agents arrived in the late 1970s who did much more for their clients than book and pocket their 10% commission. In the pre-1970s era, a few agents such as Gloria Peyton had the market 'sewn up; they didn't have to go out and actively seek work. They could just sit there, the phone would ring ...' The producer and the single agent would simply decide who would be in the production. This relatively cosy arrangement was transformed by the growth in the number of agencies throughout the 1980s and 1990s. Kristin Dale from Faith Martin, a major casting agency, estimates that there are now in excess of 150 agencies in Sydney and Melbourne. The agents who were the product of this highly competitive environment have therefore had to engage in a great deal more promotion of their clients to get them work.

As a result, professional connections to the casting agencies have become a crucial factor both for the aspiring actors and for their agents. Casting consultancies/agencies are on the other side – they work for the producers and the television networks, not the actor. The actor pays the agent to help them cross that divide. Since there may be a glut of agencies, professional reputations are crucial, as they determine which agency an actor will most prefer to represent their interests. For them, a successful agent is the first step to a successful career. The stories of how agents become successful at managing their network of connections are quite varied but often involve the agent having worked previously in some other part of the industry.

Gary Stewart of Melbourne Artists Management (whose clients include *Blue Heelers'* John Wood, and Rachel Griffiths) spent years working in live television productions such as *In Melbourne Tonight*. Sydney-based Kevin Palmer moved from acting to directing live theatre in England and Australia, before managing and then buying an agency:

> KEVIN PALMER: To be quite honest I was an alright director, I wasn't a brilliant director – but I mean being a director sometimes is not

being brilliant. Being a director is learning how to drive traffic on the stage and be able to talk to actors and communicate with actors. I was at an age where you thought, well, what else do you do. I wanted to stay in the industry so the best thing was to look for another sort of niche.

Palmer's ability to communicate with actors as a director as well as his wealth of production experience has helped to make him a successful agent, with a client list which includes Penny Cooke and Eden Gaha. Williams relied on his legal training in his move into the world of entertainment and agents. Leane began with an advertising agency and then occasional work with one of the key casting agents in the early 1970s to get a firm grasp of what being an agent entailed. She made contacts and developed what she now describes as her key asset: 'people skills'. Viccy Harper, of Hilary Linstead and Associates, worked her way into her position as director from being a receptionist when much of the firm's work was that of a casting agency. June Cann, the *grande dame* of Australian theatrical agents, was the script girl on the film *Eureka Stockade* and then did extensive voice-over work for the ABC before establishing her agency. Rebecca Williamson, who works with Cann, with her economics degree and her extensive family background in the arts (her father is the playwright David Williamson, and her brother is the actor Felix Williamson) had roots in the industry prior to becoming an agent.

As these examples indicate, broad backgrounds in the industry are undoubtedly helpful. The demands of making an agency a viable operation force the most traditional theatrical agency to recognise that they must understand the full range of possible forms of employment for their clients:

> GARY STEWART: We cover all drama. We cover radio, film, television, theatre, commercials – we have to do the lot to survive really … I think most actors need to be able to do just about anything to make a reasonable living out of it. They must be able to voice-over commercials, if they sing and dance it helps. They've got to be good actors and we just kind of feed them into all those areas.

For the writer or the performer who loves the theatre, there is still the monetary pressure to do film or television. Palmer commented wryly that '10% [commission] of nothing is nothing', and indicated that 70% of an actor's 'income is in front of a camera one way or another'. Musical theatre, although infrequent and limited to large-scale productions, pays reasonably well; Harper explained that, in the post-10BA subsidisation of the film industry,[1] her firm became more focused on cabaret and musical theatre performance and they now represent a large part of the talent that performs, writes and directs for that market (they handled *Tap Dogs*, for instance).

The day-to-day running of an agency demonstrates the high level of involvement required to stay in touch with the industry. All the agents interviewed considered phones and faxes as virtual extensions of their bodies. Much like the talent scout for professional sports, the agent is always looking for new talent and therefore must attend a great number of plays, receptions and launches to keep connected to the industry and to read what it needs. Stewart went through his daybook for us to outline a typical 'day-in-the-life'. On the day we spoke to him, he was trying to circulate some photographs and biographies of Cerrian Clements, who was in the cast of *Les Miserables* in Melbourne for six months but wanted it to be known that she was available during that time for casual television work. He had to ring a contact for tickets to *Chicago*; he indicated that he had no clients in the musical but it was obvious that it was a scouting exercise. There were continuing discussions over a new contract with an actor (Jane Menelaus) who was in a play with the Melbourne Theatre Company. And he was preparing videotapes for four of his clients to send to the producers of a television lifestyle program who were seeking a new presenter. Stewart revealed that he has a backroom of videotapes of his actors; many of them he prepared himself from hours of television tape and dubbed on to individual show reels. He remarked that glossy photographs and a bio will get you in the door, but in the current state of play you need the videotape ready to send to secure a screen test.

This level of involvement is typical of what Barbara Leane calls the 'new-wave' agent. (The generational divide between traditional and new-wave agents is also dealt with in Chapter 4.) The new-wave agent (or agent–manager) can be involved at a very personal level: Williamson acknowledged that she may be called upon for mundane support services, such as picking up her clients at the airport, and Harper admitted that she has had to make chicken soup for a client. As she recognises, this suggests that she has crossed a line into career or personal management: 'As an agent, you're a surrogate mother. We have to deal with mid-life crises sometimes. You have to deal with so much stuff because it all affects the bottom line – which is their careers.'

The new-wave agent – a response to the expansion in the size of the celebrity industry in Australia – provides probably the key example of job hybridisation. Their activities have expanded so that they now perform an analogous role to that of personal managers in the American entertainment industry.

AGENTS AS SCOUTS

One of the realities of the entertainment industry in Australia and elsewhere is that it operates on a massive surplus of labour. Unemployment for actors in Australia is a fact of life. Palmer admits that 'if you want to live comfortably you don't become an actor', and yet there is a swelling potential pool of actors to draw upon. He identified a real compulsion beyond the necessary ego ('that you are the most important person in the world at any moment') that operates 'like a drug that [the actor] cannot live without once they decide that's what they are'. The cultural value assigned to public performance of one kind or another is implicated in the constancy of this desire (but that may be another story).

Agents are part of a massive filtration system for the entertainment industry. According to Williams, many publishers also now prefer to handle only authors who have an agent. Stewart described dealing personally with at least half-a-dozen tapes a week from potential new clients – and these were the ones which were not screened out before they reached him. Similarly, Palmer received twenty to thirty letters each week requesting representation. The reality of this surplus of aspiring actors was reinforced by the number of times our interviews were interrupted by a cold call from an unknown, unrepresented talent.

The tertiary education system has built on these expanding aspirations. Initially, there was only the National Institute of Dramatic Art (NIDA), which accepted twenty-five students a year. After the Western Australia Academy of Performing Arts and the Victorian College of the Arts established competing programs in the 1980s, virtually every university and many TAFEs have developed drama studies courses and programs which service and reinforce the desire for an acting career. While this might seem out of all proportion to the opportunities available, these programs have been surprisingly comprehensively integrated into the industry system. Most agents we talked to considered it a sign of commitment if a new client has trained for three years at a given institute. In the filtering game, most of the agents follow the graduating class from NIDA very closely to see whether they want to represent any of them. Like a debutantes' ball, their final showcase performances are attended by agents looking for future stars. Because many agents come from a theatrical tradition, they expect that training for the stage will provide the necessary range of skills that a future client needs for television or film. An odd anomaly in the training system is that there are few courses on film and television acting, even though this is likely to provide around 70% of their students' future income. Most agents we spoke with were drawn to performers who could act, sing and, preferably, dance as well. This implied what could be regarded as a slightly anachronistically vaudevillian model of the entertainment industry, where versatility was central and the capacity to perform credibly on stage was the issue rather than a specific set of skills.

Even with the best eye and the best contacts, however, it is a high-risk business. Agents deal with this by serving a surplus of clients:

> BARBARA LEANE: Well, I had this dream … Wouldn't it be wonderful just to look after 50 people. That was the dream, totally

impractical dream – totally, totally impractical dream. You can only charge, well, 10%. You're never going to get rich on 10%. The only way you're going to make any money on 10% is if you're fortunate enough to get someone in a big American movie with a lot of money, or a good ongoing American series.

At the time of our interview, Marcus Graham, the star of *Good Guys/Bad Guys*, was Leane's international hope as he had just completed a US television series, *City to City*, in Miami.

Other agencies are forced to play the same numbers game. Palmer's two-person agency was lined with photographs of his clients – hundreds of images – and yet he will only take on those who have theatrical training and who pass the test of his 'gut feeling'. Not all agents are looking for raw talent. Stewart might consider a potential client if they are good-looking; they can be employed in television commercials regularly because, often, this is all that is needed in a typical soap-advertisement shower scene.

As Stewart suggests, the choice of who gets the roles is at least partially determined by looks. This influence on casting is reinforced through *Showcast* (a massive casting book composed of glossy industry photographs of actors and performers, and their credits). As scripts and casting calls go out, the agent is part of the first screening process, determining who should be sent to the audition. Depending on the strength of their links with casting services and directors, a specific agent will begin to have a certain amount of influence in a certain sphere of production. So, agents themselves are also filtered. Leane felt that she had 'made it' (that she had the confidence of casting consultants, producers and directors) when she started receiving scripts to read. This exposure to the script gives her and therefore her clients an inside track, enhancing their chance of being employed on projects. Other, less well-connected, agents will be responding to general audition calls, where knowledge of the characters required will be much more restricted. As a result of this process, a level of specialisation can develop. Consequently, Stewart was more comfortable with musical performers, while Leane tended to represent actors. Other agents, not interviewed, specialised in getting extras and, presumably, one of their key skills was getting the right look for that shampoo commercial.

Considering that the agents interviewed readily agreed that the number of agencies had grown exponentially in the last twenty years, competition for talent must constitute a major part of their daily work. They generally denied the practice of poaching – after all, the Drama Agents Association forbids the practice. However, there was some finessing about whether someone had been poached (the jilted agent's position) or had looked for a new agent (the lucky agent). Leane, while protesting her innocence of poaching, indicated that Marcus Graham is a new client who has proven to be very lucrative for her. Williams suggested that the practice was common, if not routine: 'There are one or two agents who are enthusiastically poaching, particularly amongst ... the glamorous sort of playwrights or writers'.

THE CONTRACTS

Although most agents do not have any legal training, at the heart of their responsibilities to a client is the contract. Leane acknowledges that much of her job consists of working out contracts and determining whether they are in the best interest of her client; but she laments her lack of legal qualifications and envies Williams his training as a lawyer. Hilary Linstead and Associates finally hired an entertainment lawyer because of the proportion of their business that is fundamentally concerned with their clients' contractual obligations. Most learn on the job, and much of what they learn is about the requirements of different kinds of performances. Television contracts, for instance, may not pay much up front, but, as Stewart explained, the key factor is 'residuals': the income earned from repeated screenings and sales of the vehicle for that performance. This complicates matters for the agent attempting to set a price for an actor in a television commercial, for instance; it is hard to determine the long-term value of each performance. The requirements of a particular career, too, may influence the agent's judgement about which or how many contracts to pursue. Stewart points out that he has to be selective about which endorsement or merchandising contract he advises *Blue Heelers* star John Wood to accept. Not only is over-exposure an issue for this actor, but he has also to be aware that any contract he signs now must help him deal with a period of virtual unemployability when he leaves the television series.

The level of involvement implied by the orchestration of Wood's public profile marks Stewart as occupying a transition point between the traditional and the new-wave agent. Like a manager, the new-wave agent may be involved in career building as opposed to just taking whatever money or deal is on offer. Rebecca Williamson explained the process that the actor/presenter Kimberley Joseph went through in working out her *Gladiators* television deal with Channel 7. Joseph had begun appearing irregularly on *Hey Hey It's Saturday* after the retirement of Ozzie Ostrich (Ernie Carroll). Her previous work had been as an actor on the soap opera *Paradise Beach*, but as a friend of Daryl Somers she had taken this casual, uncontracted work with his program. Although there were intimations that it might become regular, there had been no contract signed with Channel 9. In the intervening time, Channel 7 – possibly in a move to embarrass Channel 9 – had drawn up a contract for Joseph to appear in the first series of *Gladiators*. Williamson, acting as her agent, encouraged Joseph to sign the *Gladiators* contract.

The repercussions of that signing meant that the Nine Network had lost her services, just as they were using her to advertise *Hey Hey* (and promoting her in a story in *TV Week*). Williamson attempted to shield Joseph from the small-scale publicity scandal that the defection produced, as well as from Somers' wrath. Joseph did well financially through *Gladiators*, but it became clear to her agent that she wanted to return to acting, not presenting; she also did not want to become what Williamson described as 'a Seven girl', where she was contracted to perform or present whatever they were developing. Even though Channel 7 offered a longer development contract, Joseph turned it down in favour of greater autonomy and career independence. And she made a relatively successful transition back to acting through appearing as a regular character in a Village Roadshow production, *Tales of the South Seas*, which is destined for international release, and has now an American feature film behind her.

Handling and controlling publicity often falls into an agent's hands because of their contractual relation with a performer, although it is strictly speaking not part of their job. During our interview, Kevin Palmer was regularly distracted by having to screen press demands from women's magazines and daily newspapers for more information on the breaking story of former *A Country Practice* star Penny Cooke's pregnancy. Cooke did not in fact want her pregnancy to be widely known, so that requests for work would still come in, but Palmer acknowledged that the publicity at this stage (the last trimester of the pregnancy) was indirectly beneficial to her career. In general, and like most agents, Palmer felt that publicity itself was out of his jurisdiction, however much it affected a career. As we saw, though, the agent is often the first line of defence of an actor's privacy because the agent usually clears most press inquiries. They can also be placed in the position of protecting their clients from the consequences of some of their own choices and contractual obligations. When Noah Taylor, after having completed a small independent film, was being pressured by the distributors to engage in a major publicity drive, the June Cann agency tried to shield him from their demands. Eventually, this can stretch the role of the agent, even the new-wave agent, to breaking point. When a star reaches a certain level of prominence – particularly the kind of overseas interest that would surround, say, Rachel Griffiths – the agent will generally recommend the hiring of a manager.

While the overseas success of a client brings credit to an agent, it does have its downside. As a star moves internationally, contractual negotiations become more complex. According to most agents, it is the usual practice that, when an actor gets work in the United States or England, a local agent is involved. Instead of the entire 10% commission going to the Australian agent, there is a shared distribution. Occasionally, if the negotiations are done directly, the Australian agent picks up the full 10% from the international contract. Marcus Graham's recent success in *City to City* was all arranged between the casting director and Barbara Leane, who knew the casting director personally. The negotiations went on over a long period of time but, ultimately, Leane was able to claim the entire commission for the role. The usual case, however, is different; it is referred to as the 'Shanahan split' after the famous agent Bill Shanahan. If they successfully place one of their clients on an American film or television program, the local agent's share is 'two-and-a-half per cent of their [the American agent's] 10%; they hate to give it to you and you've gotta fight to get it – I always get it. If they want my actors, you've gotta do it – otherwise [they're] not coming.' Nevertheless, it has to be said that, if their actors land these large roles, even the regular 2.5% can keep an agency solvent. In the long term, though, such achievements are tempered by the reality that international stardom will move their clients out of their Australian orbit into the more elaborate agent–manager–publicist network of Hollywood.

The manager

> Management is a risk, clearly when you start the process, when you agree to manage, the best relationships between managers and artists occur when those artists have had nothing and so the growth has been together. Therefore the bad times have been shared by both, there's therefore no money for the manager let alone the artist for those years that it takes to get the income to that level.
> *Peter Rix*

Managers are much fewer in number in Australia than agents, and their clients are an equally select group. The activities of managers vary significantly in the Australian context. From our interviews and analysis of the way the industry operates, there seem to be three general types:
- the classic manager of a star's complex engagements, with both financial and personal responsibilities;
- the role-specific manager, who might be engaged to line up speaking engagements; and
- the impresario manager, who plays an often public role while orchestrating or controlling the media presence of their clients.

THE CLASSIC MANAGER

Managing entertainment figures involves an intense and ongoing relationship. Consequently, the number of clients that any manager takes on is constrained by the earning power of the client and the scale of the personal attention they will require. Customarily, a manager receives 15% of their client's income and this, given that there will also be agency fees, limits the number of entertainment personalities who can afford a manager. Mark Morrissey's rule of thumb is that a client needs to be earning in excess of $100,000 before they can afford management services. As a result, while the agency arm of his firm has around 150 clients, the management side has between five and ten clients at any one time. Only one of his staff is employed exclusively as a manager, while the others divide their time between agent business and management work. Morrissey himself manages only three clients: Steve Bastoni, Alex Dimitriades and Bill Hunter. Others in his firm are involved in the management of some of the young soap stars of *Home and Away*, *Neighbours* and *Heartbreak High*.

Frequently, in the Australian context, where the management contract emerges from an agency contract many agencies have used this as an opportunity to expand into management. Hilary Linstead and Associates, like Morrissey's company, has a management arm where clients such as Tim Ferguson, Magda Szubanski and Wendy Harmer are handled with greater attention and personal involvement. Ferguson's long-term contract with Seven and his writing and performing credits, for instance, demand a more engaged, career-building managerial role. Having an agency with a stable of talent provides the foundation for building a management business from the break-out successes of early career performers. This is clearly a process the agencies wish to encourage. Morrissey's agency offers a cut-price deal when managing becomes part of the service: instead of 15% commission for management, plus 10% for agent work, he renegotiates a reduced total commission and thereby holds on to the dual role.

Like Morrissey, Peter Rix, who has been managing entertainment personalities since 1974, has maintained an extremely limited client list. Although he engages in other activities and has been involved in a great number of Australian musicians' careers (he has been the producer of the annual award show of the Australian Record Industry Association, the ARIAs, since its inception in 1986), Rix has managed Marcia Hines, Deni Hines and Jon English for many years. All of them produce the consistent earnings that he requires. But the relationship is more than a financial one; he thinks of his role as integral to the production of their performances and their music.

Rix's take on the role of the manager is a consequence of a hands-on relationship with production that dates back to his original management of the 1970s pop band, Hush. His involvement with Hush is typical of management relationships in Australian popular music, in that it developed incrementally and relatively organically out of the individual's interest in the band:

> PETER RIX: Every Friday night I ran a club in Sydney. I was hired as the manager of a club in Sydney, a gay club in the Cross, and

> Hush was one of the bands I used to book and they would turn
> up. I lived in Paddington: they needed a place to rehearse so they
> used to use my garage. Some record company turned up and said,
> 'We want to sign you [Hush]', so they turned up at my house again
> and said, 'Look, you're at university doing a law degree. Can you
> have a look at this contract for us?' and I thought God this is a
> dreadful contract and so I helped them with that. And then they
> needed someone to drive the truck another night, their little van,
> so I drove that one night and then ...

Rix began handling more and more aspects of the business and production
side of the band as it garnered greater success. He would spend ten months
on the road, handling eighty or ninety shows a year, when Hush, along with
Sherbet, was one of the top two teen pop bands in Australia.

After years of hotel living, Rix today is able to settle into managing some of
the most successful Australian performers from his Sydney offices. Nevertheless, the experience of managing every aspect of a pop band has made
him the quintessential 'classic' manager. As he explains, the manager of a
personality/performer is involved in directing sales, keeping the accounts,
marketing the artist, working on research and future developments of the
product, and working on the image. To further complicate the job, these
various tasks are not done 'in isolation – clearly a lot of it's done very much
hand-in-hand with the band or artist that you work for; but someone has to
be the legs and arms of those decisions'.

The classic manager is clearly different from the agent (even the new-wave
agent); Rix maintains that the agent plays their part only 'after the real work'
(presumably, of creative development) is done. There is a degree of sector
specificity about his account, though, as the music industry is something of a
special case. The infrastructure requirements for performing and touring
bands demand some form of (at least) road manager, and this function can
easily expand into a more entrepreneurial and developmental role. In most
other areas of the entertainment industry, managers are rarely part of the
early career of a performer. They only become an essential element of success
as the performer's career produces a proliferation of offers and possibilities.
The manager grows with the client.

At the time of our interview, Morrissey was literally packing to head off
with Alex Dimitriades to Cannes Film Festival. Dimitriades was starring in
the 1998 film *Head On* which was part of the Directors' Fortnight screenings of the festival. Morrissey makes it clear that there were times after
Dimitriades' film debut in *The Heartbreak Kid* when his transition into adult
roles had to be carefully managed (a transition ultimately completed with the
role in the ABC series *Wildside*). But Morrissey believed that the acclaim for
Dimitriades' performance in *Head On* provided an opportunity that had to be

exploited to the full. Through his description of what he was about to do for his client, we can see the intense kind of investment that is part of the manager–client relationship at such moments:

> MARK MORRISSEY: What I will do is promote and fend off for Alex. Whatever group of offers come up, I will help determine what might be good for him. I also plan to go to Los Angeles following Cannes and meet with American agents and managers to stitch up potential deals there. Alex will hold a press conference the morning of the opening of the film and I hope to be culling out offers, once his commitments to *Wildside* are over.

Morrissey was capitalising on what Rix would call the promotion of an artist's product. The critical acclaim that Morrissey foresaw accurately in Cannes becomes the moment where a manager can make the international transition for a client.

Where managers have emerged from agencies, one sees another phenomenon developing which, on a minor level, echoes a forty-year trend in Hollywood: managers are involved in 'packaging' to get a production off the ground. Morrissey considers that holding on to the traditional roles of agents and managers does not make sense for the Australian industry. Like the Michael Ovitzes and Stan Kamens of the Hollywood film industry, the ultimate power of the manager/agent is the ability to link talent with talent. This requires powerful agent/managers who are servicing different parts of the entertainment industry.

Thus, Hilary Linstead's business, which began, as Viccy Harper explained, by representing the interests of creative people who are not on the stage or in front of the camera, has been ideally suited to managing the development of a production. Their work in theatrical productions and stage shows demanded the linking together of writers, set designers, directors, and others. Occasionally, this expanded into Linstead's taking on the role of producer. With Linstead's representing key creative talents such as Jane Campion and Gillian Armstrong from a very early stage in their careers (immediately post–film school), one can see how the manager/agent nexus facilitates the orchestration of an ensemble of talent (and occasionally money) for the industry. Indeed, although Rix did not use the term 'packaging', by his wide range of activities and his close connection to talent he has been invaluable in staging a variety of productions that have been the mainstays of the Australian music industry. Probably the most successful producer/manager of them all, Harry M. Miller, spent much of his career packaging his own projects: producing, publicising and managing large-scale musicals or promoting concert tours by major American stars. In cases such as Miller's, the line between the producer, the manager and the packager is thin.

THE ROLE-SPECIFIC MANAGER: MANAGING SPEAKERS

> If you ring Ita Buttrose she would send you to us.
> *Winston Broadbent*

Every single day in Australia, there is some kind of conference or convention running somewhere. In fact, every city sees it as a necessity to have a modern convention centre to handle this part of the tourist business, and every hotel is partly organised around facilities that appeal to corporate conferences. Conference organisation is a very big business. But every conference needs a keynote speaker, some individual who has a high public profile and the ability to convey a message that is both entertaining and useful. A support industry has grown around this need and manages the provision of their speakers to conferences.

Speaker managers, such as the Saxton Speakers Bureau, Celebrity Speakers and Speakers Network among others, are a very specific element of the celebrity industry. They do not develop the talent or the performance as a traditional manager might do; they cultivate already existing public personalities and then seek to make speaking engagements a regular source of their income. Their specific skill is developing the value of the 'touch' or proximity of a celebrity. One of the 110 speakers that Saxton's manages is Max Walker, the former Test cricketer who has made a lucrative second career as a sports commentator for the Nine Network and who, by their estimates, has been the most in-demand speaker for the last fifteen years. Walker creates an intimate 'touch' environment for his corporate clients:

> WINSTON BROADBENT: As he walks into a room to speak everybody knows Max Walker and he'll potter round the tables and chat to people individually. No airs and graces, very down to earth. By the time he stands up to speak, everybody loves him. So the user-friendly bit is a big part of the issue – so he stands up to speak and he creates these wonderful word pictures of anything from his cricketing days to his Channel 9 travelogue days to his South American trips for speaking to whatever and he just manages to create these wonderful, as I say, word-pictures.

Even though Broadbent emphasised that their speakers were principally hired for their record of achievement, and were not typically the material for women's magazines' celebrity reports, he did underline that his business is still in the domain of providing access to these public personalities:

> WINSTON BROADBENT: [People] seem to love to have touched a star. Two months ago, we had an event here where we invited 200 people from the media industry and we brought in 35

personalities ... They were just chatting to all these people that they only saw pictures of – it's a wonderful sensation. And then they go away and they talk about it for ever.

The particular craft of speaker management is to determine how a particular celebrity/personality can be marketed to the corporate world. The principal tactic is to translate the success these speakers have achieved in their various pursuits into a generic formula that can be offered to individuals within a corporate structure. Thus, the mountain climber Peter Hillary can be transformed into a speaker who talks about corporate teamwork or about reaching for transformed goals:

> WINSTON BROADBENT: Peter Hillary was doing Toyota and they'd just fallen from being number one in Australia to number two – Ford had taken over the lead. And so Peter Hillary came up with this comment of the lost summit: once you climb Mt Everest something has gone out of your life – just as once you've become the top car producer you've lost something. So you've always got to be looking for new summits if you like to climb. It's a lovely twist in what he normally does, which is climbing your own Everest, but an ability to be able to tailor is critical for a speaker to be successful.

Business celebrities who populate the business sections of newspapers are some of the most natural candidates for the speaker circuit and are actively cultivated. James Strong, of Qantas and Australian Airlines fame, is in great demand because he can talk about mergers. Others who can form their message around hi-tech or the future are also popular. Corporations are willing to pay for personalities in order to have close access to the kind of exclusive information and background knowledge that cannot be given through television or open public appearances:

> WINSTON BROADBENT: Obviously our fees are not cheap by comparison. Having said that, there's a number of ways of looking [at it] ... When you start talking fees for 1000 people and say you talk $4000 – 1000 people at $4 a head – they spend more than that on the cappuccino that comes after the event. So for somebody with enormous expertise you often are getting 40 years of experience in 40 minutes and it's the essence of success that you're actually buying in the speech and so dollar for dollar you're getting an exceptional deal. You'd expect me to say that but that's the rationale behind the whole process.

The management role in this part of the celebrity industry can encompass a great deal. Broadbent indicates that they are responsible for press releases, a degree of publicity for their speakers, and focused work on matching corporate clients to individual speakers. They are also responsible for handling the celebrity – that is, the delivery of the speaker to the event, the establishment of the itinerary and the time commitment involved – as well as for coordinating relationships with the conference organisers. The fee for their service is 25% of the speaker's fee and Broadbent explained the odd reality that is so different from other managers: there is no written contract with any of their speakers and they all work under the handshake agreement system.

Speaker agencies' close connection to the corporate world can generate other kinds of spokesperson roles for their clients. For instance, Steve Bisley's recent work as spokesperson for Telstra's Big Pond advertising campaign was orchestrated by Saxton's. Broadbent described the essential work of such a campaign as a form of personality branding, aimed at a marriage between the personality and the company. In a similar vein, Saxton's provided Ita Buttrose for a Meat and Livestock Corporation promotion: the specific focus was the value of meat in combating iron deficiency in women and the corporation wanted a high-profile and credible spokesperson to represent it in a prominent and multimedia campaign.

The management of speakers, although not entailing complete personality management, is a very lucrative part of the Australian celebrity industry. Speaker management agents identify how celebrity status can be converted into other services, other forms of information and other products, thus playing an important part in the capitalisation and proliferation of such status. Finally, celebrity speakers and company spokespersons connect corporate Australia to the celebrity industry.

THE IMPRESARIO MANAGER: 'JUST TALK TO HARRY'

> Yes, an impresario; but really an entertainment producer because we produce television as well. It's not my day job. My day job is running a business of celebrity management.
> *Harry M. Miller*

There is a third kind of manager operating in the Australian celebrity industry that does not necessarily emerge from a specific form of cultural production nor from a history of being an agent. Unlike Peter Rix, this kind of manager revels in the public sphere itself and, as part of the business, takes publicity beyond the entertainment industry and into the broadest public domain. Very few of us have heard of Winston Broadbent or Rebecca Williamson; however, if the names were Harry M. Miller or Max Markson, there is a high probability that we would be aware of their activities. Miller is certainly a celebrity figure in his own right and Markson seems bent on tracing out a similar trajectory through the promotion of his own media presence as well as that of his clients.

We have set up a category of the 'impresario manager', but, despite Markson's increasing media visibility, it is a category with only one member at the moment. The term 'impresario' does usefully connect Miller with a long line of theatrical entrepreneurs, skilled at reading public desires and presenting events and shows which capture that desire for paying audiences. P. T. Barnum, the nineteenth century master and manager of ceremonies, was precisely this kind of figure: intuitively gauging popular sentiment, he managed the curiosities and personalities of the world and displayed them for entertainment in the form of a 'museum' or a circus. The contemporary Australian impresario manager works the same public terrain, although there have been major changes in the locations where the celebrity spectacle takes place.

Harry M. Miller has built a number of careers from producing entertainments and promotional events, and has over time moved into managing key public personalities. His background as a sales representative in New Zealand in the 1950s and early 1960s, arranging a series of 'contra-deals' to link his products (mundane items such as socks, underwear and electric cookers) with other events and other products, stood him in good stead when he began to move into show business. After managing a New Zealand singing group, the Howard Morrison Quartet, he first came to public attention in Australia as the promoter of high-profile concert tours by well-known American and British performers, including the first Rolling Stones tour, Judy Garland's only appearances in Australia, and Sammy Davis Jr. He moved on to package larger and more complex shows; he developed and promoted Australian productions of the key international musicals of the late 1960s and early 1970s: *Hair, Jesus Christ Superstar, The Rocky Horror Show*, and *Boys in the Band*. Such was his prominence after the success of these productions that Miller could claim in our interview (with appropriate chutzpah) that he 'was, still am really, the most famous producer Australia ever produced and I was born in New Zealand'.

His move into celebrity management has been gradual and has only dominated his activities relatively late in his career. It has also tended to be at the request of others, seeking the kind of support and advice they saw Miller as uniquely able to provide. The element which seems to have made him an attractive manager for public figures such as Graham Kennedy, Maggie Tabberer and others is his apparent ease at working out how to do a deal with the media by understanding the nature of the media's commercial interest in a personality or information, and then manipulating that interest. Experience in promotion, production and management gives him an extremely broad understanding of the entertainment business. These days, Miller also possesses what he describes as 'leverage' in the media and business market-place. Significantly, he is probably more well known than some of his clients. His own celebrity both precedes and facilitates his work for clients by providing the necessary access to influential people. In describing how a deal was worked out between Collette Dinnigan and Audi, he relates how his name on a fax produced an immediate reaction from Audi's marketing director to help set up a coordinated promotional deal:

> HARRY M. MILLER: Fax from Harry M. Miller about a really famous person – you know she is going to ring [back] … So we're very good at leveraging that sort of stuff and that's part of our fame and when we don't know people – which is occasionally, not very often – but when we don't know people we just rely on our brand name [which] opens a lot of doors.

Consequently, the famous come to him to work out how they will be represented to the public. His first client, Graham Kerr, of *Galloping Gourmet* fame, wanted to make his unique cooking style and personality a fixture on television, radio and newspapers and Miller helped Kerr to achieve this.[2] Some of the more interesting clients have not emerged from the entertain-ment industry directly but have sought assistance when they have become the unwilling object of media attention. This is a relatively new category of celebrity, in fact, a consequence of changes in news values in the print and electronic media, and the intense competition between television networks since the end of the 1980s. While there are a number of other managers bidding for this kind of business – Max Markson and Leo Karis, for example – Miller's market dominance is significant. It is a market he is serious about serving. Unlike most other agents and managers, he admits to very little interest in representing actors or directors as an ongoing activity: 'I'd rather use them for something than be their agent'. Throughout his career, it is the deal which seems to attract Miller, and handling the accidental celebrities who are routinely thrown up by events, disasters or controversies provides plenty of opportunities for doing the deal. Not that he is entirely uninterested in packaging ideas for the entertainment industry. In our interview, though, we saw how he liked to synergise his varied interests, say, in a production deal that allows him to link personalities and figures to a given project that may have emerged from one of his clients. He described his plans for a further development out of the story of James Scott, whom he represents:

> HARRY M. MILLER: I have no interest in reading some of these scripts and saying, 'Baby, this is a great idea for you'. We are more likely to take a script to somebody and ask them. Like this James

Scott book. The film is about his sister – that's what it's about – how she persevered and finally they found him. The person to play that role is Nicole Kidman. It's a killer of a role for her, killer, and there are very few roles that are good for women. So we're saying to the guys that are developing it, 'Keep Nicole Kidman in mind when you're writing it'. And I am saying to Nicole's agent, 'Just down the road, it'll be there soon'. That's all we're doing, just keeping everybody on the case.

Far from the grassroots developmental process described by Peter Rix, all Miller's clients these days come with value and are therefore already a desirable product: what his firm does for them is 'enhance product'. Miller explains that only about 4% of his business comes from 'crisis management control': dealing with formerly 'ordinary' people who have become the focus of media attention, where his role is to control media access and to effectively organise singular deals with particular media sources. His own background has given him a heightened sensitivity to the media circus that can develop and he is ruthless in his control once a Stuart Diver or a James Scott is in his stable.

In his more regular client pool, Miller works towards what he labels a 'seamless outcome' between his client and a particular product. Deborah Hutton's recent spokesperson/promotional campaign with the mid-range and compact Holden cars is exemplary of that approach, as was her former role as Myers Department Store representative. Similarly, Maggie Tabberer, whom Miller describes as an 'icon' and someone who is 'very careful' with her image, was working with him at the time of our interview on coordinating her endorsement of Sydney's Stamford-on-Kent apartments so that they matched her public profile of elegance and concern for design.

Although there are entrepreneurial aspects contained in the development of the other managers studied, Miller is distinctive in that he considers each individual's media moment as an enterprise that requires its own form of management, its placement and (significantly) its development of ongoing desire. According to published accounts,[3] Max Markson seems to approach his management of sports personalities and other newly public figures in similar ways, in that he clearly sees the moment of media presentation of a personality as something that needs to be professionally produced. However, at this point in his career, he lacks the leverage which comes from the establishment of an identifiable public persona, an authority and celebrity that challenges those the media can invent for itself. Miller's frequent play in the scrum of the media frenzy is self-consciously designed to create the impression that he is more knowledgeable of its workings, its desires, its motives and its directions than anyone else. His interest in regulating media attention raises more than issues around publicity or promotion, however, and we will return to this in more detail in Chapter 4.

The publicist

Sandwiched somewhere between the managers, producers and agents, on the one side, and the media outlets on the other, are the publicists. As a group, they have certain clear characteristics: they are overwhelmingly female (70–80%, by one estimate); they are exceedingly accessible; they have often worked as journalists; and they are intimately connected to the network of interests that produce the Australian fame game. Listening to the publicists, you begin to see the interconnectedness of the celebrity industry. Tracey Mair employed an assistant who worked regularly for Markson; Kerry O'Brien's experience in promotion brought her into a working relationship with Miller; Georgie Brown was employed by the publicist *par excellence*, Patti Mostyn, who in turn used to work as publicist for Miller. Other professions are often associated with what we are grouping in the publicist category. The use of the description 'public relations' by freelance publicists seemed to be a strategy to connect them to potential corporate work. Generally, however, the category of publicist applied to those working in the entertainment industry; as the sphere of activity moved away from that, other terms – such as marketer or public relations expert – were employed by our interviewees.

A defining feature of the Australian publicist is that almost all contracts or positions are related to products first and personalities second, even though the personality may be the principal means of selling the product. Unlike Hollywood, where even supporting stars on a television sitcom (Cathy Negemi, for instance, from *Veronica's Closet*) might retain a personal publicist, Australian entertainment publicists rarely work for an individual. The promotion of Australian personalities and the handling of overseas personalities while touring Australia are dealt with in two quite distinct ways: either they are managed internally by the television network or the production company that is staging the show or producing/distributing the film; or they are piloted by freelance publicists who are called in to help orchestrate media coverage. Our analysis of the work that is done by publicists is divided along these lines: the freelance publicist and the media corporation publicist. Our conclusion highlights the varied roles of the entertainment industry publicist as well as their convergence with the strategies usually identified with public relations. Because the product is so central to the publicist's contract, corporate positioning is always somehow implicated in the use made of Australian and overseas personalities.

THE FREELANCE PUBLICIST

> They also know that when you're trying to find people, who's the
> one person who is going to have their mobile phone on until
> midnight seven days a week? – it's the publicist.
> *Tracey Mair*

To work independently as a successful publicist requires industry connections
of the highest order. Although a great deal of publicity is handled by freelance
companies, most have some form of background that helps to establish them
in a certain range of activities. Rea Francis' career with the Australian Film
Commission not only connected her to the entire Australian film revival, and
the variety of producers, directors, stars and distributors that were implicated
in the renaissance, but also enabled her to develop international connections
through the promotion of Australian film via film festivals such as Cannes.
When she set up her own firm in 1981, she retained the Australian Film
Commission as a client. Similarly, Brown, another Sydney freelancer, has
had substantial periods of employment with Channel 7. O'Brien worked in
promotions for Sony Music to help bolster her independent status in publicity
campaigns for tours and shows in Melbourne. So it is rare to find a publicist
who has not worked at some time for a major media corporation; their
freelance status may continue to be dependent on their former corporate
connections.

THE UNIT PUBLICIST: GIVING THE MEDIA A 'HANDLE'

In Australia, much of the entertainment industry is organised around the
individual production. Thus, one of the key contract jobs is as a unit publicist
for a film or television production. This entails any publicity that can be
achieved while the film is in production and is financed by the production
company. The collection of behind-the-scenes footage, on-the-set interviews,
and the distribution of stills from the film to newspapers are fundamental
parts of the job. Because of the size of the industry and the intermittent
patterns of film and television production, unit publicists on local films are
sometimes engaged for the complete campaign: from production to distribution and even orchestrating the promotions for exhibition. Mair, who says
80% of her work is on film and telefilm/series publicity, demonstrates the level
of involvement that a publicist can have in the promotion of a particular film:

> TRACEY MAIR: I was the unit publicist on *Shine* in the winter of
> 1995 and then I began working on the release publicity for it in
> Australia when it premiered at the Sundance Film Festival in
> January 96. And then it was released in Australia in August 1996.
> So I followed that whole process through and in fact my work

wasn't complete until after the Academy Awards in 97. So that was a very long process. It was unusual to be in a position to do unit publicity and then follow through to release. I try to do it when I can and it depends who the distributor of the film is in Australia.

The ultimate product of unit publicity is the press kit, the guide that is distributed to newspaper columnists, magazine and feature editors, and film and television critics. To coordinate with the international distribution of material on film and television, Francis has developed a second business to service the film industry: the electronic press kit, which is distributed to television networks and syndicated programs that focus on entertainment. Here television program editors can find a video interview and then intercut their local host into the footage of the interview to lay claim to what looks like an exclusive.

Publicity, whether for film or other events, has basic objectives: it must appear to be newsworthy, it must be placed appropriately and it must be timed to coordinate with the product's release. As Mair, Brown and Francis underlined, the lead actor is the natural vehicle for the representation of a particular product as new, exciting and therefore worthy of coverage – after all, they present the public face of the film or television program. Placement of film publicity depends on how its appeal is constructed and the publicist actively works on surrounding a particular product with cross-media attractiveness. With the film industry, as opposed to television, operating with very few stars who have value for magazines and newspapers, a publicist has to create clear 'events' that highlight the film's content. Mair's success in promoting *Crackers* relied on working through both the themes of the film and the awkwardness of its shooting schedule to provide a 'handle':

> TRACEY MAIR: A lot of my job is my phone conversation with the journalist, my pitch to the journalist and I'm always looking for the angle to pitch at journalists. On *Crackers* – its Melbourne stand-up comedians spent seven years bringing this script to the screen and, my God, look at the public reaction to it – they just adore it. How does someone hold onto that kind of dream for seven years? Filming in a Melbourne winter, it's a family Christmas nightmare kind of comedy. How do these actors survive sitting in bikinis in a Melbourne suburban backyard in the middle of July? You know, those kind of things that give a hook to it. What I'm trying to do is provide an excuse for a journalist to write about something, make their job easy for them, give them a handle on what the story might be.

Each media form was targeted with different interviews and different angles. Serious interviews with the director appeared in the major dailies, while Mair was able to construct an on-air Christmas lunch with the director, three of the actors and Kerri-Anne Kennerley for the *Midday* promotion. The theme: everyone would 'talk about their worst family holiday experiences'.

The importance of publicity for independent film and television producers is intensified in the Australian entertainment industry. Although unit publicists want their campaigns to be coordinated with an advertising onslaught, local films' promotional budgets are very limited. Gaining editorial coverage of a particular film or television series is therefore critical for the successful film run. A full campaign coordinates with media buys and efforts in publicity that provides appropriate background features for a given film. Publicists in these larger campaigns are liaising with the advertising agency to ensure their 'free' media coverage resonates both temporally and in terms of placement with these commercials.

EVENT PUBLICISTS: ELECTRIC DREAMS

Constructed events are the territory of all publicists. The unit publicist tries to construct events that are worthy of coverage beyond that of a critical review; however, other freelance publicists specialise in the orchestration of public events as a form of marketing. Each event has a target audience that the publicist is trying to attract and interest. At the Cannes Film Festival in the late 1970s, Francis lobbied to get Australian films into competition and then staged events that attracted international attention and critical appraisal. Because 'in those days a lot of Australian films were not pre-purchased … they needed a run press-wise internationally', so Francis cultivated as a core audience 'all the top film critics worldwide': 'I made it my business to become great friends with them and we indeed did'. An Australian barbecue on the beach at Cannes, supplying Australian directors, stars, fashion, wine, meat and cheese, became a Francis trademark.

Francis' expertise is in establishing the territory for networking. Describing herself as 'a very successful hostess', she attributes her sense of the value of this kind of interconnection to the English film producer Verity Lambert:

> REA FRANCIS: Verity is very fond of saying there are only 300 people in the world and it's not a matter of the size of this. Camaraderie has nothing to do with the size of this country's industry – it's exactly the same in New York, it's the same in England. I know most of the English-speaking players in PR and in media round the world [and] it's the same small pond in each city.

Part of the objective of glitzy premieres and grand openings is to service this network, but it is also to construct the kind of event that attracts media coverage. Promoting the opening of a new Club Med resort in the Pacific region, Francis took a group of journalists there; not only travel journalists, though, but also those writing for sports, news, and a wider feature market. She called this strategy 'widening the press net'.

Event publicity has three objectives: making a media scene, satisfying the needs of the personality or personalities involved, and selling the show. For the publicist, it is crucial that this is achieved, as much as possible, with free advertising or editorial content. Publicists like O'Brien determine their success in terms of page-one newspaper placements and similarly high-profile magazine covers; if she achieved blanket coverage in the morning papers, she might have a celebratory lunch 'and take the rest of the day off'. All saw their function as excitement generators, translating hype into media presence and, finally, sales.

Louise Carroll had a virtual monopoly on publicity for international popular music tours of Queensland for a period of twelve years. She outlined the four phases of publicising a concert through the example of the successful Dolly Parton and Kenny Rogers 1989 tour:

- Phase One – The announcement. The promoters announced the tour two weeks before the tickets went on sale and the publicists had a whole team working on the moment, capitalising on the impact of the press release. Radio and newspaper features were part of that strategy.
- Phase Two – Over-the-counter sales. The day tickets go on sale has the potential to be a media event. One of the ticket offices in the Queen Street Mall in Brisbane had queues on a scale that had never been seen before and by 11 o'clock the concert was sold out. The speed of the sellout gave Carroll's team 'ample opportunities there to work with your media in a publicity sense of the emotion'. The result was that by the afternoon a second added show had been sold out. Maintaining a certain 'emotional' momentum led to the addition of further shows and the sale of a total of 53,000 tickets.
- Phase Three – Pre-show publicity and promotion. Even when a show is sold out, there is an effort to maintain 'general public awareness' in the three-month gap between the ticket sales and the concerts. Promotions, interviews and competitions through CD and ticket giveaways (now no longer necessarily given away but usually coordinated with advertising time for the concert) become critical as the relationship to radio stations and their audience is maintained. Part of this promotion is to give further cultural value to the tickets and the performance. The point of this is a more long-term benefit. A concert is a particular moment for the personality/star to connect to an audience and to establish their continuing presence as a performer of significance. Ticket sales are the first priority, but for the record company the CD sales that can result from this extended publicity campaign are often even more lucrative.

• Phase Four – Bringing it home. The final phase involves ensuring coverage of the actual concert itself. Live crosses from a radio station to the concert could be employed; getting journalists to review the concert with an appropriate press package is also part of the final strategy.

Publicity for concerts and touring shows may be handled by a variety of freelance publicists, but most of them depend on a close and continuing relationship with the small group of local concert promoters in order to contract the assignment. Success for the publicist in this field depends on the frequency of concerts. According to Carroll, there have been fewer international acts touring in recent years. This is in contrast to 1994 when, during a one-month period, she managed the publicity for forty shows. An independent publicist has to be flexible in responding to such a demand with an expanded team and office, before trimming back to the leaner operation that Carroll's office was in 1998.

In general, we observed that most freelance publicists seemed to have very few permanent staff, preferring to employ a regular group of support staff on a contract-by-contract basis. The reputation of the service was directly connected to the name of the principal, and this may explain why all of these publicists traded under their names and not through some authoritative or generic description of the service they provided. The freelance publicity business is as much about trading in names and networks as the celebrity industry itself.

MEDIA CORPORATION PUBLICIST

The hub of the Australian celebrity industry is in the publicity departments of major media corporations. Television networks have, as Carroll indicated, expanded from the single-person operations of the early 1980s to whole 'departments' with support staff dedicated to the task of making their personalities circulate prominently in other media. At the time of our interviews, the publicity department for Channel 9 in Sydney had a director, five full-time publicists, a part-time sports publicist and two assistants. Likewise, in film, Village Roadshow Distributors had three distinct departments (publicity, promotion and public relations) dedicated to advancing the profile of their films both nationally and internationally. Suzie MacLeod, publicity manager for Roadshow's distribution interests in Greece, Singapore and New Zealand, as well as film publicist for any Australian film produced and distributed by Roadshow, organises a continuous stream of international stars on promotional tours, introducing key figures from Australian films for press interviews and providing 'colour' images and stories for newspapers, magazines and television. Once you see the inner workings of the publicity departments of these major corporations, it is easy to recognise how much material they provide for the other media.

The everyday: The media feeding the media

Heidi Virtue, who was working for the Nine Network at the time of our interviews, embodies a great deal of what is needed to be a good network publicist: taking care of your 'talent' and ensuring regular editorial coverage for your particular programs. Because of the sheer size of the Nine Network, programs are divided up among the publicity staff; Virtue's portfolio, when we conducted the interview, included *Midday* and Kerri-Anne Kennerley, the stars of *Murder Call*, journalists from *60 Minutes*, and the host of *Australia's Funniest Home Video Show*, Kim Kilbey. But what makes her job a daily source of content for newspapers and magazines is that she is also responsible for all of Nine's international programs:

> HEIDI VIRTUE: I am the sort of point of contact for the publicists in all the other states plus all the media. Whenever they want to do a story about *Friends* or *Veronica's Closet* or *Drew Carey* or *ER*, I've got all the contacts they require – the synopsis and all that sort of stuff. Then I liaise with our publicity/liaison person in our bureau in Los Angeles and he and I will come up with sorts of strategies of what we're going to place, and where, etc.

These strategies will be varied and contingent. For instance, because *Friends* had previously been screened by Channel 7, its move to the Nine Network in 1997 required a different kind of campaign than the promotion of a totally new series like *Veronica's Closet*. With *Friends*, audience familiarity with the cast and the leakage of knowledge about the stars through the United States meant that Virtue had to work on different angles and, in particular, to find a repertoire of photographs different from those provided (presumably, in the first instance, to Channel 7) by the Los Angeles distributor. Her task, then, would have involved trawling for photographs or 'trannies' (transparencies) which might be new and interesting for newspaper features. Publicity 'head shots' may end up being used for the regular television listings that appear in the Sunday paper previews, but they are not acceptable for illustrating a full-page feature about a particular show or star. Virtue would have sought more individual and less generic photographs of the *Friends* stars from such large American magazines as *TV Guide*. These shots would then have been purchased for $500 or $600 by the publicity department for free distribution to support such features. *Veronica's Closet* was publicised through a series of interviews with the cast members which emphasised its relative success in the United States. With the network publicist providing a lot of the written material used in the short features in newspaper supplements, it is clear that Virtue and her counterparts at other networks do a great deal of the work in setting up the content, style and image – and even the agenda – of the media treatment of television programs.

Interestingly, although network publicists do provide some of their 'colour', Virtue indicated that mass-market women's magazines usually do their own trawling for and purchasing of international star images. The key factor here is that a magazine's interest in gossip is not necessarily in accord with the commercial purpose of a network's publicity. Consequently, a network's energy tends to be concentrated on providing free images to newspapers, rather than to magazines, because they can be relied upon to treat the program and the stars somewhat differently in their entertainment pages:

> HEIDI VIRTUE: Those magazines are after personal life and, you know, boyfriends, girlfriends, lovers and all that stuff. Whereas newspapers will talk to them about their career, about the show they're working on, the character they're working on, you know – there might be a little bit about their personal life, but they're not after that sort of angle.

Publicity for Australian-made programs on network television parallels some of these strategies but with much greater intensity. There are regular features about someone like John Wood of *Blue Heelers*, provided by Seven publicists who will also have arranged a series of interviews. Likewise, Virtue coordinates interviews with *Murder Call* stars for background features. Some consultation occurs with the producers of the particular program, but generally the network publicist organises the publicity shoots as if the network publicist were effectively the unit publicist for the Australian market and the producers. Part of any contract signed with a television producer (usually in very close association with the network that is buying the series) is a 'publicity clause' which stipulates that the star is available for publicity; their appearances fulfil that element of the contract and no further money changes hands. The Nine Network is particularly committed to using its performers and personalities for various forms of network and program publicity. Indeed, it prides itself on being the 'network of the stars'; CEO David Leckie is reputed to like referring to Nine as 'Australia's Hollywood'.

The networks: Australia's Hollywood

> The people driving television in this country are doing it for commercial gain, ratings and revenue ... The byproduct of television is

that publicists get to work and because of those objectives they drive the household names from those soap operas into becoming magazine covers, newspaper covers, television stars, in order to fulfil the brief by television management, and that has created a very different industry here in Australia … The networks are control freaks about publicity and the network publicists insist on controlling the publicity for the stars on the shows.
Brian Walsh

The Hollywood reference is not inappropriate. In its attempt to develop stars and through them the profile and audience appeal of network programs, network publicity departments constitute the Australian incarnation of the old Hollywood studio system. Virtue describes Kerri-Anne Kennerley as a 'company woman', a star who understands the interdependencies which mean that it is in her long-term interests to loyally serve the Nine Network. History has proved that those who work within the system, including co-operating with publicity, will be rewarded with future assignments. According to Virtue, Kim Kilbey is also developing as a Nine girl, with appropriate forays into publicity ('in six months she's appeared in all the women's magazines') and an understanding of the pragmatics of network loyalty. By way of contrast, Virtue observes that some new hosts do not understand their dependence on the network for their professional profile.

Perhaps the most recent and surprising example of a (much older) personality who appears to be learning that lesson is Ray Martin. For years Martin represented the pinnacle of the studio/network system: he was Nine's brightest star and anchored its image nationally. His public comments about network decisions in 1999 (comments obviously not orchestrated through the publicity department), his complaints about the invasion of his privacy by John Safran and Shane Paxton (complaints which struck everyone as pretty rich coming from the former host of *A Current Affair*), and his ill-considered stint as the anchor for the World Cup cricket coverage show how easily a public reputation can unravel if it is not centrally managed. He was conspicuously absent from the presenting team for Nine's mega-broadcast, *Millennium Live*, on New Year's Eve, 1999.

Because of their concentration on the promotion of personalities, the network publicist is by far the most powerful single factor in shaping the celebrity industry. The Nine Network is particularly vigilant and focused on advancing its stars (presenters, journalists, and actors from high-rating drama series such as *Water Rats*) in other media, thus exploiting the cross-promotion possibilities of the Australian Consolidated Press (ACP) magazines. But it also foregrounds them through such events as its annual pre-season promotional campaign which depends solely upon images of its personalities (rather than on its programs). The Seven Network is more

dependent upon actors from its successful local drama series and so promotes itself through John Wood and Lisa McCune of *Blue Heelers* and
through teen/young adult stars such as Belinda Emmett of *Home and Away*.
The Ten Network relies on its high-profile, mostly American programs for its
targeted young adult demographic. Nevertheless, a benefit of Ten's recent
raiding of the ABC's battery of youth-oriented comedy programs has been the
development of a stable of stars with great appeal to its audience: the teams
of young comics and personalities from *The Panel* and *Good News Week*
which have become synonymous with Australian youth culture.

Other media forms, perhaps as a result of the networks' establishment of
an expectation of personality promotion, have likewise developed publicity
that is focused on the personality or the individual celebrity. Book publishing
has become more and more concerned about the nature of the author's
image/identity and how it might assist sales. Andrew Freeman, senior publicist of a team of five at Random House, explains that it is much easier to
promote non-fiction than fiction authors because they generally come with a
ready-made public profile. Established journalists, for instance, attract good
publicity. Sydney columnist Paul Sheehan's *Among the Barbarians* was an
immediate success, selling more than 40,000 copies in three weeks.[4] While
the book was easily promotable because of its controversial opposition to
political correctness, Sheehan's success, Freeman admitted, owed a certain
amount to the fact that journalists are already part of the media and personality system, and the strength of the 'journalist network' means that they
tend to be 'very good to their own' in terms of coverage.

The negotiations around the Ian Roberts biography provide a further
indication of how celebrity percolates through the Australian media.[5] Once
Random House had won the contract (which included an advance of
$150,000) for Roberts' account of his life as the first openly gay rugby league
player, Freeman sent advance manuscripts to newspapers to produce a bidding war for extracts. News Limited paid $30,000 for the exclusive rights
to publish excerpts, coordinated with the publication date of the book. The
three-month campaign was at its most intense over the three weeks surrounding the publication date. During that period, Random House arranged
displays in all bookshops – these included a full-size cardboard cutout photo
image of Roberts (which still decorates Freeman's office), book signings/
autograph sessions, and prominently featured piles of books – as well
as ensuring general reviewing in the major newspapers by both sports
columnists and book reviewers. Because of the unique spin of sportsman
and sexuality, the book had a high-enough profile that it led to features in
newspapers that might not have carried the exclusive extract and, more
importantly, it led to another battle over exclusivity for a television profile
of Roberts. Freeman indicated that the favoured television program for
author interviews would almost always be *60 Minutes*; however, in this case,

Channel 7's *Witness* flew a crew up to interview Roberts in his hometown of Townsville and thereby eliminated any interest from other networks that might have provided prominent coverage as well. Random House also organised a series of radio interviews with Roberts, designed so that they did not conflict with his playing commitments and training. In all, the publicity generated a level of media saturation that allowed Freeman to claim a publicist's success: a massive amount of editorial coverage of the book and sales in excess of 30,000.

The circulation of personalities through the celebrity industry is equally part of the business of running a large television production and distribution house. In the case of the Southern Star series *Water Rats*, for example, Lesna Thomas, from Southern Star, and the publicists at Nine work very closely to coordinate their strategies. If the series' stars are reticent about appearing on *TV Week* covers or inside posters, Thomas and her staff will try to facilitate the outcome desired by the network. Like all the other publicists, though, her general publicity goal is to move stories out of the television sections and into other areas of the newspaper and into magazines because 'this is the only way to make your audience grow'. And as was the case with Brian Walsh's mid-1980s massage of *Neighbours* into a youth program (see Chapter 4), Thomas identifies casting and script strategies aimed at drawing younger audiences. *Water Rats'* 1999 acquisition of young Aboriginal star Aaron Pederson was part of that strategy; a more concerted effort of refocusing a series on youth can be seen in the addition of Damian Walshe-Howling to the cast of *Blue Heelers* for 1998 and 1999.

One of Thomas' principal tasks is promoting and positioning Southern Star's dramatic programs internationally, and here again the marketing of the stars is important.[6] For the launch of the second season of *Water Rats*, she toured the major European buyers' markets (MIP-TV, MIP-Comm) so that star Colin Friels could talk to all of the major buyers. They followed up with a series of interviews with the principal entertainment magazines in Germany and London. Other stars used to promote local product overseas include Bryan Brown (*Twisted Tales*), Lisa McCune (*Blue Heelers*) and Gary Sweet (*Big Sky*). In a rather odd but almost universal pattern, Australian dramatic actors are more willing to expose themselves to international publicity circuits than domestically:

> LESNA THOMAS: You find the sort of productions that we do, which are primetime quality drama, you're not going to get a star going on domestic networks saying, 'Hi, I'm so and so – you can catch me on Nine'; but I can get them to do it for overseas brochures because it's not their domestic market. If you're a star in Australia ... you don't want necessarily to have [your] face out there talking to a camera telling people to watch you ... and you

won't get a Jerry Seinfeld doing that [in his home American market] either.

The various media corporations, with their permanent publicity staff, are able to construct a celebrity world for the Australian media from a blend of national and international personalities. Walsh, who is now director of programming, publicity and promotion for the pay television company Foxtel, has resurrected the large-scale promotional strategies that used to be more commonplace in Australian networks: bringing out the big American television star. For the launch of the stripped series of the *X-Files* on one of Foxtel's channels in 1997, he toured its star, Gillian Anderson:

> BRIAN WALSH: I gave her a week at the Four Seasons in Bali – because half of these Americans have got no idea, they come down here and they think they can do Ayers Rock and the Barrier Reef in one day. So they come down here – and I did with Gillian Anderson what I did with Kylie and Jason. I took her to Westfield Shoppingtown Centres, and it was mayhem ... And she couldn't believe it. She had never seen anything like it in her life, and we got unbelievable coverage from that tour ... Now, you tell me what other company in broadcasting has 30,000 subscribers and gets front-page coverage like that? ... Actually ... what is the front page of the *Sunday Telegraph* worth? It's – you know, it all reinforces Foxtel as the brand leader ... I have an entire dedicated LA office that just generates stories for me out of LA that I can then give my publicists here to resubmit to the Australian media.

The tour cost Foxtel $100,000, as did a similar tour by *Melrose Place* star Andrew Shue.

The international publicity tour is the staple activity for those involved in distributing Hollywood films. Suzie MacLeod regularly coordinates such tours for Hollywood stars and thereby provides a massive amount of editorial content for the Australian media. Tours coincide with the release dates of the films involved and combine planned public appearances with media interviews. MacLeod's job is to organise the itinerary, provide the images necessary for pre-publicity and then accompany the star throughout all of the activities. Stars are discharging their contractual obligations to provide publicity and are thus only paid daily rates ($150) – nevertheless, they are completely taken care of during their visits. Interviews are scheduled with journalists and a list of guidelines is handed to each interviewer, covering 'things like you can't ask for personal autographs' or possibly a range of personal questions that the star does not want to answer. The pattern of interview staging is all too familiar for major stars: the 'landing/arrival' press conference, followed by a day of hotel suite interviews – sometimes using two suites in order to keep to the fifteen-minute time frame for each interview. The publicist works to maintain this schedule so that the greatest number of media hits is made, and made effectively. Because the star is out of their usual territory, special rules do develop when they are promoting a film in Australia. Overseas stars, such as Matt Le Blanc who toured in support of *Lost in Space*, often have their own publicist with them. This risks potential conflicts over the presentation of the personality. The distribution publicist is concerned about using the star as the bait for general media coverage; the personal publicist is working towards managing the star's presentation as a distinct commodity that just happens at this moment to be connected to a particular film.

Column inches: Public relations and value

Publicity, while being at the very centre of the celebrity industry in Australia, suffers from the fact that its value is never entirely concrete. Because publicity, by definition, always appears to be something else (a news item or a feature story, for instance), and because it is therefore, again by definition, 'free', publicists are always looking for ways to identify and quantify the benefit of their work to the industry. One of the common ways of evaluating it is to calculate the dollar value of the coverage generated from the dollar value of an equivalent amount of purchased advertising space (column inches of newsprint) or time (seconds/minutes on air). MacLeod and Walsh regularly assess the value of their newspaper coverage in terms of column inches; hence, MacLeod could claim that a particular tour had produced over a million dollars' worth of coverage. Dollar value of exposure, however, still begs the question of effect or influence on the market; the advertising industry is notorious for not always knowing what works (in terms of generating sales) and what doesn't.

There is another way in which the publicist's function can be understood, though, a way that is more structural than commercial: they constitute a vital link in the chain of connections which enables the media to deal with the entertainment industry. All of the publicists we interviewed expressed the opinion that the media was 'very' or 'highly' or 'incredibly' dependent on their work. Georgie Brown, for instance, found that her material went so seamlessly into mass-market women's magazines that she started doing freelance writing for them. Suzie MacLeod explained that, whenever there is a media release publicising a tour, it is routinely swallowed and regurgitated by radio, with at least 'a couple of columns … always in the newspaper'. Heidi Virtue said that, although journalists will absolutely never admit it, entertainment writers and editors simply depend on her supply of content. The distribution of free images, declining staff numbers on newspapers, the 'non-news' or 'soft news' character of today's feature, lifestyle and entertainment sections, all contribute to press dependence on publicists for copy. Given the regularity of contact between editors and publicists, and the occasional junket that journalists receive through that contact, a convergence of industrial and commercial interests must develop.

Publicity has built the celebrity industry. Although the client of Australian publicists is only rarely the individual (generally, the producer is paying), the channel taken by publicists to represent the 'emotion' of the cultural product is invariably through particular personalities. Celebrities are all spokespersons in one form or another for some further commodity than themselves (think of how Southern Star has used its 'stars' to position its product internationally). The result of the increasing intensity of the competing and overlapping publicity campaigns selling various cultural and media products has been an emerging Australian star system. A register of the industrial significance of this system is the fact that, in many instances, the selling of specific newspapers, magazines and television programs is now dependent upon their deployment of these personalities as images, voices and quotes. In the media marketplace today, in a wide range of contexts, the publicity practitioners are the facilitators – the go-betweens – of product positioning and media coverage; their main tools are celebrities.

Chapter 4

Managing the Media

You don't become a star by trawling around Australia playing seven hundred jobs in two years. You become a star by manipulating the forms of media that are there to your own ends.
Peter Rix

Promotions and publicity people work with the dynamics of media exposure on a daily basis. Their capacity to manage these dynamics is their primary industrial skill. Their incapacity ever to *completely* manage them is an industrial reality which makes their daily activities highly contingent. These practitioners understand, perhaps better than anyone else, how the media can build reputations, affect careers and sell an object of desire to consumers. Even to them, however, managing this potential can be a problem. Media exposure can get out of control; it is volatile and it resists containment. While there may be no such thing as bad publicity, most publicists would agree that exposure can be dangerous if unforeseen or unplanned. Professional careers are destroyed by poor handling of media interest; and the objects of intense scrutiny, particularly from news or current affairs journalists, can become 'media victims' overnight. In this chapter, we look at the media as a problem to be managed, contained and controlled by those whose livelihood depends upon it.

There are at least two perspectives which inform this account. Let us take the more positive one first. The role of the manager, the network publicist, the publisher's publicist, or the agent includes strategic use of the media to build and shape a career, to generate box office, to excite public interest, to disseminate information, and so on. In the pursuit of all of these possible objectives, the management of media exposure – and its corollary, the restriction of the media's potential to be a problem – is quite critical. Among our interviewees who stress this are Harry M. Miller, Suzie MacLeod, Peter Rix, Brian Walsh, Tracey Mair, Rebecca Williamson and Heidi Virtue. From accounts such as theirs, we can see the positive outcomes of the publicists' efforts: the end product may be a successful career, or the establishment of some personal or corporate control over the accuracy and legitimacy of the media's representation of an individual, group or project.

The negative perspective, however, is perhaps more often canvassed in public – and in some of our interviews. Media management also involves restricting the flow of information to the public, by regulating the news media's access or by deliberately lying (through the media). This may be regarded as necessary for a number of reasons. The most common reason is, of course, the protection of personal or commercial interests: simply, it is often not in the interest of a specific individual or organisation to have their activities made public (although it may be in the interests of the public). Few of our interviewees provided us with evidence of instances where restriction of information was necessary, but none were concerned about the fact that they occurred. It was clearly a fact of life. Where our interviewees did express concern (and this implied a secondary reason for careful media management) was in relation to what they saw as the intrinsically destructive potential of excessively intrusive or unregulated scrutiny from an overwhelmingly commercial media – even when the object of this scrutiny is a celebrity and thus, up to a point, 'fair game'.

Since the death of Diana, Princess of Wales, this point hardly needs making. There have been many cases where celebrities have felt sufficiently wronged by media reports to take legal action. Famous examples outside Australia include successful actions against the British tabloid *Sun* (in the case of Elton John) and the British style magazine *Face* (in the case of Jason Donovan). Similar actions can be expected, increasingly, within Australia. Protected by distance and by their relative unimportance overseas, Australian mass-market magazines have generally been more inclined to handle scandalous stories about overseas, rather than local, stars. However, a recent action launched by Jim Carrey against *Woman's Day* suggests this will no longer be tolerated by, at least, Hollywood stars.

Concern about the potentially destructive nature of publicity, however, goes further than the issue of defamation, the invasion of privacy or the need to protect a client against malicious or false reports. The whole process of publicity, the manner in which it works even on those who believe they are its beneficiaries, is open to question. On 31 March 1998 Lizzie Gardiner's ABC documentary *Fame Game*, on the careers of television soap actors, argued persuasively that unregulated media interest – something that is now routine for young soap stars – radically overinvests in these stars as public personalities at the time of their performance in a program but leaves them totally unprepared for the automatic decline in media interest once they leave the cast. Ironically, the revelation of the 'real' off-screen self, which might be thought to be what could continue after their contract ceases, is completely in the service of the on-screen self. Once they cease embodying the fictional, there is no point to their celebrity.

There are other examples of the damage celebrity can do. In the case of individuals who become prominent accidentally, not as a consequence of their professional activities but through their implication in high-profile news events (the case of Thredbo survivor Stuart Diver was the most prominent example during our research period), the pressures of media interest can be unwelcome and frightening. Harry M. Miller is a good example of somebody who has built a reputation by intervening in such situations and regulating the flow of media interest through the manipulation of exclusivity.

Underlying this chapter, then, are concerns about the media's power to create celebrity, the predatory manner in which this power can be exercised and how this is managed by the industry. Set against this context, the role of the manager, the agent or the publicist appears to be dominated by the necessity of maintaining control: keeping material out of the press, dealing with the damage caused by unwelcome publicity, handling the difficult celebrity bent on generating unwelcome publicity themselves, and strategically regulating precisely what kinds of media attention are allowed for a particular client. Managing the media and its desires, excesses and predispositions is central to the work of managing and producing celebrities.

Product enhancement

> We enhance product, we don't go and get stories.
> *Harry M. Miller*

It is clear that there are varying views about the appropriate sphere of activity for managers and agents. Different sets of practices make it hard to predict exactly what each celebrity's agent or manager does for them. As it responds to the dramatic shifts in the structure and operation of the media industries in general, the role and character of the manager have been in transition over the last decade. The gender balance is changing (more women), the ethical orientation is changing (towards that of business rather than that of, say, the performing arts), and the range of services being offered or the degree of control provided has increased. Two decades ago, celebrity managers like Max Markson did not exist; now they dominate the public (or at least the news media's) conception of the media manager and control a significant proportion of the celebrity market.

Today's celebrity managers/agents are significantly different from those of the preceding generation. Anthony Williams does not think it is appropriate that he should get directly involved in the promotional activities necessary for developing his clients' careers (he would, instead, suggest the name of a good press agent). There is a strong theatrical/artistic tradition underpinning the industrial location of agents like Williams which slightly discourages close professional associations with networks of publicity and promotion. Indeed, this tradition leaves behind it a residue of distaste for the mass-market end of the media in general. This distaste reflects something like a high culture–low culture split, with theatre and film work carrying a cachet of legitimacy not available through, say, television soap opera. So, Rebecca Williamson, of June Cann Management, one of the oldest and best-respected agencies in Sydney, expressed reservations about her clients working in television soap opera at all: 'I wouldn't recommend people [doing soaps] ... it's almost like you don't have any acting talent to go by'. Not surprisingly, her clients can be very picky about what they think is appropriate work: Noah Taylor, for example, only accepts projects that interest him personally – 'He's not really concerned about whether they are high budget or low budget' – and avoids becoming involved in publicising them. (Williamson contrasts his involvement with that of Geoffrey Rush in the publicity for the film *Shine*.)

The other end of the agent–manager spectrum is quite different. Mark Morrissey is much more comfortable with the mass media and sees his management role as a more comprehensive one. For this generation of manager, the market determines how the client should present themselves and what career choices they make. The client is a product that requires development and marketing; they are not a unique artist whose emergence is to be facilitated. Morrissey admits that he has to control everything about his clients' activities, including their private lives:

> MARK MORRISSEY: [I decide which] functions they should be going to ... handle their bank accounts (not the funds, but just make sure they have money in their hands and in the right account), and get people to their jobs ... We'll handle their looks too, the way they present themselves, dress, hair, everything.

Necessarily, this kind of manager works cooperatively with other agents, such as network publicists, to coordinate the development of their clients' profiles. Despite the genteel charm and clear ethical position of the approach taken by the older theatrical agents, it seems inevitable that the more aggressive model of professional activity will eventually prevail, as it is more suited to the increasingly competitive commercial environment within today's media and entertainment industries. As Morrissey points out, 'Past agents wouldn't touch that end of the business – and many want to keep thinking of the job as just bookers. But you can't [just] do that – you have to work to construct opportunities for your clients.' Thus, the doyen of celebrity managers, Harry M. Miller, is representative when he claims the need to control a wide range of his clients' activities: 'We strategise their careers, make their deals for them ... In a way, we are just like a policeman: we must make sure nothing goes wrong. We guard our clients.'

Interestingly, for both kinds of celebrity managers, it was clear that they built up a strong personal relationship with many of their clients. The celebrity manager seems to deliberately encourage a kind of emotional dependency so that their clients feel able to entrust their interests, extra-ordinarily comprehensively, into their care. Depending on your point of view, such a relationship could be regarded (probably with equal justification in specific instances) as either nurturing and protective or cynically manipu-lative. Admittedly, with the more traditional agents, it was a little easier to read the relationship as benign. A theatrical tradition which emphasises verbal agreements, long-term relations with agents, and sanctions against client poaching seemed to endorse principles of operation which opposed, and probably ultimately competed with, those of commerce. But it was by no means only in these agents' offices that the conversation about the pro-fessional relationship with the client repeatedly subordinated the commercial nature of the relationship in order to foreground its personal dimension. This is an oddly contradictory, and possibly professionally delicate, aspect of the celebrity manager's activities; there must be many occasions when personal and commercial considerations conflict. Nevertheless, it is also true that the manager's reputation, and thus their own career, depends on how well they handle the clients, in terms of both professional and personal objectives. At the end of the day, though, it is clear that these clients have to be regarded as commodities, products, properties – that is explicit. Morrissey talked of packaging products, Miller talked of enhancing product, and Rix provided a very striking analogy between the role of the manager and that of the CEO of a successful business:

> PETER RIX: My long-lasting description of management is that, for example, an artist like Marcia Hines in a good year ... will have ... gross income in excess of $2 million. If it was any other industry [such a business] would have a sales manager, a marketing person, and an advertising person. Certainly it would have a CEO ... Being that Marcia Hines is the product, there would have to be some form of research and development so that the next elements that were to take place within the corporation, and the products that were involved in that, were dealt with ... All of these elements, in the business that I'm in, are controlled by the manager.

There are limits to this analogy. The process of developing the product/client can be trickier in the media and entertainment industry than in most other industries. 'Strategising' a career involves careful judgement about what is appropriate in an environment where all you may have to go on while making this judgement is, at best, a hunch. Sometimes the hunch is wrong. Rix regrets, for instance, encouraging Hines to host a variety series on ABC-TV in order to develop a broader audience at a crucial stage in her career: 'I was making her [be] things that she really wasn't and it didn't increase her stature or her audience base. In fact, it shrank.' Barbara Leane remembers encouraging Sandy Gore to do a film she thought no one would ever see: '"Why don't you do this film", I said, "it's a good role, I'll get you some good money, it'll never be seen". Wrong, came the videotape. We all forgot ... and it comes back to haunt you and it's there in Video Ezy.'

While the popular mythology of the Svengali promoter or spin doctor might encourage suspicions of the worst, it is not possible to draw general conclusions about how much the celebrity client usually contributes to 'strategising' their own development. In one instance, Morrissey wanted to move 'someone with a girl-next-door look' out of 'that bracket', and so arranged for her to pose in a bikini in a men's magazine. The result was a 'whole new list of possibilities' and two film contracts. While this irresistibly invites speculation about how closely involved the subject of this transformation was in 'orchestrating' the process, Morrissey claims that he would always get the client's approval for deals struck with third parties. Gary Stewart's stories of handling offers of work for Rachel Griffiths indicate that he tried to dissuade her from accepting a film role he saw as too graphically sexual, even when she had expressed interest in it.

Morrissey suggests, though, that there are plenty of instances ('terrible stories') elsewhere within the industry of 'a client learning after the fact' of commitments made on their behalf. While none of our interviewees admitted that they would cynically manipulate a client in this way, Lesna Thomas from Southern Star conceded that she can find herself working in conjunction with a television network to build a client's profile in ways that are more in line with the network's priorities than those of the client. In such circumstances, her task is to secure the client's assent: '[If] it's a priority for the network, we would try ... to make it happen'. This prompts the question of just who is the client in such negotiations. As Thomas says, from her employers' point of view, the network is a more powerful and important client than the actor, so, 'at the end of the day, it's the network's call about how things and how people are publicised for the shows in Australia'. It might be regarded as rather disingenuous to call both parties 'clients' in such instances: after all, the company Thomas works for sells to the network but buys the services of the actor.

On the other hand, we heard plenty of stories which demonstrate that a determined actor/celebrity does have the capacity to take charge of their career and that there are agents who will respect them for doing so. Leane was handling Sophie Lee when she decided to walk away from her contract with the Nine Network. This was the contract which had provided the opportunity of hosting the *Bugs Bunny Show* and *Sex with Sophie Lee* but which seemed to hold little prospect of anything more challenging. Lee decided she could do better away from television and declined to renew her contract. Leane recalls telling Nine's incredulous executives: 'She won't go to another network, she'll not go to do another television show. She's going to go on, she's going to study, she's going to do theatre, she's going to do other things. And she did.' As Leane points out, Lee accomplished the transition from being a 'personality' to being a respected actor, 'one of the few that's made that move' successfully. It appears to be a move which was loyally supported by her agent, despite almost certainly reducing the agent's financial return.

In most cases, the interests of the celebrity-client and those of the agent happen to be pretty well in alignment because both are pursuing commercial opportunities. Nine Network publicist Heidi Virtue reported continual pressure from men's magazines such as *Ralph* and *Max* for female presenters like *Funniest Home Video*'s Kim Kilbey to do photo shoots in lingerie. From Virtue's point of view, this is pointless: 'She's host of *Funniest Home Video*, it's a family viewing show, she doesn't need to be in underwear in a men's magazine'. It is important to note that she does not object to the idea in principle ('I wouldn't ask anyone to do it in their lingerie unless they were getting paid, or unless they were the host of a sex show, or something that was a bit more relevant'), but she did not see any commercial advantage in cooperating in this instance. 'Those men's magazines, they wanted JoBeth [Taylor], Catriona Rowntree, Rebecca Harris ... all our girls, they've asked for and, no, we just won't do it. It's not right, it's not the sort of image that we want for any of them.' (Interestingly, the comment about getting paid indicates that publicity of this kind arranged by the publicist earns no income for the performer and also costs the magazines nothing.)

Stewart reported similar requests from men's magazines for photo shoots with Rachael Blake and Rachel Griffiths; in both cases, he regarded this as not being the kind of publicity they needed (although Blake did do a nude shoot with *Black and White* magazine). Alternatively, while both manager and client may find certain kinds of media exposure distasteful, in some circumstances there is little room for refusal if they wish to work in their sector of the industry. Unlikely as it might seem to some readers – particularly in light of the exploitation of female presenters in men's magazines – Brian Walsh bemoans the need for footballers to appear on the *Footy Show* ('I know that most rugby league players hate appearing on the show because they find it demeaning'), but refusing to do so is probably not an option for a football player wanting to establish or maintain a celebrity profile, especially one with the potential to continue after the playing career is over.

Damage control

Unfortunately, dealing with the media is a highly contingent activity, and managers and agents spend significant portions of their time struggling to secure their involvement in decisions which influence the regulation of their client's media exposure. Much as they would like to, in practice it has to be accepted that they cannot guarantee control over the exposure received. No matter how much time and organisation is put into its production, publicity can be distressingly unpredictable, seeming to come from nowhere or, alternatively, resisting all the normal strategies employed to get it started. Little wonder that publicists establish rigorous systems of control: restricting access, regulating exposure and personally supervising their charges. Village Roadshow's Suzie MacLeod sets up explicit rules of engagement for the Hollywood stars she tours around Australia to promote their latest film: no autographs, no personal photographs, no endorsements, and she sits in on every interview. Most infuriatingly, even though these arrangements are in the touring star's interests, they can themselves choose not to cooperate when it suits them. George Clooney, for instance, liked to have MacLeod refuse permission to interviewers who asked for autographs, simply so that he himself could say OK: 'He said, "That way I look like the nice guy"', says MacLeod, 'and I'm thinking, yeah and I look like the absolute bitch'.

Of course, in certain circumstances, the problem for the publicist is keeping stories *out* of the news. We are used to the euphemisms used to describe uncooperative visitors from Hollywood – they may suffer from the flu, jetlag or fatigue but they are not stoned, drunk or just plain obnoxious. MacLeod's example is *Friends* star Matt Le Blanc, who was on a promotional tour for the movie *Lost in Space*:

> SUZIE MACLEOD: He got off the plane in Sydney and basically cracked the shits, to put it bluntly, and we told the media he was sick and to this day everybody believes he was sick. But what happened is that he missed his flight in New York, he missed his connecting flight in Los Angeles, and ... by the time he got to Sydney ... he was exhausted.

Virtue describes an instance where she knew there was something to hide, but 'the talent' hadn't told her what it was. All she knew was that her job was to pretend that 'everything was just fine' and to continue putting out the official, damage-control line. The unexplained disappearance of Nine Network presenter JoBeth Taylor was the subject of wide speculation in October 1997 (she ultimately left television, and gave interviews many months later which described a nervous breakdown). The official story from JoBeth's father was that she was unavailable for work because she had a mystery virus, but that didn't stop the media frenzy:

> HEIDI VIRTUE: Every day I would have two to three calls ... asking about JoBeth ... Most people thought Channel 9 had dumped her or she was a drug addict or she was pregnant or she was having an affair with Daryl [Somers, host of *Hey Hey It's Saturday*] and Daryl dumped her. But then *New Weekly* rang me and said, 'We have a photo of JoBeth in Bali with her boyfriend. You said she was ill.'

Here, the publicist was at the mercy of 'the talent', still trying to hold the line on their behalf but unaware of what the potential for damage might be.

This issue – the potential for 'damage' – is one that comes up frequently in the interviews and dealing with it constitutes a major component of any publicist's job. The likely source of the 'damage' depends on the media environment within the specific media market. In Australia, it is the mass-market magazines, the few remaining tabloid newspapers, and television current affairs – often, all working together. In one illustrative example, Channel 7's sports commentator and ex-swimmer Neil Brooks found himself in some trouble over an interview in *Max* (January/February 1999). His discussions of sex and alcohol were probably appropriate for the magazine, but his statement that the most 'unmissable' part of the Olympic Games (for which he was expected to be a commentator) was the 'after-Olympics piss-up' was not regarded as good company behaviour. The 'Melba' column in the *Australian*, among others, noted that Brooks 'has been suspended for six weeks after a rather ill-advised interview with the men's mag *Max*' (he was eventually cut from the network) and provided some indication of the content.[1] Other papers took up the story, quoting what they could. This is an instance of the way in which scandalous stories circulate even within the quality press; the appearance of the initial story in one of the mass-market magazines is treated as news within the daily press and may even be seen as ammunition in the competition between media companies. This particular issue of the magazine was withdrawn on the publisher's request over another matter, so the interview would probably not have been read by very many people, especially given that the circulation of *Max*, already low (about 24,500 at that time), was faltering. Had newspaper gossip columnists not taken it up (as well as in 'Melba', it was mentioned in the *Sydney Morning Herald*'s 'Stay in Touch' and the *Australian Financial Review*'s 'Rear Window'), few would have been alerted to Brooks' faux pas.

The Australian press tend to disavow this kind of activity, but in the United States and Britain everyone agrees that the danger of damaging media exposure lies overwhelmingly with the tabloid press. Keith Negus' work on the music industry makes the point that the tabloids have become almost unavoidable for record company publicists in Britain because of their market power. However, he also points out how difficult a problem they represent for the publicist who wants to manage media exposure. There are reasons for this (and generally they hold true for Australia as well): the tabloid press are more interested in scandal than in, say, the client's musical performances; their final version of any given story is highly unpredictable in that the use of headlines or unflattering photographs can dramatically change the spin (and this can be the result of a senior editor's late intervention, not the original reporter's intention); their level of accuracy is rightly perceived to be lower than in other media; and they are prone to conducting campaigns or vendettas against particular personalities (often in conjunction with some strategy to involve their readers, like a phone poll). As a result, Negus says, many press officers do as much as they can to avoid the tabloid newspapers altogether, despite the consequent sacrifice of exposure to their readership.[2]

At present, there is no Australian equivalent to the British tabloids in terms of their content, their market dominance or their treatment of scandalous stories about public figures. Even so, the astute management of media exposure here is a highly detailed and selective procedure. Variables involved include the selection of interviewers, photographers and media outlets. Of course, the higher the profile of the client, the more selective the process can be; with a less saleable product, more compromises have to be made, more risks taken, more mistakes regretted. Even then, however, there are strategies which can minimise the risk of damaging or unhelpful material being published. Hence Heidi Virtue's lack of interest in having her young presenters pose for *Max* and Peter Rix's distaste for feeding the gossip columnists news about his musicians.

Publicists are not afraid to veto specific media personnel if they do not play according to the established rules. Kerry O'Brien, among others, blacklisted certain photographers after clients had bad experiences with them; Sue-Ellen Topfer refuses to allow a particular photographer, known for his intrusive tactics, to enter the building; and, as we detail later, Harry M. Miller has blacklisted *60 Minutes'* Richard Carleton. However, blacklisting does not necessarily mean that magazines are unable to run stories on the relevant celebrities. MacLeod provides pictorial material to the magazines, notwithstanding such an embargo, but individual interviews or exclusives are out. Overseas celebrities circulate their preferences to their publicists ahead of their Australian tours so as to proscribe particular media outlets: Sharon Stone won't do interviews with *New Weekly*, Kim Basinger won't do *Who*, Liam Neeson won't do *TV Week* (because he had a bad experience with a magazine of the same name in Germany),[3] and presumably *Woman's Day* can forget about Jim Carrey, Demi Moore and Bruce Willis from now on (all are rumoured to be engaged in lawsuits with the magazine). Despite all this attention to detail and all this accumulation of highly specialised knowledge to prevent such a possibility, bad publicity still occurs.

At the end of 1998, it was revealed that Australian cricketers Shane Warne and Mark Waugh had accepted money for providing information to an illegal bookmaker during an international one-day series in Sri Lanka in 1994. Waugh was booed by the crowd when he came out to bat in the next Test, Warne lost his lucrative sponsorship deal with Nike, and editorial writers had a field day. Mike Colman's feature story in the *Courier-Mail* pointed out that none of it would have happened if there had been a manager around to say, 'You must be kidding!', at the time the two cricketers were approached. Interviewed for the feature, Max Markson had this to say:

> It happens. You would like your client to refer everything back to you and most athletes do. But you can't be everywhere at once. Inevitably something will get through the cracks. A few years back my client [then Test player] Greg Matthews signed to do an anti-smoking promotion. One of the requirements was a photo shoot for *Woman's Day*. I didn't go to the shoot – but Greg and I were to wish that I had. The photographer got Greg to crumple a packet of cigarettes. Unfortunately, the pack he chose was Benson and Hedges – who just happened to be Australian cricket's No. 1 sponsor.[4]

In the Matthews case, the negative effect fell, not on the celebrity himself, but on the relationship between him and the endorsed product. As the consequences for Warne and Waugh suggest, the individual dangers of unwanted publicity are real enough. Nevertheless, we occasionally heard stories where the compulsion to control and manipulate publicity appeared excessive and, to an outsider, disproportionate both to the benefits it would bring and to the damage it would prevent.

Brian Walsh was the mastermind behind the success of *Neighbours* on the Ten Network as well as the related promotion of Kylie Minogue and Jason Donovan as teen stars through the mid to late 1980s. In particular, he proved outstandingly successful in turning publicity into news: 'I was a lot more interested in newspaper coverage than I was magazine coverage ... the newspaper gave it a sense of news. Magazines [were] wallpaper.' The photograph of Minogue and Donovan kissing on the beach, which made the front page of the Sydney *Daily Mirror* in 1985 (headlined, 'TV Shock: Teen Sex on *Neighbours* Tonight'), was a publicity event Walsh turned into news. It revived the fortunes of the soap opera in Sydney at a point when its axing was imminent, and helped to cement the celebrity of the two actors. Their secret romantic relationship was central to Walsh's promotional strategy. While it continued for more than four years, it was strenuously denied throughout that period. Rumours and speculation flourished, though, and the continuing press interest in discovering evidence of their relationship was expertly manipulated. Walsh would deliberately alert the paparazzi and the news-papers to where Kylie and Jason were going to be and what they would be doing; the resultant coverage would take on the news value of an exposé rather than a planned promotional photo-opportunity.

Without the secrecy in the first place, of course, there would have been no story. Press interest was excited and maintained by the possibility of a juicy revelation, something that was definitely never an option to those in control. Curiously, though, Walsh does not present his *manipulation* of this secret as a masterstroke of media management. Rather, because he believed that it was essential to protect *Neighbours'* ratings, Walsh takes pride in his success at *keeping* the secret. He described the lengths he went to: 'I took [Kylie and Jason] overseas every year for four weeks for a holiday, so that they could get away and just have time together out of the glare of the public spotlight, and we kept that secret for years'. Greater devotion to the client could not be imagined but it is difficult not to wonder if just, maybe, it was all unnecessary. Certainly, a major enticement to the press would have been sacrificed, but *would* the ratings have suffered if the relationship had been revealed all along? One cannot help recalling the promoters' orthodoxy from the early days of rock'n'roll that insisted rock stars should never admit to being married because it would alienate their fans. There aren't too many cases when it did, and lots of cases when it didn't. In light of that, this instance looms as one of the more exorbitant investments in celebrity management in Australian television history.

Stories like this one highlight an attribute of promotional culture about which some of our interviewees expressed concern. The allure of the pro-motional opportunity, the tendency for media attention to flatter their subject into revealing more than they should, the displacement of personal priorities by those required to present the celebrity to the public, the uneven distri-bution of media savvy between the celebrity and their handlers – all conspire to create an atmosphere which is unduly responsive to opportunity and readily incited to excess. In the instance Walsh describes, two teenagers spent four years protecting themselves from the press in order simply to continue their romantic relationship without producing a dip in the ratings of a television soap opera. Within the industry, that is not seen as excessive or disproportionate – rather, it is an example of a highly efficient orchestration of media exposure. Outside the industry, we suspect, it would be regarded quite differently. Indeed, instances such as this reinforce what is clearly a widespread mistrust of publicity, demonising 'spin doctors', publicists and others as cynical mercenaries employed to do whatever is necessary to advance their clients' interests.

There's no such thing as bad publicity

While this may be an unfair assessment of the industry as a whole, there is a more substantive concern which underlies and informs popular suspicions about what we have been calling promotional culture. At some fundamental level, we would suggest, people outside the industry regard publicity – and its product, celebrity – as potentially dangerous. As noted earlier, celebrities are often marked by their relatively sudden elevation to celebrity status; one of the key attributes of the celebrity is the slightly eruptive, unpredictable, or even arbitrary, nature of their acquisition of a high public profile. Because such a profile is, definitively, in excess of their particular professional skills or achievements, the resultant publicity is always likely to be read sceptically by the public. The individual celebrity's meanings shift, as they are represented and read across a spectrum from the authentic and 'true' to the unauthentic and 'false'. This presumes a public which critically assesses what it sees and hears, and implies that there is much put at risk when exposed to the judgement of that public.

Against such a view is the old nostrum: that there is no such thing as bad publicity. The cynical point this makes is that visibility is all: it matters little what you are famous for, but it matters a lot that you are famous. In our interviews we heard something reminiscent of that line only once, from Random House publicist Andrew Freeman: 'Mostly, controversy is good for sales'. He cited the example of Bob Ellis' *Goodbye Jerusalem*, which had to be withdrawn from sale for legal reasons, but 'as soon as the news got out that we were butchering it ... people rushed into book stores to get it ... before it could be withdrawn'.[5] In general, however, the managers we interviewed took much the same line as, we imagine, the general public – that publicity, and those aspects of the promotional culture which sustain it, are dangerous.

At the most limited and instrumental level, this translated into an informed scepticism about the notion that any old form of publicity will work for people attempting to gain a profile in the entertainment industries. For example, Rix explained why some gossip stories in Australian Consolidated Press (ACP) magazines, which linked Deni Hines with James Packer, had a negative effect on the sales of her first album:

> PETER RIX: She was [now] no different to a soap star [but the music on] the album didn't reflect that. It was not a pop record, it was an R&B record ... People viewed her not as a singer or as a musician or as credible ... Rather, she was the daughter of [a] very famous woman who went out with all these very rich and famous men. Married an INXS and went out with a Packer and a Murdoch.

Rix went on to make the point that when the album was released overseas, particularly in Japan where the media flow and publicity of her 'other' celebrity status would be non-existent, it did very well. He also argued that it is possible to overstate the effectiveness even of relatively appropriate publicity. His example here was the Kerri-Anne Kennerley version of *Midday*: she is 'very lovely ... and ... someone who Channel 9's publicity machine [sends] to openings, they get her photograph taken at the Cointreau Ball. But the television show is rating, like, 3s, and the Channel 7 movie rates 10s.' Shortly after our conversation, *Midday* was cancelled and Kerri-Anne went on to 'special projects'.

Rix was particularly critical about the use of publicity for simply maintaining visibility, for promoting celebrity itself. His preference, borne out by what he has done with his artists, is only to do publicity when you have a new product to promote:

> PETER RIX: There's a great danger for someone like Marcia [Hines] or Deni [Hines] or Kylie [Minogue], that you are only famous for being famous ... That you are not famous for your work ... If you're not selling records you can still be on the front cover of *Woman's Day* because you're Michael Hutchence, because you committed suicide, because you're Pamela Anderson and Tommy Lee. I mean, Tommy Lee is in a band that no one's actually seen for the last ten years so he's only famous for beating up his poor wife ... That is not a process I particularly agree with.

According to Rix, much publicity – particularly in the mass-market magazines – actually detracts from the desired focus on professional performance in order to serve the media outlet's commercial interests rather than those of the celebrity performer. This is a view which is fairly generally held in relation to actors who do stage and cinema work as well as television, and to those musicians whose livelihood depends more upon live performances than recordings:

> PETER RIX: If you want to maintain your life as an actor, if you want to maintain your life as a musician ... [or] ... sportsman, you have to produce performances to do this. Nothing about [rugby league player] Solomon Haumono that appears in the press over the past month of his life with 'the pleasure machine' [his then girlfriend, model Gabrielle Richens] is ... in the long term going to increase his ability to make money from anything other than selling that story ... It's an enormous mistake to see the short-term potential of a story like that against the long-term potential of his life in football.

The conventional wisdom used to explain the sudden erratic behaviour we are used to witnessing from celebrities – such as that of Solomon Haumono and soccer player Mark Viduka (both of whom fled their clubs in 1998 for personal reasons) – is that the pressure of their public role has proved too much.[6] Certain categories of celebrity are seen as particularly susceptible in this regard. Since the 1960s and 1970s, rock stars have been the prime targets, especially vulnerable because of their relative youth, the appropriateness of scandalous behaviour to their professional image, and the consequent scale of public interest in their activities. Nervous breakdowns, drug or alcohol dependency, and suicide become the signs of the excessiveness of their celebrity and their difficulty in coping with it. In Australia, over the last decade or so, the most endangered of the celebrity species, though, is the young television soap star. There are two major concerns about these young actors: first, reservations about the scale of their implication in promotion and publicity campaigns for their networks; and, second, misgivings about their level of understanding of the process itself.

The first concern responds to the omnivorous appetite of the daily press and, particularly, magazines like *Who* and *TV Week* for stories about young soap stars. Promoted as the public faces of soaps such as *Neighbours* and *Home and Away*, categorically central to the demographics targeted by the network publicists, these kids can do as many *TV Week* covers as they like. As Rebecca Williamson says, 'There's no limit to how many they'll want you to do once they get a taste for you'. Stories about their work in England (albeit seasonal provincial pantomime), or their affairs with English society or industry figures, imply international prominence. This is highly flattering, of course, but it exposes them to a level and character of detailed media interest that they are relatively unprepared to deal with. According to some interviewees, the soap stars' naivety is deliberately exploited by their publicists. 'Publicity companies will have them do anything', says Rix. 'My particular favourite is the photo shoot where a pretty young blonde thing models a whole bunch of outfits and talks about her relationship with her mother and the fact that she was molested as a child by her father.'

There is no doubt that such stories feature regularly in the media in this country. Revelations of potentially embarrassing personal information from young soap stars include numerous examples of child molestation, sexual harassment, anorexia, and various forms of addiction. There can be little doubt that these stories will have long-term negative effects and that their publication, given the youth of the celebrities concerned, is exploitative. The journalists we talked to accepted responsibility for the impact of their stories on celebrities and thus made the decision occasionally not to run with a damaging story. As Jane Nicolls, from *Who*, put it, 'It's their life – this is just next week's magazine' (this remark was explicitly in the context of local, not overseas, stars). Nevertheless, these stories appear, someone places them, even if no one we talked to would admit to doing so. (Nor are we implying that they had. Our sample was skewed to the top end of the industry, where we would expect stronger ethical standards to be maintained and stated as normal policy.) Indeed, most of what the publicists and managers had to say was about protecting their clients from precisely this kind of pressure. Lesna Thomas, for instance, stressed the importance of publicists' carefully managing their young stars:

> LESNA THOMAS: When we were doing *Echo Point* we had very young stars and one of the things I stressed to our unit publicist [was] that we have to teach these young kids ... just how much to give away and how much to keep for themselves ... [Our] role is educating the stars and you're talking about some very young people. Eighteen. Now, say your father bashed you up all your life, you know if you go and say that in your first interview ... that is going to follow you throughout your entire career, never mind the damage it might do your family life. So what we say is that you have to think very carefully at this moment in time, how much of yourself is appropriate to give away and how much isn't.

Even with the best of intentions, however, it is clear that stories about soap stars – some of them scandalous, most of them not – constitute a significant proportion of the celebrity-related material published in the press and aired on television. Little wonder then, given this level of exposure, that the young actors in the soaps – most of whom have had no sustained training as actors and little other experience in the industry – begin to think of themselves as stars. This raises the second problem, that of dealing with the sudden evaporation of their celebrity status, the withdrawal of media interest after they leave the cast.

This problem is not confined to these actors, of course. What makes it of particular note is the fact that, more than most actors, soap stars are celebrities because of the context within which they work. They have been chosen as the faces to promote because of the show's audience demographic, but they are part of a large ensemble cast within which each individual actor is pretty easily replaced. (That seems to be among the lessons networks have learnt about keeping their production costs down in successful soap operas.) Without professional training or a track record outside the soap they are in at the moment; they are very hard to employ elsewhere. They have a familiar face but it is identified with another, maybe even a competing, product in an industry where soap operas represent the bottom of the barrel. Working in a soap for a long period does nothing for their credibility as an actor. Hence the frequency with which the more ambitious of them try to break out of the mould while still within the cast and therefore still guaranteed a level of visibility. Soap stars have sought to establish themselves as singers – Melissa Tkautz, Craig McLachlan, Jason Donovan and, most successfully, Kylie Minogue and Natalie Imbruglia – or in some cases have left the cast to train in more conventional ways for their profession – as has Isla Fisher. But it is likely that few of them understand that, as Williamson puts it bluntly, 'the only reason ... they are in front of the public is because ... the networks they have worked for are owned or affiliated with the newspapers'. When they no longer have access to this arrangement, they fall from view.

Gardiner's *Fame Game* documentary explored this situation in some detail. Taking a group of ex-soap stars, she examined how much difficulty they had experienced in continuing their acting careers after leaving the cast. Isla Fisher had decided to seek proper training, Ashley Gordon had left the industry altogether and was working as a bar manager, and Bruce Samazan was continuing, fruitlessly at that stage, to seek employment as an actor. Gardiner argued that the industry should accept more responsibility for helping these young people to understand the unauthenticity of their celebrity status, preparing them for its sudden withdrawal and, with it, the promise of a glittering career in television.

It is a view that we heard several times in our interviews. Walsh agreed that, 'at the end of the day, you still have got to feel some sort of responsibility for where those young kids ended up', while Rix said, 'If I have sympathy for anyone, it's those kids that are in the television shows. Because they actually think they are stars ... I've watched the damage that's done to them after they're not in the television show anymore, because they're no longer stars.' All agreed that it was not television that was the problem, it was the way in which these young actors were embedded in a publicity process that advanced the interests of the program while it damaged their prospects of future employment in the industry. This process actively encouraged them to misrecognise just how little interest was excited by their own personal qualities, and thus how little was tradable in further advancing their career sometime down the track.

Publicity is the villain in this part of our story, not because of its lack of authenticity – although that certainly needs to be understood – but because of its excessiveness. One thing the celebrity industry is ill equipped to do is to think about proportion, to calibrate its actions against some scale of relative importance, however that might be defined. (Significantly, much of the publicity mentioned above is free; promotional budgets set a limit to activities which cost, but, in such cases of pure publicity, expenditure is not an issue.) Everything about the industry works to foreground the immediate, the latest, the pressing, as deserving of new and unprecedented levels of publicity. To be a celebrity manager, agent or publicist is to inhabit a world where (to borrow from H. G. Nelson) too much publicity is barely enough.

Accidental heroes

So far we have been talking about media and entertainment industry professionals, about those who accept the necessity of using the media in order to develop and maintain their chosen careers. However, one of the key aspects of the expansion of the celebrity industry in recent years has been its incorporation into the operation of news and current affairs. The fees paid to ordinary citizens accidentally involved in extraordinary or newsworthy events have been built into the cost structure of mass-market magazines and television news and current affairs programs. (At the time of writing, an agreement between representatives of the television networks and magazine publishers is reported to have renounced this kind of activity. Such agreements have failed in the past, and it is expected that the same fate will befall this one.)

The intensity of competition within magazine and television markets has reinforced the importance of exclusivity. When most products in these markets are involved in matching each other's commercial strategies, actual differences in content or format between individual magazines or television programs are both extremely limited and extremely important. The key point of differentiation occurs when *A Current Affair*, say, has a story that is both high-profile and exclusive. Exclusivity is purchased, usually, and commits the subject of the story to an exclusive deal with one television network and, usually, one magazine outlet (the Nine Network, say, and an ACP publication such as the *Australian Women's Weekly*).

Despite all the public and regulatory agonising about chequebook journalism, despite the obvious ethical conflicts it involves for journalists who claim to be disinterested in their reporting of news stories, this kind of deal has become a fundamental component of the operation of the media in Australia. For an enthusiastic supporter like Max Markson, 'it is purely a commercial transaction' like any other:

> You've got Channel 7 or Channel 9 fighting a ratings war and a point to them is worth $50 million at the end of the year. Magazines like *Woman's Day, New Idea, Women's Weekly* and *New Weekly* are competing for readership. If one of them thinks that by spending $10,000 or $50,000 on a story they can pick up readers, then they'll do it. You only have to read the financial pages to see the sort of money the media companies make – it's substantial. Obviously, they have budgets to buy stories.[7]

Notwithstanding Markson's endorsement of the practice, from the point of view of journalism (as distinct from business) ethics, the issues of principle raised by such practices are substantial. Modern journalism defends itself, still, by claiming its democratic function as the 'fourth estate', as the independent watchdog serving the public interest above all else and impervious to corruption by commercial considerations.[8] Chequebook journalism makes a mockery of this notion and there are certainly plenty of journalists who regret and resent its widespread adoption.

It has to be said, though, that there are other regrettable practices within journalism itself, practices which have also developed as a response to the intensification of media competition since the mid-1980s and which have necessitated some method of protection for those who become the accidental celebrity. The tactics employed by the modern version of television current affairs – the adversarial style of interview, the use of hidden cameras, the carpark interview, the office invasions, and so on – have made it very difficult for the average citizen caught up in these events to protect their own interests. There is no adequate system of redress for victims of media misrepresentation in Australia and the power of commercial television programs to protect themselves, legally and otherwise, is far greater than that available to ordinary citizens. Anyone who watches television regularly knows that it is hard to come across as an innocent, reasonable person when confronted without warning by a television crew and Mike Munro as you are getting into your car. Because of its efficiency in generating a plausible story with lively pictures, and because it constructs a flattering image of the crusading reporter, the aggressive outdoor confrontation has become a routine performance in current affairs television. It is, though, a performance which reflects the demands of the television genre rather than the likely guilt or innocence of the person being interviewed.

Consequently, as publicist Tracey Mair points out, it is not surprising that people should want to protect themselves. The media has become 'trickier and people are more fearful of dealing' with it unassisted. 'People are scared of journalists, people are scared of picking up the phone and talking to a journalist.' Instead, 'they want to employ people who can actually manage the media'. Whereas once this was an option only exercised by those with some kind of professional connection to the media, it is now being employed by a broad range of people from all walks of life. Nicolls expressed surprise at the extent of this when she called a woman who had become newsworthy through a victory in a passive smoking lawsuit:

> JANE NICOLLS: I thought … good on her, that's great … It was just going to be a page-one story [i.e. brief], it wasn't a big deal, and so I rang her up and she said 'Oh, you ring Harry M. Miller', and I just nearly fell off the chair. She said, 'Oh, I've had so many requests, I just thought it easier to go through an agent … I'll be donating the money to [an anti-smoking lobby group].

While one might understand Nicolls' surprise at the commercialisation of a relatively high-minded cause, it is worth thinking about this situation from the other woman's point of view. It is in fact very stressful to be pursued by the media on the scent of a hot story. Ironically, though, the very competitiveness which makes exclusivity an appropriate commercial strategy for the networks also makes it a very effective means of personal protection. Once exclusivity has been won by one organisation, it is no longer in the interest of competing organisations to publicise their competitor's property. The media frenzy can in fact be closed down by the introduction of an agent capable of cutting a deal with one or other of the major players.

An example of this process comes from August 1998, when a 54-year-old woman gave birth to triplets following IVF treatment. She had grown-up children from a previous marriage but no children with her current partner. While they were both delighted, her age and the fact that she had made use of IVF technology created a lot of media interest. Much of this was insulting and upsetting. The couple lived in a small country town, which was besieged by the media, its citizens repeatedly bailed up for *vox pop* soundbites for the evening news and the tabloids. By all accounts, the townsfolk were supportive of the couple and defended their right to do what they had done, but the media pack cruising the town and obstructing the entrance to the couple's property was an unwanted intrusion. Miller was engaged and effectively closed things down by negotiating exclusive contracts with *A Current Affair* and the *Australian Women's Weekly*. The couple were understandably relieved that their ordeal could be brought to an end. Miller describes his method of dealing with people's apparent helplessness in such a situation:

> HARRY M. MILLER: The real lesson we teach people is that you don't have to answer any questions at all. They don't have to pick up the phone, they can put the answering machine on, and they can walk past anybody and say nothing, zilch, not even 'No comment', just keep walking.

Easier said than done, apparently, on the evidence we see on television virtually every night. Consequently, Miller says, it comes as a 'big revelation to people like the father of these triplets. He felt compelled to speak, [but] all he has to do is keep walking and say, "Excuse me, you're trespassing".'

As Miller recognises, sometimes it takes more than that. Regular viewers of *60 Minutes* may recall a special program, entitled 'Has the Media Gone Too Far', hosted by Jana Wendt in 1993 and featuring an invited group of journalists, commentators, and some subjects of media interest. In a particularly ugly exchange during this special, Joanne Robertson, the sister of Dr James Scott (the so-called 'Iceman', whose survival in the Himalayas was the subject of a Richard Carleton/*60 Minutes* exclusive negotiated through

Harry M. Miller), was bullied by Carleton and Jeff McMullen, apparently because they felt Scott never told them the 'true' story of his ordeal. Robertson was obviously deeply distressed by the behaviour of the media at that time, including the beneficiaries of the exclusive deal, *60 Minutes*. When a public contest erupted over the rights to Stuart Diver's story in 1997, Robertson wrote to the *Courier-Mail* to express her sympathy for the family and also to remind readers of the 'dreadfully intrusive nature of the media at that time and their complete disregard for everything and everyone except their need to secure a story'. It is no wonder, she wrote, that the Divers – 'another family that unwittingly has been thrown into the centre of nation-wide media attention as the result of a misfortune – have also sought the services of Harry M. Miller'.[9]

All of that granted, the activities of some agents/managers can be cynical and predatory too. We have seen copies of some letters sent to Diver the day after his rescue, seeking to manage his media affairs and offering him the promise of 'lucrative' rewards, which plumb new depths of crassness and insensitivity. The upbeat marketing tone breaks through even the most sanctimonious expressions of sympathy and must have been deeply offensive to Diver and to his family. This does seem to be a section of the media in-dustry where standards of practice vary considerably and where there seems to be room on the range for more than one cowboy. One interviewee happily referred to certain competitors as 'sleaze bags', while outlining their view that there are standards of behaviour to be observed which these competitors ignored.

This is fair enough, but also, perhaps, a little disingenuous. (As those mem-bers of the press usually denied exclusivity are keen to point out, standards do seem to be a little flexible, even for the best of them. Miller was quoted by the *Age*, with evident relish, as saying that it would be inappropriate for the media or an agent to employ chequebook tactics to secure Diver's story.[10] This was before he had been contracted – through the intervention of the Salvation Army! – to represent Diver.) The fact is that, even in cases such as Diver's, what is being contested is a commercial property; the story of his survival becomes a commodity which can be bought and developed. As Miller says, 'If you pick up a Stuart Diver … you can strategise with them until they're old. Even if they've gone out of their first life … they can become something else, they might become a television commentator.' So, while these agents may now be a necessary form of assistance to people who become the accidental objects of media interest, no one pretends that the service they provide is anything other than a commercial opportunity.

It is by no means clear that these deals will always produce outcomes that people are happy with. Swimmer Hayley Lewis' mother, for instance, has been quoted as regretting the exclusive deal the family negotiated with the *Australian Women's Weekly* to cover Hayley's wedding: 'It was meant to keep everyone away but I think it just attracts attention'. (Hayley, too, suggests there is a downside to the endorsement potential of the sports star: 'I used to be known for my swimming, now I'm known for washing machines'.)[11] As mentioned above, the James Scott deal produced an interview that angered the Scott family and also Miller, the negotiator of that deal:

> HARRY M. MILLER: No matter how much money they offered us, I would never agree or advise a client of ours to be interviewed by Richard Carleton ... I don't want to put at risk any of the clients with somebody like that. Here's a guy who decided before he interviewed James Scott that he wasn't really sick and I said, 'We'll do the deal but we don't want to talk about the chocolate bar'. We just thought it [Carleton's pursuit of the name of the chocolate bar] so stupid in the context of someone surviving 39 days in an ice cave.

If Harry M. Miller cannot guarantee satisfaction out of an exclusive deal with *60 Minutes*, what hope do the rest of us have?

Regulating the 'mad dogs'

What we have described as the process of managing the media does not, cannot, have the interests of the public as its primary concern. At times, it may be in an organisation's interest to enhance the public's access to accurate information; at other times, it may be in their interest not only to deny access to accurate information but also that it ever existed. Managing the media can involve telling barefaced lies; mostly, it has to be admitted, these lies protect powerful people, but they can (and sometimes do) protect vulnerable and powerless people too. Given the shifts in media ethics over the last couple of decades, it is not surprising that the ethics of some celebrity industry practitioners are proving flexible as well.

A more fundamental concern, however, is the fact that the celebrity industry is now so pervasive, so broadly implicated in so much of the activity of the public sphere in Australia. That may be as much a product of a decade of government deregulation of the media industries as of the celebrity industry's expansion. Consequently, it should now worry us that the job of protecting ordinary citizens against unwanted, intrusive and, in many cases, unwarranted attentions from the news media has passed over to celebrity management. Without appropriate provisions for privacy protection, or any method of redress against misrepresentation or entrapment other than the very limited (and expensive) opportunities provided by libel and defamation laws, the ordinary citizen who becomes an accidental hero (or villain, for that matter) is pretty much at the mercy of a media driven by the pressures of commercial competition to behave cynically and irresponsibly. As Miller says, sometimes they can behave like 'mad dogs'. That would not be such a problem if it weren't for the absence of any kind of regulatory dogcatcher to round them up from time to time.

Chapter 5

Core Territory: Celebrities and the Women's Magazines

When you open a current issue of *Women's Weekly, New Idea* or the more gender-neutral *Who Weekly*, what strikes you first is simply the number of images of personalities. The faces which occupy these pages need little introduction as the captions often imply that we already know the people who have been captured (usually quite willingly) by photographers. Openings and premieres abound and jostle with gossip-driven exposés and supportive pieces that try to tell the star's 'side' of a current scandal or health risk. The familiarity of the faces and stories is a product of, and intersects with, their coverage in other media forms as well, but the regular backgrounding of what is occurring with particular celebrities is the natural territory of these publications. The mass-market women's magazines, which also include *NW* (once *New Weekly*) and *Woman's Day*, construct a continuing serial which informs conversations throughout the week. Celebrity reportage in these magazines, gently but definitely, assumes both continuing knowledge and interest, drawing the reader back each week for the latest developments.

As acknowledged earlier, women's mass-market magazines are often the target of criticism for the character of their representation of women's interests, criticism that probably these days they knowingly provoke. Their television advertisements, for instance, leave us in no doubt about how they conceptualise their audience's desires. For example, in a long-running commercial series, *Woman's Day* depicts its readers as sneaking off into a fantasy land removed from the flows of everyday life. Their magazine is a refuge from worldly demands – and definitely not an earnest politicisation of women's thinking. Accordingly, it is not surprising that Susan Faludi was able to mine American and British women's magazines for evidence of the backlash against feminism with their stories of female celebrities and 'health' articles concerning the biological clock working against the corporate and publicly engaged trajectory of the female achiever. Similarly, Germaine Greer's opinion of end-of-millennium 'girls' magazines is predictably dismissive. In her reading of *Sugar*, a British magazine aimed at early teen and pre-teen girls, she attacks its misdirected focus: 'Nothing in *Sugar* magazine suggests a girl can have a life apart from lads, that she has any interests of her own beyond make-up, clothes and relationships, that she will ever get a job or travel, that she plays any sport, that she has ever read a book'.[1] According to Greer, girls' magazines – notwithstanding the rhetoric of 'girl power' – are as complicit as women's magazines in providing the wrong kinds of information and emulatory identities for their readers.

Our intentions in this chapter are not primarily concerned with damning the state of mass-market women's magazines, as the popular press is given to do, nor with celebrating an overdue reintegration of the feminine and the personal into mass media content, as certain feminist readings of popular culture have done. Rather, we want first to understand them a little better by identifying how they work so successfully for their readerships. Part of that success must be related to the fact that these magazines are the classic location of celebrity journalism. As our surveys have indicated, celebrity stories have become a major component of all media, but these magazines have turned more categorically to celebrity-based content than any other Australian media form. In Australia, they represent the core territory of a celebrity industry and this chapter maps that relationship.

Women's magazines in Australia

> There is such a feeling of excitement on a Monday morning that there is a new magazine out there with the latest gossip, and they're down the newsagent buying it.
> *Bunty Avieson*

Australians are reputedly the highest per capita consumers of magazines in the world,[2] and Australian women buy more women's magazines than do women of any other nation.[3] If sales figures were averaged across the population, every man, woman and child in Australia would buy sixteen magazines a year – and that is without considering those they might read which have been purchased by other people. In 1998, for the first time, the total sales of magazines exceeded the total sales of newspapers.[4] New titles come and go so rapidly that it is impossible to say how many magazines are available in Australia at any one time, but 1998 estimates suggest a total of 5500.[5] While the four top-selling magazines (in order: *Australian Women's*

Weekly, Woman's Day, New Idea and *Reader's Digest*) have maintained their market leadership for many years, since the late 1980s their total circulation figures have fallen substantially as many more titles become available. Among the most successful new titles are two specifically devoted to celebrity gossip: *Who Weekly* and *NW*.

Of course, not all successful magazines concern themselves with celebrity (*Reader's Digest*, for example). Keeping company with the new celebrity gossip magazines are two (*That's Life*, the fifth highest in circulation, and *For Me*) which explicitly avoid celebrities, instead publishing stories about events in ordinary people's lives, together with puzzles and competitions. The remaining magazines in the top twenty are a mixed bag: three dealing with domestic pursuits including gardening, a downmarket male sex magazine, a news magazine, and three glossies pitched at 18–30-year-old female readers and containing a small number of items about celebrities (*Cleo, Cosmopolitan* and *marie claire australia*). The overwhelming majority of the other magazines sold in Australia are special-interest publications (on such topics as computers, cars, travel, financial advice) and do not have an interest in celebrity.

While the celebrity-oriented magazines do not quite constitute a majority of the top twenty titles (nine, according to the 30 June 1998 audit, were concerned with celebrity),[6] the high public profile created by the intense competition between them produces a misleading impression about the importance of celebrity to the magazine market as a whole. That said, however, the cultural prominence and high circulation figures of such magazines indicate the effectiveness of celebrity journalism in attracting a mass market. As already noted, celebrities constitute an important category of women's magazines' content, interest in which (though probably not deep) is shared by a large percentage of the population. The importance of celebrities to television is similarly broadly based (the Nine Network's market dominance is related to its well-planned promotion of its network personalities). As an indication of this widespread popular interest, the total circulation of the nine celebrity-focused titles (*Australian Women's Weekly, Woman's Day, New Idea, Who Weekly, NW, TV Week, TV Hits, Dolly* and *Girlfriend*) is significantly greater than that of the eleven with very little or no interest in celebrities.

Not all of the nine titles deal with celebrity in the same way. A major discriminator is the extent to which the interest in celebrity includes an interest in scandal. *Who Weekly* attempts to distinguish itself from *NW* by a more limited attention to scandal and a claim to a substantial proportion of male purchasers, though it is still counted as a women's magazine in the biannual reports of circulation audits. *Australian Women's Weekly* (as a monthly magazine and the market leader) affects slightly more gravitas than either *Woman's Day* or *New Idea*, so it too publishes less scandal. The two television magazines, inevitably concerned with celebrities, rarely carry scandal since the purpose of *TV Week* is to detail the schedule and to promote programs, while *TV Hits* is, like *Dolly* and *Girlfriend*, a teenage magazine addressing an audience of young fans and focusing on pictures of singers and soap stars accompanied by relatively innocuous text. To our industry interviewees, the differences between the mass-market magazines were highly significant, but the intensity of the competition between publications in the two age-based markets, and the significant fluctuation in sales reported in response to particular covers, suggest that readers may not feel the same. Even if there is not a lot of brand loyalty, this is nevertheless an important and lucrative market.

The content of mass-market women's magazines can be divided into two sections: service and personalities. Service covers the regular articles on fashion, beauty, health, cooking and other home-making activities as well as the columns of advice, tips and psychic phenomena. Personality material refers both to celebrity stories and to those about ordinary people who have in some way become prominent – stories of ordinary people doing extra-ordinary things. Bunty Avieson, speaking of *New Idea* in 1998, noted that, while the service section was very important and popular with the 50-plus readers, the celebrity gossip sold the magazine each week since it was there that 'the excitement' was generated. The celebrity personality story obviously occupies a very important position in the magazine's marketing strategy, but it has been suggested also that the combination of both the celebrity and the 'ordinary' personality stories serves an important function. Discussing the value of using celebrities and ordinary people for stories in magazines in Britain (where the mass-market weeklies have much less celebrity gossip), Marjorie Ferguson has commented:

> The repeated use of real readers and celebrities demonstrates deeply held professional beliefs about the audience gratifications assumed to derive from satisfying curiosity about, while supplying bases for feeling the same as, quite other people. This is the vicarious living or voyeurism syndrome of popular culture and is not confined to women's magazines ... The message that such rich, powerful or beautiful people are employed to communicate is that 'you may not be exactly like me, but there are aspects of me that you as a woman may wish to share or emulate' ... [Yet] fascinating as the royal, rich and beautiful are, they present problems of economic and social distance which do not arise when 'people like us' are given the 'treatment'.[7]

Publishing stories on both categories of personality aims to address both sets of audience 'gratifications', as, in a different way, does the provision of magazines concentrating either on celebrities or on ordinary people.

Gossip magazines like *NW* have smaller service sections than such mass-market women's magazines as *Woman's Day*. *NW* makes a minimal attempt to address the home-maker because its target audience is much younger and more decidedly inner urban (as against suburban). Yet it still has sufficient fashion, beauty and cooking items to enable readers to regard it as just another style of women's magazine. In comparison, *Who Weekly* carries such items only when it can tie them to celebrity photographs. It is probably true to say that the separate entertainment sections in both of these magazines constitute their versions of the service function, although they also carry horoscopes and puzzles. (At the other end of the spectrum, of course, there are best-selling women's magazines which contain no personality material of any kind and which publish only service information; *Australian Family Circle* is the prime example.)

In terms of these broad categories of service and personality, it may appear that there has been little change in the content of the long-running Australian women's magazines since their establishment. In 1976, then editor of the *Australian Women's Weekly* Ita Buttrose noted:

> With the Royal Family (perennial favourites), Jackie Onassis ('About two years ago you couldn't go wrong with her, today she's not so popular') and Princess Caroline ('Always good, you see, she's young, she's romantic and she's just about to set off on her life'), the *Women's Weekly* offers patterns, knitting, crochet, fashions in the shops and cooking. It's a successful formula which has served over 41 years.[8]

The continuities between the content Buttrose describes and that of today's magazines, even in the celebrities instanced, are remarkable. Closer observation, however, reveals significant shifts since the 1970s. Some of these shifts are also implicated in the appearance and success of the newer arrivals, the celebrity gossip magazines, and the increase in the number of titles targeted at teenagers.

During the 1930s, the *Australian Women's Weekly* carried a surprising amount of political content, initially reflecting both the presence of E. G. 'Red Ted' Theodore as one of its founders and a level of feminism which today seems rather improbable.[9] This was largely displaced by patriotic material during World War II when the magazine dedicated its content to supporting the war effort.[10] Virtually all overt political content had disappeared by the 1950s. In these early days, the three leading women's magazines (*Australian Women's Weekly, New Idea* and *Woman's Day*) were more readily distinguishable from one another than they were by the late 1970s. Until the mid-1950s, *New Idea* was predominantly a magazine of short fiction, and letters and columns, but few features and comparatively limited use of illustrations.

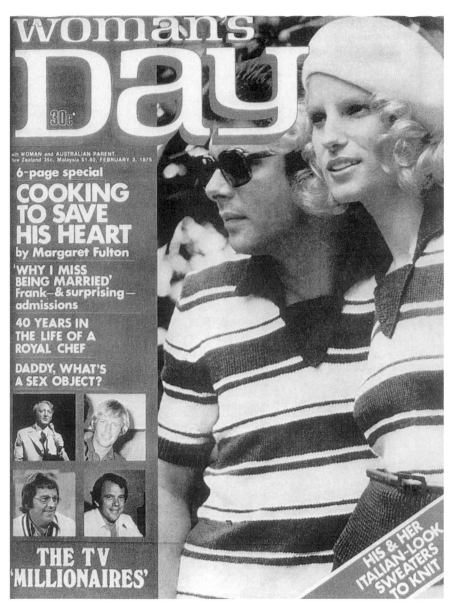

Woman's Day, 3 February 1975, shows beginning of shift to celebrity covers. Anonymous models promote knitting patterns in main picture, while side-bar features 'TV Millionaires' Graham Kennedy, Paul Hogan, Ernie Sigley and Mike Willesee. (with kind permission of ACP Publishing Pty Ltd)

Woman's Day started as a fortnightly in 1948, became a weekly in 1949 and went through many changes of title as it absorbed other magazines in the 1950s and 1960s. According to Beatrice Faust, during this period it had a provocative style, more interest in film stars and a 'veneer of novelty and smartness'.[11]

By the beginning of the period which is the core of our concern here – the two decades from 1979 to 1998 – the differences between the big three magazines had largely eroded under the pressure of competition.[12] Although the *Australian Women's Weekly* broke step to become a monthly in 1983, the changes that are most relevant to the current study all occurred later in the decade. They involved a reduction in the length of feature articles and an increase in the proportion of content (in all three magazines) that was devoted to health, celebrities and superstitious beliefs. The number of articles on health in the *Australian Women's Weekly*, which had grown steadily during the 1950s–1970s, nearly trebled during the 1980s. Also over the same decade, there was a substantial increase in the number of articles which featured celebrities talking about their health.[13]

This account accords with perceptions from within the industry. For instance, when asked about the changes in Australian women's magazines over the period of her involvement with them, Avieson, editorial director of *New Idea* (and, before that, editor of *Woman's Day*), nominated two changes which she dated to 1988. One was the change in advice columns, from the more traditional 'Dear Dorothy' style to 'things like Feng Shui and clair-voyants'. The other was the greater attention paid to celebrities. Significantly, she related this latter development to a change in editorial direction:

> BUNTY AVIESON: The quantum leap would have been when Nene King left *New Idea* where she was deputy editor and went to *Woman's Day* where she became editor and ... she thought that people wanted more stories on Australian or on showbiz celebrities.

Qualifying the 'quantum leap' phrase, Avieson suggested that 'it was more like an evolution, but [King] then accelerated it'. Humphrey McQueen has suggested that it was Ita Buttrose who, as editor, doubled the frequency with which entertainment celebrities appeared on the *Australian Women's Weekly* covers. Other sources place this kind of change in the early 1980s and stress the appearance of scandalous stories more, but the influence of particular editors is usually regarded as significant.[14]

One of the reasons for this is the high profile taken by some of the leading women's magazines' editors, as they became celebrities themselves. Although devoted readers may well have always known the name of the editor of their favourite magazine, the editors themselves had no significant profile until the

1970s. There was none of the current practice of a highly personal editorial, with accompanying photograph and signature, and even if their names were known, the editors most certainly were not celebrities themselves. This changed when Ita Buttrose took charge of the *Australian Women's Weekly*. She was made editor in 1975 and left Australian Consolidated Press (ACP) in 1981; during that six-year period she became one of the most famous women in Australia, in part through her appearances in television advertisements for her magazines. She used her own celebrity – constructed through newspaper interviews, television programs, social pages, even in a song by Cold Chisel as well as in her own editorials – to promote and personalise her magazine. (Dawn Swain, who followed Buttrose, maintained the personalised editorial message but neither sought nor achieved personal celebrity.)

The second editor to claim and market her celebrity status was Nene King. King is not quite as categorically identified with the celebrity-editor model as with the shifts towards chequebook journalism that accompanied the intensification of the competition between women's magazines for exclusive celebrity stories. She outbid her competitors by paying $165,000 for the Fergie toe-sucking photographs, and she was the editor-in-chief of *Woman's Day* when it paid between $100,000 and $150,000 to Kym Wilson for her story on Michael Hutchence, 'Michael's Final Hours'. King has not achieved the personal, nationwide, popular recognition that Buttrose did, nor has she ever been 'voted' 'most admired woman in the country'. But she has a social and news presence in the daily press, significant exposure on television and, of course, whether she was editing *Woman's Day* or *Australian Women's Weekly*, she was a distinctive personal presence in their pages.[15]

When an editor is a celebrity in the manner of Ita Buttrose or Nene King, the person and the magazine become interchangeable: each identity advertises the other. The strategy looked to have achieved its apotheosis when Buttrose created and published the magazine *Ita*. When, after a few successful years, it failed to attract sufficient advertisers to continue, despite the intense loyalty she had established with her readers, there was an expectation that Buttrose too was doomed. But, notwithstanding her close identification with the magazines she had edited, Buttrose's celebrity proved to be far more broadly industrially based. She is now managed by the Saxton Speakers Bureau and Management Group and, in our interview with him, Winston Broadbent used her as an example of a speaker in high demand whose 'every speech is a work of art', who is a 'very solid business speaker' and whose celebrity is still a tradable commodity.

The contemporary pervasiveness of celebrity which has facilitated Ita Buttrose's public career – her sponsoring of celebrity journalism in women's magazines, her deliberate and well-planned construction of her own celebrity, and her attempt to literally capitalise that celebrity through the establishment of *Ita* – should not blind us to the fact that journalism's interest in celebrities is not in itself new. For the entire twentieth century, magazines have carried articles about celebrities, usually entertainers or royalty. As far as mass-market women's magazines are concerned, prior to the mid to late 1980s, celebrities were just one part of the content mix but not a major one. In quantitative terms, they were certainly less important than knitting patterns, advice on childcare, or recipes. So, while the changes in the representation of celebrity in Australia during the 1980s did not introduce celebrity coverage to magazines, they substantially increased the proportion of content devoted to such material as well as the proportion of celebrities who were themselves Australian.

The enduring value of scandal

Criticisms of the tabloid register of contemporary celebrity journalism have suggested that the tone of celebrity coverage has changed in recent years, becoming much more scandalous and much less respectful, but the situation is not quite that simple. The language of popular journalism has itself become much less formal, so that most feature material from twenty-five or more years ago sounds rather stuffy and longwinded. An *Australian Women's Weekly* article on soprano Elisabeth Schwarzkopf in 1949 provides a useful comparison. The personal interaction between the reporter, Helen Frizell, and the star is very evident, as is the reporter's familiarly privileged access into the personal space of the celebrity:

> At nine am I knocked on the door of soprano Elisabeth Schwarzkopf's hotel room. There wasn't a sound for a moment and then I heard a sleepy Viennese voice call, 'Come in'. Pushing the door open, I saw the startled face of a very pretty girl looking at me from over the top of an eiderdown.

A very long interview ensues over breakfast and many details of the soprano's health and beauty regime, as well as her musical history, are provided before an obligatory fashion note: 'Miss Schwarzkopf has brought out to Australia some French and Austrian model gowns neatly packed into the six small suitcases she carries. One is white, trimmed with mink, another is a Christian Dior model, another is lavishly sunray pleated.' Apart from an absence of reference to romantic liaisons, this content is very similar to what we would expect to read about a visiting celebrity today. The stylistic differences, especially the slight wordiness, are what make it strange.[16]

Yet, even when the language is elaborate or formal, the content could still be scandalous. One of the standard figures of 1950s scandal was that of the runaway heiress – although, then, these were scandals about unsuitable romantic liaisons or marriages rather than about, say, drugs or sexual abuse. While not all such heiresses or their parents could reasonably be described as celebrities, the stories functioned very similarly to today's celebrity coverage. A feature article in the *Australian Women's Weekly* in 1956 about the life of 'Jimmy' Goldsmith (the late British tycoon James Goldsmith) and the daughter of his runaway marriage provided the opportunity to revisit the deeds of the rich and famous and deplore them, while observing how tragedy was obviously making him a better person. This structure remains highly contemporary, reminiscent of the recent adventures of the princesses of Monaco, Caroline and Stephanie. The opening paragraph reads: 'A tiny two-year-old girl has come to be the "happy-ever-after" part of romance to Jimmy Goldsmith, wealthy company director, whose runaway marriage in Scotland to Isobel Patino, daughter of the Bolivian tin multi-millionaire, two years ago enthralled the world'. The bulk of the story details the visit of the reporter to the house where the child, her father and nurse live, provides information which enables the reader to work out that the child was conceived before the marriage occurred, tells us that the mother died giving birth to her daughter, and at the end of article recaps the past scandal, recounting how Patino's father 'sent Isobel off to Casablanca to forget her lover, but Jimmy chartered a plane and flew to her, only to find she'd escaped and flown back to London. Jimmy joined her and they fled to Scotland with Don Patino's private detectives on their heels.'[17]

Similarly, gossip columns were not an invention of the 1980s either. Mass-market magazine gossip has always circulated around people who were likely to be familiar to the majority of readers, and who more likely to be familiar than celebrities? One of the most popular writers for the *Australian Women's Weekly* during the 1950s and 1960s was Dorothy Drain (who edited the magazine briefly during the 1970s). Her principal regular contribution was a gossip column called 'It Seems to Me'. A sample item from a 1951 issue reads:

> One of the doctors attending Franchot Tone, whose face was damaged in a brawl with Tom Neal over actress Barbara Payton, says Tone's profile will be as good as ever, that maybe he will look even better than he did before. Seems a drastic sort of beauty treatment, just the same.[18]

Wordier, again, than the captions to the photographs in the 'Famous Faces' or 'Hot Gossip' sections of the current weekly magazines, but both content and style seem contemporary. It is necessary to bear this evidence in mind when reading such claims as Sian Powell's that celebrity coverage prior to the 1980s was uniformly gentle and admiring.[19] Material about Australian figures and overseas celebrities visiting Australia may have been overwhelmingly brief, but celebrity scandal was still to be found.

Finally, one area where we are entitled to claim a dramatic difference between the current and previous generations of women's magazines is in their visual appearance. Women's magazines are now much more pictorial and much more colourful. The layout of the covers more comprehensively advertises the (putative) contents with banners and teasers, while using the full resources of colour and design to generate a sense of excitement. Inside, very few pages are predominantly print; the one regular exception is revealingly called 'Big Read' (in the *Australian Women's Weekly*, where it precedes the longest of the surviving instances of magazine short fiction). Most notable has been the transformation of what were once society pages or collections of photographs of 'What People Are Wearing Overseas'. Today, these are more often composed of unflattering celebrity photographs, with running titles like 'The Good Goss', 'Star Style', 'Hotline' or, in the newer magazines, 'Paparazzi with Attitude' or 'Star Tracks'. Some, but not all, of these reveal the other change in celebrity coverage: captions that can be snide, flip or just plain insulting. This is one area where the distinctions between the competing magazines become significant. *Who Weekly* may print photographs in 'Star Tracks' showing famous people caught off-guard or looking less than their best, but the captions still provide little more than identification and an anodyne quotation. The *Australian Women's Weekly*, though, uses this section for less flattering comments. A regular component of its 'Star Style' is a page or even two of celebrities caught wearing the same dress, with captions commenting on which one (if any) is wearing it successfully.

In the following section, we examine some further aspects of contemporary women's magazines in an attempt better to understand the nature of their appeal: the central discursive territory of 'the personal', their idiosyncratic but highly successful redefinition of 'news', and the importance of the promises offered through the magazine cover – whether or not readers actually believe them.

The personal, the new and the exclusive

> The celebrity may fascinate, but the trace of ordinary habits of life, from domestic friction to eating disorders, connects even the most worldly celebrity to the mundane.
> *McKenzie Wark*, Celebrities, Culture and Cyberspace

THE PERSONAL

The revelation of the personal life is a central consideration for women's magazine stories. Our interviewees persistently claimed that the demand for the personal is what distinguishes the magazines from newspapers and other media outlets. A survey of actual newspaper coverage reveals a slightly greater convergence of media concerns than such claims might suggest: the 'Stay in Touch' page of the *Sydney Morning Herald* is probably as personal and gossipy as any part of *NW*. Nevertheless, while they are not the only places we can find it, in the magazines 'the personal' dominates. The covers routinely foreground personal revelations as their primary category of information, and details of domestic or personal life clearly figure as more important than, say, a new professional opportunity for the celebrity concerned. Nine Network's Heidi Virtue said that the emphasis on the personal was a particularly noticeable component of the interest in local celebrities:

> HEIDI VIRTUE: Personal angles, that's what the women's magazines want. They want deaths and marriages and births, they love babies, they want sickness, recoveries, fitness, light weight loss, giving up smoking, anything like that, that's what they want of local people.

As an example of the kind of demand that is, in a sense, always going to be insatiable because of its personal nature, Virtue said that she is asked at least once a week, 'Why won't Kerri-Anne have children?', although this is something Kerri-Anne Kennerley has never talked about, despite her openness on most other matters.

While it is easy to read the emphasis on the personal off the billboards, the covers and the list of contents, it is instructive to see how fully institutionalised this is – how it is embedded into the production practices of the magazines. In this context, the stress on the personal is most clearly exemplified by the insistence of *Who Weekly* on the home-take, the interview and photo shoot with the celebrity in their own home. *Who*'s stories of the celebrity in her or his intimate space are the closest that Australian magazines come to a local edition of *Hello!*, the Spanish-based celebrity-at-home interview and photograph magazine with many local European editions, which is the favoured European site for negotiated celebrity exclusives. In *Who Weekly*, the trade-off between intrusion, revelation and celebrity promotion is at its most obvious. Although not as blatantly sycophantic as *Hello!*, its greater propriety and avoidance of scandal make it a highly desirable outlet for celebrity promotion.[20] In return for the guarantee of a respectful story, both reporter and photographer are allowed inside the celebrity's home and the reporter is licensed to go after personal revelations. Even so, *Who* tends not to be chasing scandal. Intimate titbits are the aim, and their deliberate ordinariness is well represented by an article on comedian Glenn Robbins which devotes quite a bit of space to his boarding his cat with his parents while he goes on holiday.[21]

Trivial they may be, but untrammelled access is demanded in order to get such details. Jane Nicolls recalled when one of her journalists went to interview comedian Julia Morris and found that, contrary to the standard terms of a *Who Weekly* interview, one of the publicity people from Channel 9 (where Morris was appearing) was present. The result was that this interview appointment was used for the in-home photographs and an interview performed entirely for the publicist's benefit. The reporter took Morris out to lunch alone the following day for the interview that would actually be used in the feature. Nicolls admitted that, by insisting on the in-home photo sessions, the magazines were asking a lot of their subjects:

> JANE NICOLLS: What we're asking for is a huge slab of time to shoot an interview at home. It would rarely be less than four hours, I suppose that would be the minimum, whereas you can have a quick hit with a newspaper journalist and get them out of your hair in 40 minutes.

The fact that celebrities were still willing to invest this amount of time indicates their estimation of the importance of a feature in the magazine, as well as their interest in generating the kind of stories such an approach tends to produce.

Despite the importance that we (and Nicolls) have placed on the home-take as an exemplification of the mass-market magazine's concentration on the personal, these stories constitute only a small proportion of *Who Weekly*'s content. Further, and even with the extended interviews, there were significant exceptions to its insistence on interviews being conducted at home and accompanied by photographs taken at the same time. Nicolls instanced an interview with Jack Nicholson: 'We got a hotel room interview with him which we thought would be just "Inside Scoop", but … it was a pretty good interview. We just ran it as a straight Q and A.' Sections of the magazine are exempt from the home-take rule; in practice, it applies only to the feature stories. The issue which carried an interview with Pamela Anderson's estranged and abusive husband on his release from prison – a story that Nicolls admitted would have run even if they had not received the home-take – had three other features, all of which obviously had involved home access.[22]

The importance of the home-take lies not so much in its dominance of the prevailing practice of the publication or of its content but, rather, in its capacity to signal to readers the magazine's focus on the personal, the domestic and the intimate details of the subjects' lives. Consequently, the home-take features are always highly self-conscious, deliberately foregrounding the signs of privileged access. The Glenn Robbins story not only describes 'his (spotless) renovated open-plan living room in bayside Brighton' in the text, it also captions an accompanying photograph with a reference to his being 'flat out at his Melbourne home'. The domesticity revealed in this way also displays the 'ordinariness' of the Australian celebrity, while his contrasting 'extraordinariness' is conveyed by the other details of the story:

his professional performances and an accident with an ultra-light plane during filming.[23]

NEWS AND THE EXCLUSIVE

> We are a news magazine.
> *Bunty Avieson*, New Idea

In our interviews with them, Avieson and Nicolls both emphasised the importance of news as a content category in their magazines. It turns out that what they mean by news is what we had thought of as celebrity gossip. News for them is what is published in such sections as 'Hotline' (*NW*) or 'Hot Gossip' (*Woman's Day*) or, most explicitly, 'News Flash' (*New Idea*), as well as in the features following up (more traditionally defined) news stories – such as the day-release pregnancy of a Queensland woman dubbed the 'black widow' because she bought a black dress, allegedly for the funeral, before murdering her husband.[24] The inclusion of this kind of news is held to distinguish the weekly from the monthly magazines.

The focus on news did come as something of a surprise to us, indicating the usefulness of analysing this industry through interviews with practitioners rather than relying on secondary sources. Academic and most other analysts of women's magazines do not normally categorise 'news' as among the content found in them. For such analysts, usually, news is identified only in magazines which are specifically devoted to this category of information: the *Bulletin* or *Time*. While traditional journalistic definitions of news (the definitions underpinning most academic analyses of women's magazines) do allow for articles about the break-up of famous people's marriages, for instance, to be considered news, the classification of such articles tends to relegate them to the less important categories: 'soft news' or, to use Galtung and Ruge's categories, 'negative news of elite people'.[25] Also, the periodicity of magazines – weekly, monthly or quarterly – is out of step with the dominant time frame of what is more conventionally considered news (that is, daily). More importantly however, daily newspapers, not to mention the more frequently broadcast bulletins of radio and television news, regularly scoop magazines on timely events. The lead time of magazines can be several weeks, and in the case of glossies like *Vogue* may be several months, which makes the idea that magazines can *break* 'news' improbable.

There are, however, many occasions when the mass-market women's magazines can claim to have done just that. During our survey period, there was a series of incidents involving *Footy Show* host Sam Newman. He was assaulted by the ex-boyfriend of a woman he had been seen with; his ex-girlfriend, Leonie Jones, was fined for not reporting a car accident in which she had run over Newman and broken his leg; and, finally, there were

I NEVER MEANT TO HURT HIM

Leonie Jones says she's having Sam Newman's baby and the couple were planning a secret wedding. Then one night it all went horribly wrong . . .

Being dubbed "Sam Newman's fiancee" has made Leonie Jones from the past eight weeks has been one of the few women the 51-year-old shows a quick glance above the surface of his private life and the tears welling just below the surface.

It's obvious from her age alone that Leonie has not been well. She's had a lot on her mind lately. She has no job, no home, no partner, no prospects and will around December this year she was two-and-a-half months pregnant with TV larrikin Sam Newman's child – whether they are together or not and despite the fact that Leonie has refused to publicly acknowledge the child as his. Yet for all that, you don't want to feel alone. You don't want to bring a baby into the world with no partner, and I'd get by with my family and friends.

Leonie is a 23-year-old, who met The Footy Show star and former Geelong champion at just 18.

"In a small country town we all worked ourselves into a frenzy over the woman who killed the footy star," she says.

The whole time Sam and her man has made her have refused to comment.

Leonie's agent says that her apology gets that her baby is her and she is not broken now – not Sam now, or his broken leg. She says she and there he together become a media melodrama, and has been trying, about without success, to piece their life back together.

If you believe the press she's had a go at Leonie deserve every-thing she gets. She broke Sam's leg and did a runner. Not so, says Leonie. And despite an argument between Leonie and Sam at his Melbourne home on May 24, it was about the pregnancy, she claims nothing could be further from the truth.

"Sam got a bit flustered and said, 'Just stop the car or I'll walk the rest of the way,'" I was sitting there mumbling to myself. He got out of the car and began walking. He saw that I was still mumbling and appeared really approached the car and I didn't really want to

Caption: Leonie and Sam's volatile relationship has been public property, especially since the accident.

continue, because neither of us was getting anywhere with what we had to say.

"While most people would recall in vivid detail the argument that sparked off such a traumatic experience, Leonie is adamant she does not. "I know it's hard to believe, but we had a dispute and it was just so trivial I don't remember what it was." In all fairness, it was not unlike any dispute we had in the past."

Leonie decided she was going to drive home – but

drive straight into a night-mare. "I took my foot off the brake, I didn't go to speed off, he wasn't in front of the car, he was at the side and I thought he was clear of the car but the car made contact with him. I didn't think that I had actually hurt him. I heard him yelp. I saw him in my rear-view mirror. I wasn't very far from him, maybe a house away. He was trying on the ground on the road. I put the car in park and left it running, the lights were on, I opened the door, got out and ran to him.

"I said, 'Come on, get up,' this is enough, step being so silly. It wasn't until then that I realised that I had made contact with him with the car, it was purely an accident."

Leonie says she was stunned and horrified and was unable to take in what had happened.

"I got into the car to go back to watch over him as he was near the road, a little bit. I saw a man in his dressing-gown and reversed the car and drove away. I came back to watch Sam and said to the man that said to the man to call for an ambulance."

Contrary to all reports of the accident so far, Leonie adds "I was with Sam when the ambulance arrived."

She describes the "devastation" as she realised that she had run over the man she loved.

Arriving at Melbourne's Alfred Hospital's casualty ward she says Sam held her hand and assured her he knew it was an accident.

"I sat there for about an hour and when I was allowed to see him for about 15 minutes, he said everything was going to be okay. I felt horrible," she says.

Leonie says that while Sam is aware of the accident, many of those around him aren't so sure. And she says the Nine network has made it clear to Sam that any further "incidents" would not be good for his television career.

Sam de-cided it was not worth the risk and shortly after the accident he asked Leonie to leave his $1.5 million Brighton home.

Leonie who did not make a court appearance last Thursday to answer a charge of failing to report the accident, entered a plea of guilty through her solicitor and was fined $250. No conviction was recorded.

"It's been horrendous. I've lost the person who I was going to make a life with. I don't have anyone to live for the moment," she says.

It's quite a turnaround at just nine months from what she had planned – a future with her fiance – to becoming an adventure, just the two of us," Le-

"But I suppose I got cold feet. I was worried he wasn't just jumping into a fourth marriage. I wanted to make sure he had been as it 100 per cent."

Leonie is the first to concede that the few would have tipped their relationship to blossoming so readily, particularly given their volatile history. In June last year, when she and

New Idea, on 2 August 1997, devoted four pages to the 'real story' about *Footy Show* celebrity Sam Newman and ex-girlfriend Leonie Jones. (with kind permission of *New Idea*)

rumours that, despite their well-publicised differences, Jones was pregnant to Newman. The story of her pregnancy was put on the news agenda by its publication in a mass-market magazine, *New Weekly*.[26] Technically, television scooped the magazine, as the story was actually carried on television before the magazine hit the streets, but, since the television items explicitly referred to the magazine both as a source and as a means of legitimation each time, one could argue that this was an instance of magazines breaking news. There are limits, of course. This story was not acknowledged as news by the more serious outlets, although popular newspapers and television bulletins carried it (it produced 11 stories in total: 7 in newspapers, 1 in the magazine and 3 on television). But it does provide further evidence of the extent to which the traditional distinctions between 'soft' and 'hard' news, and between newspaper and magazine news content, are shifting and blurring.[27]

As part of differentiating her magazine from others, Nicolls argued that *Who Weekly* was much more driven by news values and responsible journalism. The story she chose to demonstrate this was the exclusive interview with Tommy Lee, a story with the cover line 'Tommy Lee Tells All' but entitled 'Home Alone'.[28] It does follow a traditional journalistic style – the 'as told to' confession – but for newspapers this is a feature format, not part of the news, and indeed is in any case very much a standard form of magazine journalism. What emerged from Nicolls' discussion of this story, though, was a forceful demonstration of the importance of the term 'exclusive' to the magazine industry. When the editors of the magazines talk about 'news', it does not necessarily refer to the content of the story or even to its level of importance. Rather, it tends to indicate whether the story is being carried elsewhere – the extent to which it, or some part of it, is 'new' and 'exclusive' to this magazine.

The Tommy Lee story came about because the Los Angeles Deputy Bureau Chief of *People*, Todd Gold, had a contract with Lee and was able to persuade him to do the interview. *People* included a small item on it in its 'Scoop' section and there was a television interview which ran with Fox in the United States, but this did not negate the exclusivity, which has a medium as well as a geographic component: *Who Weekly* was not claiming a 'world exclusive'. As Nicolls said, 'It ran on some TV show over there, but we were just able to say exclusive because we knew he hadn't talked to anyone else in the print media, and we knew that he wouldn't be. You know, I mean, that's just a sales point.' Because no money changed hands, exclusivity here seems a rather fluid concept. In other situations, where stories are bought and sold, the rights to exclusivity are contractually controlled. *Who Weekly*'s use of the home-take produces one avenue for exclusivity because it can at least guarantee that the photographs will not have appeared elsewhere.

It would be hard not to notice the amount of energy expended on cover design and in current issue advertising aimed at producing the sense that the latest hot gossip printed inside is news and available only in this magazine. This has become a major means of differentiating not only between magazines but also between individual, competing issues of the magazines. Among the changes in format in the last decade and a half, then, the appearance of the word 'exclusive' or 'world exclusive' on the cover is a significant one. What it establishes is an imperative reason for buying *this* magazine, *this* week. Clearly, it works. Avieson reports that half the sales for each issue of *New Idea* occur on Monday, as soon as it appears, with the rest being spread over the rest of the week. Such a purchasing pattern supports the idea that readers are indeed buying news.

Does the classification of these kinds of celebrity stories as news mean that less attention is paid to what we might conventionally think of as 'serious' news items? This is a standard element of complaints about the 'dumbing down' or tabloidisation of the media, as it turns away from the public and the political and towards the private and the personal. From one point of view, the answer to such a question is 'of course'. But there may be a number of ways of looking at this. McKenzie Wark gestures in one interesting direction when he argues that 'one of the things that connects the cultural to the political is celebrity', referring to the fact that all kinds of representations of political leaders will circulate and contribute to their political and cultural significance within the public sphere.[29] Wark is implying that the practice of turning political or business figures into celebrities, or treating part of their activities as if they were celebrities, means that political coverage is continued, although its focus is altered.

Cheryl Kernot's appearance on the cover of the April 1998 edition of *Australian Women's Weekly* in a flirtatiously red frock can be considered an example of this. The cover line read: 'Exclusive interview – Cheryl Kernot's dark and disturbing times'. The first page and part of the second concerned her reactions to finding out the previous December that a scandal from her past was about to be published in the press. That story had had its day, but the magazine coverage itself became a newspaper and talkback radio scandal because it raised other concerns about the manner of Kernot's representation on the cover. As the article said, 'She accepted our invitation to be pampered and posed in two very different gowns chosen by Fashion Editor Deborah Hutton'.[30] Kernot's acceptance of this invitation became a point of contention. Should she have allowed herself to be presented as a clotheshorse? As someone who spoke politically for the rights of women, should she have appeared on the cover of a women's magazine in a red and black evening dress with a feather boa? The *Australian* carried an article by one of its lighter columnists, reporting responses to the single image which had been released prior to the magazine's appearance and attempting to locate the real cause of all the fuss: 'It's the scarletness, the frou-frouness of the frock that has most whistling through their teeth, especially after the scrutiny Kernot's private life

Politician Cheryl Kernot on April 1998 cover of *Australian Women's Weekly* in the glamour shot that caused argument about the propriety of (female) politicians dressing up for magazine coverage. (with kind permission of ACP Publishing Pty Ltd)

has borne'.[31] In the *Courier-Mail* of the same day, Peter Cole-Adams noted that Kernot had to accept 'the consequences of what was undoubtedly attention-seeking behaviour'.[32] Apparently, she was asking for it.

In some respects, the scale of the fuss was surprising. However, it does seem related to the fact that Kernot had lent herself to what was a quintessential women's magazine celebrity story. It was a sympathetic interview with a woman in the public eye, which focused on her family life as much as on her public prominence; it had scandalous content but presented this in the guise of letting the subject talk about the impact of the scandal on her family; and it used an 'attention-seeking' stunt to ensure both exclusivity and the kind of controversy which might lead to increased circulation. On the other hand, it was not especially exploitative, nor did it distance itself from Kernot's political significance. In the long-running tussle for the moral high ground between magazines and newspapers which we encountered many times in our study, this was an occasion when the magazine could present itself as highly responsible by publishing Kernot's commentary on political muckraking. For Kernot, who was campaigning for an ALP seat in the House of Representatives, the cover of the highest circulation magazine in the country, a monthly magazine furthermore (which means a much longer time on the newsagent's shelf), plus a feature article in which she could present herself in several favourable lights, were understandably attractive. In addition to using the opportunity to put her side of the long-past sex scandal, she was also able to address another piece of negative coverage: losing her temper with reporters over their stories of damage inflicted on her home by a removalist's van. That the three-page story had very little that could be regarded as overt political content does not negate its political usefulness or pertinence. The Kernot cover demonstrates that celebrity coverage can promote a great range of products using the same basic tools.

Just as it would be a mistake to assume that the celebrity coverage of political personalities necessarily, temporarily, depoliticises them, it would also be a mistake to assume that all coverage of celebrities from non-political occupations is frivolous, apolitical or purely self-interested. The reverse, in fact, has been particularly noticeable in recent years over the issue of race. At the 1997 AFI Awards – clearly a celebrity-driven promotional event – there was an organised campaign to demonstrate industry support for Reconciliation. This was reported even in celebrity-based coverage. A 1998 article on Aboriginal athlete Cathy Freeman in *Woman's Day* provided an example of how the personal celebrity story can prove a conduit for (muted) political comment. The cover line, 'Exclusive: Cathy Freeman loses her Diamond Rock', directed the reader to a two-page article in the front of the magazine that enlivened a predictable 'return to competition' interview with the 'exclusive' information that she had misplaced her engagement ring. The second half of the article started with a discussion of her political ambitions.[33] The comments she made were certainly no more than conventional expressions of distrust of current political practices, but the celebrity story here provided the opportunity for the women's magazine to speak positively of Aboriginality as a politicising identity.

Political issues are not the only ones that are inflected differently, rather than erased, by celebrity involvement. At least as important is how public health education campaigns and less formal health promotion activities are conducted through celebrities. The increase in women's magazines' attention to health was raised several times in the interviews, especially in terms of the desirability of celebrity health stories to vary the rather standard formal advice offered in the service sections:

> BUNTY AVIESON: For us to write stories endlessly about breast cancer, the facts, how to have a mammogram, why you should do it; [it's] boring scary stuff. You read about a celebrity telling their story, it's far more palatable, it's far more emotive, it's far more engaging and it's what will appeal to the readers. The same with AIDS.

Even so, Avieson went on, it was a fine line for an editor to tread. Celebrity coverage of health issues could still become predictable and unappealing, but then a fresh angle would surface through the specific character of the celebrity. The example she used was Belinda Emmett, the young soap star afflicted with breast cancer: 'Because she was so young, so appealing, and was so happy to talk about it, [it] had enormous cut-through ... So to have her there and to portray her as brave, fighting, glamorous, full of life, that achieved so much.' What Avieson meant by 'achieving so much' was clearly a social rather than a commercial objective.

Emmett is a prime example of the 'good' celebrity, the kind of figure who can be played back against the standard criticisms of celebrity journalism as cynical tabloidisation. Her involvement enabled the production of a story with considerable social and news appeal, with good pictures and a degree of resonance across other news outlets. Furthermore, she had it handled properly – going through her agent and a (network) publicist to offer exclusivity to an appropriate choice of magazine. *New Idea*, despite Avieson's concern about there possibly being too many breast cancer stories, was heavily committed to breast cancer research as its main charitable activity for the year. The magazine gave at least $1 million in 1998 for research, as a result of a tithe on the cover price.

Jane Nicolls, too, was impressed by Emmett's appeal and told how other magazines deal with the problem of exclusivity: 'We would have loved to have done that story. In fact we did do that story as a write-around.' While indicating that editors did not much like the practice, she explained that a write-around involved taking the core piece of data, in this case the published fact that Emmett had breast cancer, and producing a story around it from other sources. Rather than dealing directly with Emmett, *Who Weekly* 'talked to breast cancer experts about what was the likelihood of anyone this young suffering breast cancer'. As this example indicates, and notwithstanding the criticism that the content of women's magazines in general reinforces shallow and demeaning conceptions of women's interests, there is some social as well as commercial benefit from a blurring of the distinction between the celebrity story and traditional news.

THE COVER

In 1980 *Woman's Day* started to be sold in supermarkets, where, previously, only the home-maker title *Family Circle* had been placed. Until that time, women's magazines, like almost all others, had been sold only by newsagents or by subscription. Other women's magazines followed suit. This move intensified the importance of the covers, since it was these which attracted the impulse buyer browsing while waiting at the checkout. Covers had always been important in attracting the eye of 'swinging' purchasers in newsagents, and the newer, more aggressive covers continued to serve this function there. The customer of the newsagent, however, had the print media in mind when entering the shop. The supermarket customer, on the other hand, may have gone in just for detergent; they had to be offered something more attention-grabbing, more sensational to be moved to add a magazine to their grocery purchases. A cover promising several racy stories about the lives of a range of celebrities proved capable of achieving this very successfully. The tactic worked elsewhere as well; the sensationalism of the 'supermarket' tabloid in the United States is built on similar foundations.

Given the importance of the cover in persuading the women's magazine reader to choose this magazine, this week, the choice of who to feature on the cover is crucial. For a start, no magazine devoting a sizeable proportion of its content to celebrity coverage would consider using a cover image that was not a celebrity. Indeed, one of the ways in which magazines can be differentiated one from another is in these terms: if there is a face on the cover but it isn't named, then the magazine is concerned either with fashion and beauty or with sex; if the face is named, the magazine will have a significant focus on celebrity (and maybe sex, fashion and beauty as well). Industry practitioners agree that it is the cover which draws the purchaser to the magazine and few magazines dealing with celebrities can rely on subscriptions for anything more than a minor proportion of their circulation. A particularly attractive cover can make a major difference, and editors track the success of each issue by checking the sales figures produced by the chosen celebrity. (Interestingly, these will vary from state to state, so a national magazine such as *New Idea* can do as many as six different covers for one issue – a different cover for every state.)

This does not just apply to mass-market women's magazines. Ross Dimsey, chairman of the board of directors of the company publishing *Cinema Papers*, explained (for a History and Film conference panel in 1998) how important Leonardo DiCaprio had been for the magazine. Subscriptions to this specialist film title are around 2000 and, for it to continue to appear, approximately 6000 copies per issue need to be sold at newsagents. A DiCaprio cover guaranteed a profitable issue and so, despite not being an Australian actor, DiCaprio appeared on the front of both the February and December 1997 issues. Sue-Ellen Topfer, editor of *Girlfriend* and *TV Hits*, also reported how valuable he was but emphasised that the photograph had to be one that had not appeared elsewhere, since the magazine would be bought only if it delivered a photograph that a young fan did not already have in her collection.

For Nicolls, DiCaprio was an exception that proved the rule. She did not regard product-related covers, especially of male movie stars, as strong performers for *Who Weekly*. (Product-related covers are those which promote a particular project, such as a new movie, rather than just the celebrities themselves.)

> JANE NICOLLS: You put Mel Gibson on the cover pegged to a *Lethal Weapon*, it doesn't sell that well … [But for DiCaprio] when *Titanic* was so huge, we ran Leo on the cover, I think, three times … It was so hot, it was so huge, and every time we would run a cover on the magazine, it just sold.

The mass-market women's magazines rarely run directly product-related covers either. In these outlets, a celebrity is given a cover on the basis of 'news' or a personal story and it is this that the chosen image will reflect. So distant can the product relationship be that celebrities with no product other than themselves can still generate commercially successful covers. Among the most prominent of those Australian celebrities who are 'famous for being famous' is Dannii Minogue. Avieson discussed this in a way which shows how the key elements of the personal and the newsworthy are more fundamentally accessible through the persona of Dannii than through her more famous sister, Kylie:

> BUNTY AVIESON: An interesting aside is that Kylie was never as successful as a cover as Dannii. Kylie always had more street cred and was cooler … [Dannii] was married to Julian McMahon. Older readers … are aware of her because she was married to Sonia McMahon's son. She has got the older sister who was more successful, she is constantly putting on weight and taking it off.

Now she has all the changes. So her life is more of an ongoing soap opera than Kylie's ... Dannii has all those sorts of other layers that actually make for an intriguing personality.

We will refer later on to Joke Hermes' account of the melodramatic repertoire through which some readers of gossip magazines discuss their reading. Hermes explicitly draws on soap opera to describe this repertoire and notes how the magazines 'appear to offer the pleasure of fiction in the guise of journalism'.[34] Avieson's account would suggest that Dannii's career provides, more reliably, the melodramatic 'pleasures of fiction' than does that of her more professionally successful sister.

FABRICATION

Why would I not believe, when Ita tells me to?
Don Walker (Cold Chisel), 'Ita'

In both popular and critical discussion about gossip in magazines – be they women's, entertainment or the new men's magazines – it is common to encounter the conviction that much of the material is fabricated. This conviction can produce reactions which range from outrage to amusement. Among those who profess not to read the magazines, it is sometimes advanced as a reason for not doing so. This can be a version of what Stuart Hall terms the 'cultural dope/dupe' belief, where the speaker is confident of their ability to see through the wiles of the manipulators of mass opinion but holds other consumers of mass media texts to be passive and gullible readers unaware of the 'real' state of affairs and at the mercy of the ideological practices of the producers of the texts.[35]

Listening to those who do read and enjoy the magazines, it becomes evident that belief in the factual status of their claims is, to quite some extent, immaterial. Whether or not the man pictured escorting Kate Fischer is or is not really her new boyfriend, as the caption claims, makes no difference to the reader, for whom 'Kate Fischer' is a figure who moves in a world which is entirely constructed of mediated appearances and who never enters the materiality of the reader's day-to-day existence as a flesh-and-blood individual. 'Kate Fischer' provides entertainment and pleasure as a subject of gossip, an object to lust after or a performer to laugh at. The truthfulness of the information according to which she may be enjoyed, envied or pitied may well matter to her and those close to her, but, for many readers, stories questioning whether the separation settlement from Jamie Packer was really $2.75 million or only $500,000 are followed as a form of narrativised spectacle. The structure of belief being described here is close to the classic formulation of disavowal: 'I know, but even so ...'; 'I know that this may be a beat-up, but even so I'm enjoying it'.

Magazine producers know this, but it does not mean that misleading or false stories are openly condoned within the industry. Especially for outlets claiming the status of journalism, fabricated stories contravene the ethics of the profession and are one of the factors leading that profession and those others concerned with the production of celebrity into disrepute. Accusations of the dumbing down of the popular media, accusations which usually explicitly cite the increasing proportion of personalised stories focusing on scandal and celebrities, gain support from such practices. Despite its claim to the status of news, cultural critics such as Andrew Wernick would certainly see celebrity coverage as just a part of the promotional culture which turns advertising into news,[36] albeit lacking even the minimal regulatory requirements for truthfulness that paid advertising is meant to observe.

The media practitioners did admit that fabrication occurred, although no one suggested that they themselves were among the culprits. Importantly, as they pointed out, it is not feature articles that are most likely to be the sites of fabrication, though they can be subject to exaggeration and misrepresentation. As far as features are concerned, the principal practice complained about by subjects and readers alike is the use of misleading cover lines. Screamers on the cover, promising salacious revelations inside, draw readers to innocuous stories dealing often with the character being played rather than the actor herself. In general, though, fabrication is most likely to affect the shorter pieces, the seemingly ephemeral snippets such as the captions on gossip file page photographs.

Suzie MacLeod, Village Roadshow publicist, said that, when she reads magazines, 'I just think, "How much of this story is accurate?", because we've seen so much stuff made up, all the time'. Her example involved the American actor Samuel L. Jackson's second tour of Australia to promote *Jackie Brown*. After having a drink at a club with him, she read that 'Samuel Jackson was seen at a club surrounded by a bevy of beauties and his bodyguards'. MacLeod commented: 'It was quite hysterical because the other two publicists and I were the bevy of beauties and the bodyguards were our husbands'. The triviality of the instance is part of the point; no one would bother to (or could) sue and such a minor misrepresentation hardly matters, since the focus of the story itself is elsewhere – on the simple fact of Jackson's presence, and the journalist's recording of his brief entry into the same world as the reader.

Significantly, as the conversations with magazine personnel revealed, fabrication is not just something the *magazines* are accused of. When *New Weekly* carried a three-page article about fabricated celebrity stories, it was not about the media making stories up but about celebrities duping the media. Most were accused of presenting the appearance of a happy relationship while either not being 'really in love' (Claudia Schiffer and David Copperfield, Michael Jackson and Lisa Marie Presley) or while negotiating their separation (Michael Hutchence and Helena Christensen, Richard Gere and Cindy Crawford). The article concluded with an interview with publicist Max Clifford asserting that celebrities involved themselves in these activities for the predictable reasons: for money or to conceal secrets about their sexuality or, more generally, just to further their careers.[37] Similar points were made in our interviews when Avieson complained about the hypocrisy of celebrities decrying media intrusion while using it to further their own ends. She claimed that Paula Yates alerted the photographers to her spending the night with Michael Hutchence as a way to separate him from Helena Christensen. She also drew attention to the bizarre behaviour of celebrity couples who engage in passionate kissing while surrounded by press photographers – usually on a red carpet at the entrance to an opening night. This, Avieson indicates, seems to happen more often when the couple in question is rumoured to be unhappy:

> BUNTY AVIESON: So they turn up, photographers everywhere, knowing that the shot that the papers use will be of them kissing, and then you have all this lovey – you know, they're actors, they're performing ... Bruce [Willis] and Demi [Moore] did that just before they split up.

Celebrities, as readers have always suspected, are not above manipulating the media to misrepresent their lives if it suits them.

Magazines and the celebrity industry

> There are really greedy people out there.
> *Bunty Avieson*

Clearly, there is a strong industrial relationship between the magazines and the publicists: they each depend upon the other. There are three principal groupings at work here: the performer and their agent/manager; the product promoter (such as the network or a film exhibitor); and the outlet, the magazine editor and her staff. They can operate harmoniously or with different levels and sources of reluctance. As Peter Rix indicated, and as discussed in Chapter 4, the product promoter and the magazine may have interests which are not necessarily shared by the performer. The promoter needs the magazine to publicise a project and the magazine editor needs new celebrity stories to generate the exclusives and the 'hot' items which draw the fickle reader to purchase this title rather than another.

Their sharing of a common purpose with the magazines is one of the reasons why publicists frequently find themselves charged with persuading the reluctant performer to seek publicity through these outlets. Certainly, some publicists described what sounds like a process of training their clients in publicity (or softening them up), by starting them off with smaller circulation magazines. Lesna Thomas suggests: 'If you have a star that is a little resistant to publicity, there are certain magazines they love themselves, so you have them in those ... and that gets them more experience perhaps'. Cases in point were *HQ*, *Harper's Bazaar* and *Vogue*.

As this suggests, some performers may not be reluctant to engage in publicity per se but are simply choosy about the outlet. Avieson told us that, when she was editing *Woman's Day*, she had been persuaded by a publicist for *Muriel's Wedding* to do a story on the (then) unknown Toni Collette rather than the (then) higher-profile Sophie Lee. After she had become famous through the film's popularity, Collette refused to appear in *Woman's Day*, declaring that she would henceforth appear in *Vogue*. Avieson, who regarded this as major ingratitude, insisted that the publicist's duty was to encourage the actor to do the *Woman's Day* story: 'What her publicist is telling her is "Yes, but *Vogue* isn't mass market, your film is mass market. Your pretensions may be that you would like to be seen in *Vogue*, but that's not going to help your career".' Georgie Brown may have been describing just this kind of situation when, speaking more generally and hopefully, she said: 'You are also almost obliged by the nature of the game to appeal to the egos of your clients or subject matter ... but ... once somebody has got a taste of publicity and can see what it can do for them, they want it'.

Even so, the relationship between product promoter and magazine is not always without its own problems as well. Kerry O'Brien recalled one disappointment when a magazine interviewed her client ostensibly about a current project, but eventually produced a story focusing on a past scandal:

> KERRY O'BRIEN: *New Idea* or *Woman's Day* interviewed [Moira Dougherty] the producer of *Riverdance*, and I was hoping that it would be a real story of the woman, as she's such a successful woman, and it was just turned into – it was just, you know, [Dougherty] sacks Michael Flatley and the lead photo was Michael Flatley ... but you take what you can get.

Others reported the irritation of celebs who find that the headline or cover line advertising their story has turned out to be very different from what they thought had been agreed. Jane Nicolls commented on how misleading cover lines had particularly annoyed Liz Hayes and Jana Wendt who were at the time contractually required to do publicity for ACP magazines: 'A lot of them get incredibly pissed off about how the headlines end up'. The shock–horror banner on the cover most often leads to an innocuous story inside, but to the object of this publicity the misrepresentation is a serious matter.

Notwithstanding the ACP/Nine Network examples of Wendt and Hayes, the most harmonious relationships between performer, product promoter and media outlet generally seem to occur as a result of cross-media corporate integration: when, for example, the performer is a television presenter and the network and magazine are owned by the same company. The promotion of Nine Network personalities in ACP magazines makes commercial sense to all parties concerned. It is unusual for a presenter to have an agent or a publicist who is independent of the network, so in such conditions harmony is obviously easier to maintain. Another factor contributing to a cooperative relationship in this context is that presenters operate in their own personae. Actors play parts, so the person publicly displayed in their work is a character. Personal stories, then, expose someone who has not previously been (or intended to be) shown and, more disturbingly, frequently try to close the gap between actor and character. This implicitly denigrates the work the actor does, while intruding upon what the actor thought was their private life. Presenters, on the other hand, can largely be seen as company people; without their exposure on television, they have no base from which to operate. They need the network to survive.

The strongest example given of this vertically integrated, industrially harmonious relationship was Kerri-Anne Kennerley. At the time of the interview she was still presenter of Channel 9's *Midday* live talk show. Kennerley was a favourite of the network's publicist because she understood the desirability of publicity and cooperated fully. Heidi Virtue referred to her having been on three recent *Australian Women's Weekly* covers and in many more stories: '[Kerri-Anne is] from the old school, she's a company woman, she knows the value of publicity, you know she's not gonna say "Hey, give me some money", she's been in the game too long ... [she's] professional'. The overlap between the *Midday* audience and *Australian Women's Weekly* readership was not coincidental, nor was Kennerley's agreement to publicity in the *Weekly*, the most respectful of the mass-circulation women's magazines.

To see the extent of cooperation, it is useful to briefly describe one of the magazine cover stories. The June 1997 issue has Kennerley on the cover with the pointer: 'Wow! Kerri-Anne – My amazing NEW body – ALL her slimming SECRETS'. This particular edition was billed as a special health issue and Kerri-Anne led the personalisation of this (although, if the magazine's intent had been to feature weight loss as the lead, the story it had on Colleen Hewett, who had lost 10 kilos compared with Kerri-Anne's 2, should have been more significant). Nor was Kerri-Anne's weight loss something that had already been accomplished and was then seen as worthy of a place in the story, as Hewett's was. The second paragraph reads: 'So when we asked her to star in this special health issue of the *Australian Women's Weekly* by committing herself to a month-long fitness routine, she jumped at the chance'.[38]

This is what Virtue means by cooperative. The article seamlessly brings together the magazine, the television program and the celebrity's public–private life. It traces the fitness regime designed in part by the magazine's regular nutrition columnist (shown with Kerri-Anne in one of the accompanying pictures), who at one stage recommends a low-fat cookbook published by the *Australian Women's Weekly* Home Library. The story also reports Kerri-Anne's recollection of a *Midday* studio audience member's comments about the way television makes people look larger than they are; comments on her strenuous work routine and how her eating is organised around the filming of *Midday*; and reminds readers of continuing stories about her husband (such as his bowel cancer, which had featured in a story in the magazine in February 1997). The end of the story also includes a promotional line about the 'Good Health' section later in the magazine.

Even without synergistic arrangements such as these, the relationships between magazine and celebrity range over a great variety of possibilities. Avieson spoke about the preliminary discussions with publicists to establish the boundaries of an interview, saying that these are especially important in two instances. The first is when celebrities have been treated harshly previously, and the second is when dealing with local celebrities with whom magazines need to maintain ongoing relationships. Some celebrities are able to negotiate the terms of their appearance in magazines from a position of considerable power. Nicolls told us that no photograph of Nicole Kidman and Tom Cruise is allowed to run without approval from their publicist or agent: 'It doesn't matter that the shoot is costing money, we have to clear it before you can run it'. Topfer mentioned Jim Carrey's solicitor's simply refusing access to any of his photographs. Certain American stars negotiate 'cover or nothing' deals: they will only be interviewed if they are guaranteed the cover. The example of the Kennerley weight loss story is a version of this: the negotiations over her appearance included her being on the cover. Another aspect of coverage that may be negotiated is final approval of the copy. One celebrity who has this is Lisa Curry-Kenny, one of the most accomplished of the Australian sports stars to have maintained celebrity status after leaving the sports limelight. According to a 1998 full-page article in the *Australian*, Curry-Kenny is proud of being able to promote her business activities entirely through personality pieces and without using paid advertising.[39] To keep control over her representation, however, she maintains final copy approval through an agreement with both *Australian Women's Weekly* and *Woman's Day*.

Celebrity and gossip

Of all the publications which concern themselves with celebrities, the mass-market women's magazines and the gossip magazines (whether or not they are seen to be different categories) are the most castigated for their focus.

Cross-promotion on cover of June 1997 special health issue of *Australian Women's Weekly*. Kerri-Anne Kennerley was host of Nine Network's *Midday* program at the time. (with kind permission of ACP Publishing Pty Ltd)

Interestingly, a number of our interviewees delivered much stronger denunciations of these magazines than are normally found among academic or media criticism. Rix, as we have already seen, expressed strong reservations about whose interests are served by this kind of publicity, while theatrical agents Kevin Palmer and Rebecca Williamson made it very clear that they would advise their clients not to have anything to do with such outlets if they wanted their work to be taken seriously. While one might expect that the major critics of these magazines would be outside the industry, that is not actually the case. Indeed, one of the many peculiar characteristics of the media world is that the attack on mass-market women's magazines and their exploitation of celebrity material can be charted most readily through articles published in newspapers owned by the same companies as the magazines they condemn. Furthermore, the editors whose practices they denounce have often themselves worked on those very same newspapers (and if the reporters writing the articles are freelance, they may also sell stories to the magazines).

Regular articles on the fluctuations in mass-market magazine circulation and the proliferation of new titles are concerned with charting broader industrial movements in the media, but they also routinely include criticism of the women's magazines' salaciousness and their use of chequebook journalism. Powell, for instance, writing in 1994, asked 'whether the shrill celebrity scandal and the sex, drugs and booze stories – which drove circulations up in the mid-1980s – [would] maintain their pulling power'.[40] In 1996, Elizabeth Wynhausen accused magazines confronted with falling sales of trying 'to titillate readers with celebrity stories and salacious gossip, administered in ever larger doses', adding:

> The plot is straight out of the serials. Characters are no sooner built up than they are brought down. One month our heroine is thin as a rail but happily married, the next she has anorexia and it's all over, but that's far from the end of poor Pamela or poor Dannii, resurrected again in May, supposedly after cosmetic surgery. *Woman's Day* says she hates her new breasts. *New Idea* says she looks bigger and better than ever. Does anyone care?[41]

There is an ethical or taste agenda behind such criticism, not a question about the commercial effectiveness of the strategy. Powell's report, it is true, dealt with *New Idea*'s attempt to boost falling sales by printing less gossip because surveys had revealed readers' distaste for and disillusion with it. By the time of Wynhausen's story, however, this strategy had failed and it was widely accepted that gossip was integral to the women's magazines.

There is also an element of hypocrisy and opportunism in some of this media criticism. Avieson seems to have nailed down one reason for the media's own interest in the women's magazines when she accuses the *Sydney*

Morning Herald's David Dale of routinely 'having a go at what is in the women's magazines – "Aren't they ridiculous?"', so that he is then legitimately able to get their content (the lead gossip story for the week, for instance) into his newspaper.

Women's magazines have been subjected to more intense criticism than other kinds of magazines which publish celebrity material. Entertainment magazines, whether of the more functional kind like *TV Week* or *Premiere*, or the more stylish like *Face*, are not usually attacked for intruding on people's privacy, focusing on the trivial or inventing stories. Nor are sports magazines or those concerned with music or musicians. It seems fair to suppose that an association of the personal and the trivial with the feminine legitimates much of the attack. As a medium, magazines may even be seen as themselves predominantly targeted at women; certainly, the majority of contemporary magazine scholarship is conducted by women and from a feminist perspective.

Those who work from within this feminist perspective point out that the disdain for women's magazines and the pattern of their critical evaluation is remarkably similar to that attracted by other media genres targeted at women. 'Women's films', romance fiction and television soap opera have all served to represent mass culture at its most worthless. With the arrival of second-wave feminism, all of these forms were subjected to a similar cycle of critical treatment: denunciation as an instrument of patriarchy, re-evaluation for their contribution to the idea of women's culture, and finally celebration for the pleasures they make available to the female consumer. Initially, this consumer was regarded simply as able to negotiate the contradictions in-volved in reading popular texts marketed to women – that is, as able to derive pleasure from culturally denigrated textual forms. More recently, it has been suggested that the female consumer is positively empowered by the repre-sentations she encounters in these popular culture 'women's texts' because they implicitly value the specificity of women's experience, no matter how ironically or self-consciously. Despite such critical shifts, there are still many writers who argue that these texts do not serve women's interests particularly well and who see them as complicit in women's continuing subordination.[42]

Certainly, early second-wave feminist analysis overwhelmingly perceived women's magazines as part of those discursive patriarchal structures which oppressed women. Consequently, it advocated the production of alternative, more serious magazines which could be targeted at women. (This occurred in such Australian studies as those of Patricia Edgar and Hilary McPhee.)[43] When *Spare Rib* and *Ms* were developed in response to such calls, they were included in analyses of the media field by Janice Winship and by Ellen McCracken to demonstrate alternative possibilities (in the British instance), or continuities (in the American).[44] More recent, so-called 'post-feminist', analysis also accuses the mass-market magazines of complicity in the oppression of young women. Naomi Wolf's *Beauty Myth* develops a broad and popular critique of women's entrapment in the pursuit of impossible ideals of femininity and beauty, and of the commodification of this pursuit in the various fashion and beauty industries.[45]

Against such a position, we have an almost equally popular post-feminist tract which accuses the women's movement of a form of repressive puritanism: Rene Denfield's *New Victorians*.[46] Within this debate, at present, there are widely diverging views on the extent to which media representations of women and their interests are denigratory or harmful. In Australia, Catharine Lumby's *Bad Girls* finds little to recommend either camp, as she accuses both Wolf's book and Susan Faludi's *Backlash* of complicity with politically conservative critics of the media and popular culture while offering a dated, 'pro-censorship' version of feminism. Her own account of popular culture celebrates the incursion of the unrespectable, private, domestic and feminine discourses that she finds in tabloid television like *Ricki Lake* or in the playful and confident representations of female sexuality in mainstream magazines such as *Cleo*. What Lumby wants us to see is not women's continuing objectification but a reshaping of the public sphere in ways which more than ever before recognise and accommodate the feminine.[47]

Little of this work has dealt specifically with celebrity journalism (Lumby's *Gotcha* is an exception).[48] Despite the significance of the term 'role model' for early feminist analysis, the role of the celebrity material we have focused on was not seen as particularly significant for these debates. Occasional references to royalty and even more occasional allusions to film stars are all that can be traced in the British studies. In such references as can be found, the point made is that celebrities – both royalty and the aristocracy are the prime instances given – are presented as being models of the ideal ordinary. Whether queen or film star, their lives are really just 'like ours'. Ferguson refers to the way in which the majority of British women's magazines have perpetuated the 'regal myth' but sees this as primarily (and, ironically, from our point of view today) through the way the royal family represents the 'happy family'.[49] Later in the 1980s, Winship noted the Princess of Wales being shown as the ideal wife and mother in *Woman's Own*.[50] Magazine scholarship such as this reminds us that the British royal family's operation as a model of dysfunctionality is relatively recent.

McCracken mentions 'celebrities and stars' in passing but includes them within broader content categories, such as 'Fashion and Beauty', where she refers to an article on Meryl Streep in *Bazaar*:

> The celebrity remains a superior being to imitate, at the same time humanised to facilitate identification with her. She gives testimony about beauty products and techniques ... Like the fashion features, these pieces allow utopian identification with

what is impossible to purchase (the beauty of celebrities) while establishing a pole of the real through a few accessible items.[51]

The remarks provide a very strong example of what has long been a conventional academic view: that the gap between the celebrity and the ordinary person is closed through buying commodities. It is also typical in that the tone in which it discusses celebrities is mildly dismissive, rather than seriously critical, and in its relatively superficial interest in what kind of social function might be served by celebrity gossip.

Most Australian studies of magazines operate similarly, although with only slight emphasis on the identification between the celebrity and the reader that Ferguson assumes to be at the core of the relationship. Edgar and McPhee note only that magazine content includes 'the society pages where we can find out what all the wealthy wives of influential citizens are doing'.[52] Bill Bonney and Helen Wilson argue that Hollywood 'was the American version of royalty as a source of fantasy for women and was presented as in fact a more democratic model, for many classic Hollywood stars were presented as having a background in poverty'.[53] This, however, was just a small peripheral observation within a larger argument about the centrality of America to the heightening of consumerism after World War II. Only Keith Windschuttle has regarded celebrity as a major category of magazine content. Writing in the mid-1980s, he continues Bonney and Wilson's theme by focusing on the celebrity's appeal to readers' fantasies: 'The dominant fare of the weekly magazines is the personal lives of famous people, who are displayed in clothes and settings and with companions to which their readers could never hope to aspire'. He lists the three most common types of famous people as, in order: British royalty, Australian television personalities and Hollywood stars.[54] No detail is given of the methodology used to generate this information and the results comprise solely a list of the categories in order of prominence, but it is of some use in mapping the historical shift towards this form of journalism.

There are two detailed pieces of Australian work which are more valuable for our purposes here. One that is referred to across Australian research is Shirley Sampson's study of the *Australian Women's Weekly* of 1971. This was designed to focus specifically on the representation of education, but as a byproduct it provides the only thorough statistical data from the period about relevant magazine content. She noted that '59% of all [feature] articles on women were about beautiful women, stars of film or TV or royalty',[55] and, if one added in artists and sportswomen (to constitute a category which could be considered as overwhelmingly one of celebrities), then 71% of all women mentioned in feature articles could be regarded as celebrities. As we saw in Chapter 1, however, this still constitutes only a small proportion of the content of the magazine compared with the levels of celebrity material today.

The other valuable study is Humphrey McQueen's essay on the *Australian Women's Weekly* in the 1970s. He is most directly interested in the inter-relationships between the magazine and the world of work, but he does examine how covers changed under the editorship of Ita Buttrose. He notes little increase in the use of British royalty, a major decline in models and animals, and a substantial increase in foreign royals and 'screen and stage stars'. Appearances of the latter grouping on the cover doubled in frequency, to thirteen times a year.[56]

Celebrity, then, despite the dramatic increase in the proportion of media content devoted to it over the last decade or so, has not been a component of magazine content regarded as worth major academic investigation. As a result, there is little available research to assist our understanding of the appeal and function of celebrity journalism. Textual and content analysis can substantiate claims for the presence and content of celebrity stories and their varying prominence in the women's magazines of different countries. Industrial experience enabled Ferguson to refer to an editorial conference about the availability of particular celebrities for the process she calls 'mythicisation'.[57] But the Australian and other studies which suggest that readers vicariously identify with celebrities can call on no evidence to support their claims. Some attempt to examine actual readers would help to clarify this, but there are only two studies which use any ethnographic work to explore the nature of magazine readership. The first is a more general study – by Ballaster, Beetham, Frazer and Heron – which does not ask its readers about celebrities (though they include without comment a student's observation about the inappropriateness of an article on Rob Lowe in a magazine aimed at younger teenagers).[58] The second is of more use to us in this project, and it was conducted by Joke Hermes.

Hermes' is the most recent full-length examination of women's magazines and looks at both British and Dutch examples.[59] It separates gossip magazines from women's (and feminist) ones, noting that while mass-market women's magazines reduced their coverage of film stars and royalty in the late 1970s, specific gossip magazines were introduced and became successful. The English language titles she instances include *Majesty, Chat* and *Hello!*. Despite the notional separation between gossip and women's magazines, Hermes notes how, for most of her sample of readers, gossip magazines are seen to be women's magazines anyway: 'Reading gossip magazines is very much like reading traditional women's magazines: it is pleasant to look at the pictures, to read photo captions, the more so because the pictures are of people we are familiar with through television'.[60] The mediated familiarity of the celebrity being read about is important, but at no stage does Hermes suggest that the reader 'identifies' with the celebrity, even in fantasy. Instead, the vicarious pleasures provided through reading the magazines are produced through the 'enjoyment of the glitter' (something along the lines of the spectacular narratives discussed in our earlier section on fabrication) or, arguably more substantially, the enjoyment of being privy to insider information[61] (a pleasure which resonates with the industry view of celebrity gossip as falling into the category of news).

Hermes' discussion deals with three different kinds of gossip: 'malicious gossip and scandal, friendly stories about celebrities (usually with a focus on babies) and royalty'. The third appears necessary because of the presence in her magazine sample of one British (*Majesty*) and one Dutch (*Vorsten*) magazine specifically devoted to stories about royalty. Unfortunately, these categories do not match up particularly well with those we find in Australian magazines. From our point of view, stories about royalty appear similar to stories about other celebrities – they are either malicious or friendly – and friendly stories range far more widely than babies. More useful is Hermes' suggestion that 'written gossip tends to create closeness or familiar faces in a wider world by helping the reader to bring celebrities into her or his circle of family, friends and acquaintances'. For Hermes, all gossip – written and oral – must be seen as a wish for, or a forging of, community, but she has a far from sentimental notion of what communities are. She analyses her respondents' comments, especially as they defend themselves against criticism of their devotion to gossip magazines, as belonging to one of two repertoires: the extended family and melodrama.[62]

The first of these is linked to the 'circle' idea, where information of a personal nature about familiar people is assimilated and the interest shown in it is relatively benevolent. The second is more complicated and involves a much more 'distanced', spectator-like relationship with the object of the stories. Here we find more of the malicious kind of gossip, which involves taking delight in misfortunes or, alternatively, wallowing in the misery of others. 'The repertoire of melodrama is as outspoken in its indignation as in its sentimentality', Hermes says, highlighting the importance of distaste and disapproval as components of the reader's pleasure in this form of news.[63] This is a long way from perceiving magazines as providing the identifying reader with just the right beauty tips to close the gap between them and their favourite film star.

Among the reasons, one suspects, for the durability of the assumptions that women form fantasy identifications with those they read about in the gossip columns, or that they purchase magazines in order to find models upon whom they should fashion their appearance, is a denigratory view of the female audience. Certainly, as suggested above, one factor in the castigation of celebrity coverage in women's magazines is the link between gossip and the feminine, both being seen as soft and trivial and contrary to the hard masculine world of work and other matters of public importance. But this has not always been the case. One of the earliest and most famous of English language magazines, Richard Steele's *Tatler*, published since 1709–10, took its title to reflect its interest in the gossip of the coffee houses of eighteenth century London ('tatle' being a variant spelling of 'tattle'). Its readership and its subject matter were overwhelmingly male, as were the frequenters of the coffee houses. Barrell and Braithwaite suggest that, despite a short break in publication, the *Tatler* is still 'Britain's oldest living magazine', although they make no mention of when its exclusive address to men ceased.[64] For Cynthia White, it can 'justifiably rank as the ancestor of modern women's magazines', despite its earlier gendered positioning.[65]

The role and function of gossip itself have been analysed to reveal its considerable social utility and to emphasise that it is (as women have long been aware) by no means an activity limited to, or particularly characteristic of, women.[66] Men gossip too. They may call it something else, but it inhabits the same territory. Men's magazines carry gossip. Sports or music (even some computer) magazines are permeated by the coverage of celebrities and gossip about them. In such magazines, one can certainly trace a fetishising of equipment that parallels the women's magazines' emphasis on fashion or interior design, and sports results as detailed and tedious to the uninvolved as knitting patterns, but it is difficult to find stories other than those concerned with the life of the musician or athlete and his or her performance.

At the core of all celebrity stories, irrespective of gender, are two lines: the performance and the life. Stories about Shane Warne's various shoulder injuries and operations parallel those of Debbie Byrne's depression (as those about his weight mimic those of the majority of women in the public eye). Stories about celebrities which are targeted at men may well emphasise different aspects from those which are targeted at women, but we would not want our concentration here on women's magazines to indicate support for the belief that celebrity is exclusively a feminine interest. Women's magazines do have higher circulations and the number of celebrities mentioned, if not featured, may also be larger (especially for those magazines which publish pages of captioned photographs of celebrities at functions). But, in addition to the way in which the celebrity focus of male-targeted magazines is customarily disregarded, significant numbers of men read mass-market women's magazines. Furthermore, television magazines – which do not have circulations based significantly on gender but, rather, on social utility – use celebrity as the primary means through which particular programs are recommended in editorial content.

All of that said, however, it is undeniably the case that mass-market women's magazines carry more celebrity stories, in terms of their overall number of items, than other media outlets, except for televised celebrity chat shows. We have argued against a view that this kind of media content is necessarily trivial or demeaning to those who are its objects or to those who consume it. Nevertheless, it is also clear that the magazines are businesses, exploiting a particular market for commercial purposes, not for any more elevated social benefit. There is little doubt that, for the last ten to fifteen years, mass-market women's magazines have used stories about celebrities, largely salacious in content and tone, as the principal device in their circulation battles. The entry of two new magazines devoted to gossip, and with little if any of the service sections which continue to characterise the three older titles, can be seen as further demonstration that celebrity stories do have an appeal to readers, especially the younger ones who dominate the *NW* and *Who Weekly* demographics. While many of these stories serve positive functions, they are not in the majority nor is that the primary reason they are published.

On the one hand, then, conventional criticism of celebrity journalism in these magazines tends to privilege elite views of popular culture and potentially misogynist conceptions of a passive, gullible female reader. On the other hand, though, it is difficult not to feel that the dominant register of prurient and hypocritically self-righteous commentary which frames so many of the celebrity features, as well as the predominantly unflattering snippets of gossip, participates in constructing a model of women's interests that does not, cannot, assist in such interests being taken seriously within the rest of the public culture. It may be that this is the price which has to be paid by those who wish to bring the private, the domestic and the feminine to the forefront of our media cultures, but it seems to us that the accounting should be very precise in its attempt to see if too much is being surrendered for too little.

However, such criticisms as these rarely come from the readers, who know better than to take magazine gossip seriously. It is significant that they are most commonly made by other media outlets and we have already suggested what might be motivating such attention. While there may be a number of different judgements made about the cultural function being served by these magazines, it is important to recognise that they are not just a sideline to the main game. The coverage of celebrities in mass-market women's magazines is a fundamental element in the process through which celebrity is produced and circulated in Australia. Ultimately, what we are describing in this chapter is not a separate case of bad practice but an account of an integral part of the celebrity industry: it is integrated through networks of ownership and through discourse. Magazine stories typify the basic forms of celebrity gossip, and their coverage is essential to the processes through which celebrity profiles are built and disseminated.

Training the reader: Teen magazines

One of the few bright spots in the story of magazine circulations of recent years has been teen magazines – which means especially those aimed at young girls. For many years a market segment occupied solely by *Dolly*, competition was introduced during the 1990s, particularly by the titles *Girlfriend, Smash Hits* and *TV Hits* (though it needs to be noted that about a third of the readers of each of the latter two are boys).[67] With the competition came an increased attention to celebrities. We noted earlier that Sue-Ellen Topfer had claimed a massive increase in the celebrity material appearing in *Dolly* since she left the magazine in 1993, to the point where it is 'almost 60% celebrity driven'.

The treatment of celebrities in the teen magazines is of a very different order from the way in which it is handled in the magazines we have been focusing on. It is, for example, very much more integrated with the service sections. In the September 1999 issue of *Girlfriend*, each of the letter-based advice pages carried a comment from a pictured Hollywood celebrity, the lead fashion story was modelled by four *Neighbours* actors, and other fashion pages were dedicated to 'stealing Milla Jovovich's look' or included shots of American celebrities in clothing similar to that being advocated. A column giving hints on eyebrow shaping was predicated on readers wanting to look like celebrities such as Geri Halliwell or Claire Danes.

Until 1997, young magazine readers were surveyed only if they were 14 or over, but in that year surveying of a younger age group (7–13) revealed how exposed they were to the magazines – which may have entered households as the purchases of older siblings. The readership of *TV Hits* was almost doubled by adding the younger readers; *Dolly* and *Girlfriend* added about a third more. Chantal Kershaw, then publisher of ACP titles *TV Hits* and *Girlfriend*, stressed how important it was,

> hanging on to this new generation of magazine buyers, who are obviously hungry for more … There has been an overwhelming shift in attitude in fashion, movies, music and television towards the younger end of the market and away from the older grown-up grunge attitudes that sees the youth at the end of the century once again embracing fun, frivolity and their favourite magazines.[68]

A year later, the circulations of the more music- and television-focused titles had fallen, allegedly on the decline in popularity of youth-oriented groups Hanson and the Spice Girls.[69]

Despite the circulation slips, the readership data reveals a very substantial penetration of the age range which, combined with Kershaw's comment and the way in which the magazines address their readership, suggests that the approach to the treatment of celebrities here is one of training readers for media products and engagements to come. This is not to suggest that it is in teen magazines that the first encounters with celebrities are made. Children have their own performers, and events featuring Bananas in Pyjamas or the

Typical celebrity fashion shoot, from teen magazine *Girlfriend*, September 1999, in which young *Neighbours* actors model ski clothes. The hand-lettered captions and the use of 'we' unite magazine and celebrity. (with kind permission of *Girlfriend*, Pacific Publications)

Wiggles reveal certain similarities to the encounters between a slightly older cohort and whatever boy or girl group is currently reigning. The child audience, though, is unlikely to care for details about the lives of the occupants of the Banana suits and it is their parents who read the prehistories of the Wiggles members.

The shift seems to come in mid to late primary school – before puberty but after the arrival of the recognition that puberty will come. Gender-differentiated reading habits are in the process of being established. Despite the significant male readerships of titles like *TV Hits* or *Smash Hits*, the majority of their readers are female which, together with the overwhelmingly female readerships of the highest-circulation teen magazines *Dolly* and *Girlfriend*, indicates that the force of the entertainment celebrity industry (as far as the young are concerned) is directed at girls. Boys may read sports-oriented magazines like *Tracks*, which use celebrity endorsements and feature interviews with celebrity surfers, but magazines like these are not (yet) central to the celebrity industry, in part because of the characteristically irreverent tone but also because of the poor-quality paper on which they are produced and the fact that it is entertainment rather than sport which produces the majority of Australian celebrities.

The first sign of magazines' interest in Australian teenagers, as noted in Chapter 2, was the 1954 introduction of a special column in the *Australian Women's Weekly* which in 1959 became a liftout section called 'Teenagers' Weekly' that lasted until 1964. Lesley Johnson notes that a number of stand-alone magazines for teenage girls were launched in the late 1950s but few succeeded.[70] The longest-running of the teen magazines is *Dolly*, which began in 1970. It was not initially all that much interested in celebrities, being far more concerned with fashion, beauty and romance.

One of the continuities from 'Teenagers' Weekly' to current publications has been the importance of the pin-up (although the word itself has little currency today) to the magazine's content and design. Teenagers then, as now, were seen as capitalising their emotional investment in celebrities through the display of their images. The poster is at the heart of this and of the magazines, especially for those aimed at boys as well as girls. No longer is a single poster enough; *TV Hits* for April 1999 boasts on its cover of 'Ten Hot Posters to Stick Up'. The term 'poster' covers images that range from full page to double spread to unfoldable four-sheet size; of the ten in *TV Hits*, two were four-sheet and one was double-page. Topfer, acknowledging that both *TV Hits* and its main rival, *Smash Hits*, are 'very, very poster-driven', stressed the importance of the exclusivity of these to the magazine's circulation. Readers remembered images and would say, 'Oh, I've seen that shot before, I don't need to buy the mag'. *Girlfriend* usually restricts itself to one four-sheet image and a number of full-page images which are graphically distinguished from the rest of the magazine by having little, if any, print on the page. Typically, teen mags have a busy appearance, often using apparently handwritten captions to 'personalise' coverage. This continues the intimate relationship which the magazine promotes through its pervasive referencing to the production team: 'we' go skiing with actors from *Neighbours*; 'we' get excited at meeting a particular celeb; groups about to launch their first single walk into the *Girlfriend* office to meet 'us'. Hermes' suggestion that stories about celebrities can operate to bring them into the reader's 'circle of friends' needs to be expanded in these circumstances to include the prior facilitating presence of the magazine staffers themselves.[71] When there is no encounter between magazine and celebrity, a break-out box can be used to detail a parallel with a staffer (such as an improvement in 'fashion sense'), reversing the practice of the service sections.

TV Hits, April 1999, full-page pin-up of *Neighbours* soap star Jansen Spencer. The Q&A section is on a separate page, leaving the photograph clear for use as a poster. (with kind permission of *TV Hits*, Pacific Publications)

The magazine offers itself as a friendly intermediary between reader and celebrity. Readers are continually addressed as 'you', and 'we' tell you all about the great time 'we' are having hanging out with celebrities on 'your' behalf. The happy, breathless tone is designed to catch the spirit of idealised young teen speech with as many of its (more respectable) transient slang terms as manageable. 'Idealised' in that, unlike the mass-market women's magazines, there are rarely uncomplimentary remarks passed. The snide, carping tone noted elsewhere is very rare. In this regard, teen magazines provide only a limited preparation for the different approach to come. The most negative example found (photographs of Britney Spears with a comment noting that it might be a good idea if just sometimes she wore a top that wasn't cropped) did foreshadow the kind of gratuitous fashion advice that is a common feature of the more 'adult' outlets. Criticism of Australian celebrities – even this mild – could not be found. The 'fun' that Kershaw detected pervades celebrity coverage and results in what Topfer sees as a fondness for 'quirky' captions.

The apotheosis of the magazine's role in bringing reader and celebrity together comes with the competitions where the prize is a date with a celebrity – overwhelmingly, male celebrities. Although these are a similar kind of celebrity activity to the much more common 'breakfast with the stars' or fund-raising dinner with celebrity speaker, the use of the term 'date' as well as the selectivity involved does mark these out as particular kinds of access to a celebrity. What is on offer is not just the celebrity's presence and speech but a much more blatant conflation of celebrity-as-commodity and celebrity-as-fantasy, focused on the physical body of the individual and on the continuing fantasy of an actual (or nearly actual) relationship made possible by and through the magazine.

Surprisingly, academic analyses of teen magazines have largely ignored their celebrity content. There is a common preoccupation with the way in which they prepare their readers for appropriate gender role behaviour, especially in heterosexual femininity, and the importance of consumption behaviour to producing a desirable appearance (even when the import of the article is in the main to contest this).[72] But the place of the celebrity in these matters or the proliferation of celebrity coverage in the magazines themselves is generally overlooked. Tineke Willemsen, taking advantage of the recent availability of a generalist teenage boys' magazine in Holland to examine the similarities in teen magazines across the gender divide, concentrated on relationships and appearances. Although her content analysis revealed that the two largest categories in the boys' magazine were celebrities and hobbies, compared with the girls' fashion and beauty, she dismisses celebrity from further consideration on the grounds of its 'stereotypic masculinity'. (It seems that this is because of the celebrities' prominence in what she calls the 'public life sphere', thus implying that it is the public status of these figures that is the most important aspect for the male readers.)[73] Given Hermes' comments on Dutch magazines, this is an idiosyncratic judgement but strangely in keeping with the celebrity-free vision of teen magazines provided elsewhere.

An important exception to this dismissal of celebrity is provided by Angela McRobbie's work on British girls' magazines, especially those of the 1980s in which she notes that information about the 'real lives' of celebrities mediates the close relationship between the magazines and the music industry. Though one would now have to also include television soap and sitcom actors, her observation that the 'magazines increasingly play the role of publicist for the various bands who fall into the teenybopper camp' remains accurate and of direct relevance to Australian magazines. It applies also to those magazines which have significant numbers of male readers, though this is not her concern. Yet it is her assertion that 'it is pop rather than romance which now operates as a kind of conceptual umbrella giving a sense of identity to these publications' which, again with the addition of the world of television and film, provides the key to understanding the role these magazines play within the celebrity industry.[74]

The most basic message of the teen magazines is that celebrities are important and omnipresent; indeed, that they are more important than any other aspect of life, since they are part of everything the magazine deals with. Fashion and beauty involve looking like them, having fun involves doing the kinds of things they do and consuming their products, and self-actualisation is presented in terms that use the 'ordinariness', the 'like-me-ness' of the celebrity as a touchstone. Education is mentioned only if celebrities recall being at school. Even the most-referenced relationship, friendship, is presented through celebrities. This is not just as a consequence of the illusion that, through the graces of the magazine, celebrities are part of the reader's circle of friends. It is a persistent line of questioning, as interviewers regularly ask about singers' and actors' friends, but is a topic that disappears as readers age.

Teen magazines provide the clearest picture of a world made over by the celebrity industry, a world in which meaningfulness is given by a celebrity's attention and identity revealed by the choice of which celebrity image to display. This is not to make claims about teenagers' actual acceptance of or belief in the material – they undoubtedly do more than choose to follow A rather than B or to buy this CD rather than that. But in the teen magazine there is hardly ever an indication that a situation could arise that the celebrity couldn't solve.

Chapter 6

Changes in the Media Landscape

There have been major changes and shifts in media and cultural production in Australia over the last twenty years as a result of transformed industrial practices around the construction and promotion of public personalities. The entertainment industry has fostered the development of a celebrity system that allows newspapers and magazines to have a ready supply of 'local' content, and the television networks to have successful public events populated with their own developed personalities and a ready-made system to fabricate celebrities from news and current affairs. This support industry has developed in conjunction with the growth of public relations and publicity agencies, and it constitutes a (possibly, the) principal means through which Australian media content is now generated and organised. Regarding contemporary media culture from this vantage point allows us to read popular cultural forms differently and to better understand how the production of the Australian celebrity has permeated our understanding of public life.

The red carpet treatment

> If you don't want to be photographed with your new girlfriend/ boyfriend, don't turn up.
> *Bunty Avieson*

Promotional culture is now structurally embedded into the media and entertainment industries, and among their industrial outcomes is the production of celebrity. While a celebrity may perform functions that are, in a sense, cultural rather than merely industrial – that is, it is possible to see them as satisfying desires that they themselves have not created – there is little that is natural about the process which puts them in the public eye. This process involves a great deal of work: it is the activity of an industry.

Two events in the latter part of 1999 provided our study with rich examples of how the currency of celebrity operates in Australia and how an industry organises itself to build, and then trade on, that celebrity value. One was the inaugural Noosa Film Festival in Queensland, held over the first week in September, and the other was the opening of Fox Studios in Sydney on 7 November. Both called on film actors as their prime celebrity currency and both featured at their centre one of the great motifs of the celebrity industry: the red carpet arrival of the stars. Both were staged for the promotion of films, though at different stages of the production process: the film festival targeted distribution and exhibition, the Fox opening concerned the contemporary duo of film production and theme park. Both had as their immediate audience journalists, photographers and television camera crews, through whose stories and pictures the promoters aimed to reach the wider audience of potential customers. Both used an actual audience of fans as a backdrop for their activities.

In the outcome, the two events demonstrated the importance of other factors in the mix, the importance of those things the publicist cannot control. Unsurprisingly, the power of geopolitics was one. No matter how popular Noosa might be as a beach resort for the rich and famous, Sydney is a much more valuable location for a staged media event. The other aspect was also unsurprising. The most important component in a media event is the media. The film festival was organised by a committee of actors, producers and writers, many of whom were celebrities themselves, who had employed very experienced professionals (including Tracey Mair, one of our interviewees) and gained sponsorships from, among others, the Seven Network, pay TV channel Showtime, and *Who Weekly*. As good as these connections were, Fox Studios, as part of a huge media empire, could call on a vast array of stars and guarantee their appearance and red carpet comments. Unlike the Noosa festival, they were thus able to secure a live national broadcast of the opening via the Nine Network and thereby produce a successful media event.

Both occasions generated stories and pictures on television, in newspapers and in magazines, but, in column-inch terms, the six or so hours of the Fox event was as successful as the six days of Noosa. The film festival was unfortunate to have been chosen as the event at which the *Sydney Morning Herald* launched its stand on ethical reporting: the paper refused to accept the airfares and accommodation offered in expectation of coverage. It had instituted a new code of practice designed to protect its journalists from 'infection from the PR dollar'.[1] This was in the wake of the Australian Broadcasting

Authority announcing its inquiry into the 'cash for comment' scandal and was the first in a number of responses from journalists trying to restore faith in the ethics of their profession. This action effectively scuttled the prevailing rules of engagement and thus reduced the amount of coverage the film festival could expect, especially in the Sydney market. (News Ltd seems to have treated it mainly as a Queensland story, for it received much heavier coverage in the *Courier-Mail* than in the *Australian*.)

While the Fox opening was, as one would anticipate from the corporate connections, front page (and continued inside) of the *Australian*, it was still too central a Sydney event for the Fairfax press to ignore entirely. Nevertheless, Dennis and Maddox did spend much of their article quoting the instructions which had been circulated to journalists and which emphasised the highly orchestrated nature of their media rival's event and the centrality of contractual obligations to its structure, as well as the precise calibrations of degrees of celebrity required: 'Fox Studios Australia contracted celebrities will stop ... to speak with the assembled media ... Other celebrities have accepted invites to the Grand Opening, however they are not contracted to stop on the red carpet.' The article was accompanied by illustrations showing the arrival of celebrities Kylie Minogue and Nicole Kidman, but the largest picture was reserved for Rupert Murdoch and Wendi Deng.[2]

The Noosa Film Festival provided an opportunity to observe the all-important red carpet in operation at the core event: the dinner honouring festival president Jack Thompson. A bank of floodlights bathed a red-carpeted walkway leading into the venue, and a crowd of photographers and television crews positioned themselves around it to capture the parade of dinner guests. The celebrities arrived, smiling and engaging in 'spot interviews' for the camera and waving at the small group of onlookers. Organising committee celebrities Jack Thompson, Gillian Armstrong and Rachel Ward arrived early, followed by the night's master of ceremonies, *Blue Heelers* star John Wood. Rising star Hugh Jackman, promoting *Erskineville Kings*, Michael Caton, leading actor from *The Castle* and about to host the television show *Hot Property*, and Jacqueline McKenzie, whose Hollywood film *Deep Blue Sea* was soon to be released – all appeared, posed and chatted to television crews. The publicists connected to the event were at one side, intermittently prompting journalists as the next celebrity arrived. Occasionally, they regulated the flow so that the various personalities were given their relative due. The teen stars of *American Pie*, including Alyson Hannigan, better known for her character, Willow, from *Buffy the Vampire Slayer*, provided a mini-climax, before the parade culminated in the arrival of American actor Billy Zane, the festival's 'big name'.

The hierarchy of the red carpet, which saves the biggest names till last and sends the local soap stars in early, reveals particularly starkly the order of importance in the promotional world. American stars, even those of quite a low ranking within their own industry, still outshine any Australian ones, while overseas exposure correspondingly raises the ranking of Australians. McKenzie's fame had all but vanished after her AFI award for *Angel Baby* in 1995, but her supporting role in an American film was sufficient to return her to public prominence for this event. The extent to which film outranks television in this hierarchy is not quite as clear. Hannigan was more important than her film co-stars because of her television exposure, and the choice of Wood as host of the President's Dinner acknowledged his long-running presence on television.

These are core, generic events in the production of celebrity. The pages of photographs and snippets that appear in the mass-market women's magazines are filled with 'red carpet' moments, as are news bulletins, television entertainment shows and newspapers. They provide concentrated access to a range of celebrities in dressy clothing and (usually) in couples, which itself can be a point worth reporting. They also provide the illusion of actual access to the individual celebrity in the continually recorded spectacle of adoring fans lining the street and the sides of the red carpet. For all participants – celebrities, publicists and the media – the red carpet event is an efficient use of time. It is also, to use an old-fashioned term, most emphatically a 'pseudo event', something that has no reason for existence beyond being reported.

Yet, even when Daniel Boorstin coined the term 'pseudo event' in 1961, in the full flow of righteous indignation about the misuse of news, it was a hopeless cry against what was already the norm.[3] News bulletins are full of events staged *for* news bulletins. As argued earlier, and as politicians have proved for decades, the staging of events does not negate their newsworthiness nor their ability to be part of the political process as it is now. The Fox red carpet was laid down to create a promotional opportunity and that it certainly did, but the parade of the popular, the pretty and the powerful also provided opportunities for other kinds of commentary.

The national referendum on a republic had occurred the day before and many celebrities were asked for their opinion about its defeat. Aboriginal actor Deborah Mailman and her partner agitated for the retention of the South Sydney football team, under threat from a Murdoch-backed reorganisation of the National Rugby League. Even at their most focused, celebrity and promotional activities are never necessarily outside the political process. At Noosa, the morning after he had closed the red carpet event, Billy Zane was part of another promotional event: a 'spontaneous' get-together with Michelle White, the Aboriginal film-maker of *A Sacred Celebration*, while an artist painted the 4WD-van which had featured prominently in the documentary. It looked remarkably like a politician's electioneering photo-opportunity, as camera crews, publicists and photographers gathered for the Hastings Street improvisational theatre, all aware of the political dimension being added to the promotion. And there were others benefiting too: the

Noosa Film Festival street theatre, September 1999. Actor Billy Zane talks to Michelle White, director of *A Sacred Celebration*. (with kind permission of Louise McBryde)

President's Dinner had a charitable component through its sponsorship of the Children's Make a Wish Foundation. Even as these events attempt to construct their own cultural meanings, they must do so by making use of those that are already in circulation.

The meanings of celebrity

Clearly, the ironic suggestion with which the previous chapter ended – that celebrity is expected to provide the solution to the problems of contemporary life – should not be seen solely as the misconception of teenagers. It has a broader relevance than that. Celebrities are called on to (and do) carry meaning in situations far beyond what might reasonably be seen to be their professional expertise and to audiences far exceeding those who might be supposed to be interested in the products they represent. Celebrities may act as exemplary citizens, endorsing political parties, advising on constitutional referenda, exhorting governments to adopt new foreign policy positions or to change laws on environmental issues. They are used to promote health awareness and the benefits of multiculturalism. In many instances, this can be regarded as a core part of keeping their names and images before the public to enhance their earning power, but it is far from invariably the case. Increasingly, celebrities are being asked to take on a certain amount of cultural activism as among the obligations which come with their visibility. They perform, in some cases in spite of themselves, the public roles which have in the past been filled by other categories of eminent person.

It is worth considering this a little further. In a lecture on the current state of the arts, given at the University of Western Australia in October 1999 and reprinted in the *Weekend Australian*, theatre critic Katharine Brisbane lamented how, with the highly notable exception of Aboriginal artists, the arts in Australia have 'no spokesmen and women, no revered figures who engage actively with public issues and speak for their profession'.[4] She suggested that this role had been supplanted by celebrity. Although she does not expand on the point, there are elements that are instructive about the distinction.

Implicit in it is the assumption that, once, the prominent cultural figures were the artists, the clerics and the jurists, and it is unfortunate that their 'legitimate' eminence (that is, based on their knowledge or institutional position) has been displaced by something which is commercially or 'artificially' produced. Implicitly, again, this understands celebrities as vacant ethical spaces, unengaged with public issues or their profession, always only at the service of promotion. It is an understandable, probably an orthodox, position. One can readily find instances where celebrities function as little more than glossy add-ons to campaigns, designed to attract their own demographic to the cause, although one would also have to acknowledge counter-examples like Midnight Oil's Peter Garrett in his role as spokesman for conservation. When the public visibility of the celebrity is precisely what seems to be excessive, phoney or implausible about them, it is easy to see why their qualifications to speak on behalf of even their own profession might be questioned. Nevertheless, even politics employs the discourses of celebrity to represent its positions to the public. What Brisbane speaks of regretting may not be the replacement of one class-based cultural elite with another more commercial elite but, rather, the establishment of a less transparently institutionalised system whereby public figures earn the right to speak and gain access to the media. Simply, it is no longer easy to understand how they got there.

Underlying Brisbane's comments, though, are other questions. Does the excessiveness of the discourses of celebrity drive out socially necessary but less pervasive discourses? If celebrity is now the way that arts (and sports) figures operate politically, is this solely or inappropriately a commercial activity? Our research suggests that the answer to both questions is 'not necessarily'. Mailman's cheeky advocacy of the case for continuation of an autonomous South Sydney football team signified her membership of a grass-roots campaign against big business and, in particular, media companies controlling the destinies of local sports teams. Other celebrities, like comedian Andrew Denton, have also been usefully visible activists on this issue, but Mailman signals more. South Sydney has traditionally been a club with a long line of Aboriginal players and a place where Aboriginal and non-Aboriginal people operate with shared aims. Mailman's Aboriginality, her irrepressible ebullience and perhaps her current place of residence align her with the spirit and the argument of the campaign. Celebrities may now be instrumental in carrying issues and this may affect how these issues are ultimately articulated through the media; but, because their presence is often about identity and simple emotional commitment, they can rarely be reduced to the status of pure promotional devices.

More fundamentally, why is it that celebrities are so inescapable in contemporary culture? Why are their stories and representations consumed with such detailed avidity? Further, given their apparent constructedness or lack of authenticity, why is it that they have to be *meaningful* rather than merely spectacular? There are a number of possible reasons: the media's interest in provoking class-based jealousy or resentment at their success, the audience's romantic identification with glamorous figures, the individual's incorporation of the story of a celebrity's life as a means of enriching their own circle of social relations, or the fundamental fact that they are now part of the cultural process through which we construct contemporary social identities.

One reason, in particular, is that the celebrity has considerable explanatory power in a time of great complexity and contradiction. A defining characteristic of contemporary times is what is popularly called 'information overload', and celebrities can be seen as one way in which to short-circuit this. As advertisers all know, the individual celebrity persona provides a powerful condensation of meaning which can be attached to commodities and issues; similarly, celebrities can act as prisms through which social complexity is brought back to the human level. Bunty Avieson's comment about the usefulness of Belinda Emmett in discussing breast cancer is a case in point. Emmett demonstrates the relevance of the condition to a younger age group, the importance of a positive attitude to dealing with diagnosis and treatment, and the desirability of openness about one's experience – all just through being a young woman getting coverage through her celebrity status. The downside of this, of course, is a point implicit in the reference to Thomas Elsaesser's argument in Chapter 1: that popular culture's practice of reducing large-scale change to the level of the personal may help the individual in coming to terms with it, but not necessarily in understanding or intervening in it.

Celebrities clearly have representative qualities – Richard Dyer's 'type of the individual' is semiotically embedded in the nation's stars.[5] This does not mean that they are typical, of course; the 'type of the individual' is an ideological construction which registers a range of preferences and desires, not the result of a demographic survey. They comprise a sample skewed on most demographic dimensions, being more likely to be male, white, young, Australian-born and able-bodied than the population as a whole, not to mention that non-demographic category, better looking. For the minority of celebrities who are outside these demographic heartlands, the way in which they differ may operate to give them a more specific, if marginalised, representative function and may even do so powerfully. Ruth Cracknell, for instance, especially at the height of the popularity of *Mother and Son*, was used to make observations about older people. This more specific representative function can be seen most graphically, though, in the case of Aboriginal celebrities.

The example of Mailman is of someone who has only recently achieved a degree of celebrity. Cathy Freeman and Ernie Dingo are two longer-term contemporary instances, though one could cite earlier examples like Lionel Rose or Evonne Goolagong Cawley. The high proportion of sports personalities in this (short) list reveals how similar Australia is to other contemporary western societies where sport is one of the few avenues to success available to racial minorities, indigenous or not. As an actor, comedian and television presenter, Dingo indicates the other main category for such advancement: the entertainer. Freeman and Dingo are subject to the conventional celebrity treatment: stories about their private lives are readily used to promote their professional activities, and they appear as celebrity figures in advertisements (Dingo was the first person used in the Ozemale/Ozemail ad campaign). But both are also required to act as spokespersons for Aboriginal people generally.

The cultural attraction of the celebrity figure, and the importance of the celebrity industry, mean that a celebrity spokesperson (notwithstanding Katharine Brisbane's discomfort with such a phenomenon) can be a very powerful political device. Freeman's famous celebratory lap of honour, draped in both the national and the Aboriginal flags, after winning the 400 metres at the Commonwealth Games in 1994 actualised her double representative role. Her subsequent censuring by Arthur Tunstall produced a debate about Aboriginality, framed by that most powerful of Australian national discourses – sport. Even though Freeman herself is customarily reticent about political issues, her actions and her prominent media presence inevitably act as a vehicle for political sentiment. Thus, a quite trivial magazine story, such as the one about the lost engagement ring, can also involve her responding to a question about whether her future will include more formal political activity.

Ernie Dingo, possibly because he does not have the formal double articulation of an international representative of Australia and of Aboriginality, may not appear to immediately evoke political arguments. However, his performance as 'Robert Gottliebsen' in television's *Fast Forward* certainly carried a strong political message through the unlikely spectacle of an

Aboriginal face dispensing stock-market advice. More generally, Dingo plays out an indigenised version of the emblematic function of many stars discussed by Richard Dyer: the star's personal success testifies to the openness of a society.[6] Specifically, Dingo's celebrity is a sign that it is possible for Aboriginal people to find fame and fortune. The politics of his representation can also work in less consoling ways, however. Dingo operates in his own persona as a presenter, but as an actor he also plays other characters. Some of the political work which the celebrity Ernie Dingo performs comes through the characters he plays – such as in the 1988 made-for-television movie *Tudawali: Release from Sorrow* where he portrayed Robert Tudawali, famous for his role as Marbuk, the 'renegade' doomed lover in Charles Chauvel's 1955 film, *Jedda*; or the policeman Vincent Burunga who falls in love with Beth Ashton (Cate Blanchett) in the ABC's 1994 social problem drama series, *Heartland*. Promotional work for productions like these requires actors to talk from the perspective of their characters and to discuss the issues that the dramas explore, issues which for Dingo always involve the conditions of being Aboriginal in a white-dominated society.

The distinction between the celebrities who operate only in their own personae, and those who act and thus exist as characters as well as themselves, is an important one. The former group includes sport figures, musicians, ex-politicians, accidental celebrities, and television presenters and reporters; the latter includes those who specialise in film and theatre, and actors in television drama. Our research identified the active work of an industry, often uncomfortably, trying to position these two general categories of celebrities. Television networks and their powerful publicity departments are expert at making their presenter-personalities into celebrities, while film and television production units sell their feature films and drama series nationally and internationally through publicising the stars. Agents and managers often work on both sides of the fence with their talent: sometimes they protect their clients from publicity that is not related to actual work, as Peter Rix does with his musical stars; and sometimes they are complicit in the development of the public, as much as the working, profile of their actor/personality.

Although it is possible to distinguish between these two kinds of celebrity personae – and it is probably easy to tell which one you would rather be – the activity of most aspects of the industry is concentrated on strategically manipulating this distinction. In some cases, the industry sets out deliberately to obliterate the distinction between the public and the private persona; at other points, it deliberately creates or defends it. The celebrity persona, whether emerging from Australia or internationally, is all about playing with the differences between the 'work' and the life. A celebrity figure is encouraged by the industry to allow their work to generate a second life – a second skin, perhaps – which can provide the content for the publicity which surrounds the television program or film. The 'life' that is presented in feature articles and television interviews is designed to appear to reveal some element of the celebrity's 'actual' private world which is thereby made public. In this process, the promotion of the persona dovetails with the needs of the cultural product and, as a result, the distinction between the performer and the role, the public presence and the private life, is routinely being dissolved and reconstituted.

The naturalisation of this second life of celebrity for the working public performer has been well established over the last fifteen years in the Australian industry, so established that the most reluctant person with a public profile can rarely avoid the publicity pull. Speaking on a panel about celebrity at the Brisbane Writers Festival, Kate Langbroek, best known for her regular appearances on Channel 10's *The Panel*, was insistent about her desire for what she did there to be treated as work in the same way that her 3RRR radio show was. She did not want to be turned into a celebrity and paid 'for being' (to use her term). Nonetheless, she admitted that, in a small way, she had not been able to resist completely. She had agreed to an interview with *Who Weekly*, after which the magazine persistently called her for 'celebrity comments' on trivial things like the popularity of new fashion items.[7]

A final point in this discussion of the meanings of celebrity is probably necessary as a kind of reality check. While the cultural function of celebrity needs to be better understood, it must also be remembered that close, avid attention to specific celebrities is not necessarily the norm for most of the population. The publicity machine certainly offers a kind of intimacy with the celebrity-as-commodity, but there are plenty of people who are simply not interested. The consumption of publicity is most often distracted, diluted and so deeply embedded in the everyday that it is to all intents and purposes invisible, rather than generating a moment of focused and conscious identity formation. But, on the other hand, for most consumers, the publicity is all that they take of the celebrity – the film or the CD, the play, the book or the sporting contest is never encountered of itself – and the reported entertainment 'news' is absorbed (or not) as what one should know about that particular moment of popular culture.

For many of the targets of promotion and publicity, the celebrity is the only commodity being consumed: there is no mystery in the recurrent coverage by mass-market women's magazines targeted at suburban women over 35 of such figures as Courtney Love, whose records are pitched to a totally different demographic. Love is of interest as a scandalous celebrity and her music is irrelevant. Similarly, the Spice Girls, omnipresent in newspapers during the late 1990s despite their appeal being primarily to children and adolescents, precisely the groups least likely to read newspapers, were instances of publicity successful in generating column inches that seem unlikely to have led in any direct way to sales. In a full loop, it could be said that the pretence that a story about a celebrity exists for reasons other than product promotion is less honest – and certainly less 'pure' – than a story that is about someone who is famous for being famous and has only themselves to promote.

The critique of promotional culture

> In the future everyone will be famous for fifteen minutes.
> *Andy Warhol*, Diaries

Not all celebrities have products to promote, however, and not all celebrities are interested in promoting themselves all of the time – the 'accidental heroes', for instance, for most of whom the time spent in the public eye is an unwanted intrusion in their private lives. These are the ordinary members of the public who find themselves inadvertently 'celebritised'. The destructive power of celebrity is manifest in such cases. Since the distinction between ordinary people and celebrities is the principal way in which individuals are categorised by the media, when individuals emerge from ordinariness for one reason or another (good fortune, bad fortune, valour or criminality), they are treated as if they have crossed the line into the other grouping whether or not this is appropriate or beneficial to them (or to us).

Examples include Thredbo survivor Stuart Diver; convicted criminal Chopper Read, who was interviewed as a celebrity on Elle McFeast's chat show and led to talk about his crimes within the same framework that singers talk about their latest chart-toppers; and Shane Paxton, who was demonised by *A Current Affair* as a dole bludger and subsequently used by a succession of media figures to advance their own agendas. These are instances where the mobilisation of the discourses of celebrity was inappropriate, offensive, destructive – and deliberate. Confronted with such opportunities, journalists, producers and media audiences seem content to forget that these people are not an Elle Macpherson, model and underwear company owner, promoting her own and other companies' products through appearances, interviews, and staged and stolen glimpses of her private life; or a Jeff Kennett, ex-premier of Victoria, promoting his political agenda through press conferences, fashion shoots and websites. These five differ on almost any dimension of public interest one could care to construct, yet the way that they are presented to the public obliterates those differences. An intimacy is constructed between the person and whatever kind of media employee is acting as the intermediary and surrogate for the public eye, their family lives are scrutinised and changes in them brought into the open, while their activities are monitored, not so much for political or criminal news as for personal trivia.[8]

Such instances are occasions when the dominance of celebrity as a media discourse, as well as the ethical regime within which the news media currently operates, is rightly exposed to criticism. It is hard to see what defensible interests are served by such a pattern of representation applied to such objects. That is only the beginning of the critique of celebrity, however. The development of the public relations and publicity industries has been seen by many in journalism as a negative influence on the democratic operation of the press, in particular. There is also a long tradition of moral critique of the media which sees media celebrities as intrinsically inappropriate as cultural representatives of any sort. And the body of arguments around tabloidisation suggests that we are witnessing a general trend towards the intrusive and the sensational across all media forms for which the promotion of celebrity is tailor-made.

The problem is not merely that such modes of media promotion exist; the problem is that they are seen to be progressively displacing other, perhaps more socially useful, forms of reporting, programming, information or entertainment. What results, the argument goes, is a diminished public culture, where one mode of representation, one discursive pattern – and one commercial objective – prevails. Andrew Wernick has discussed the homogenising character of promotional culture at length, noting how 'regardless of whether its manifest function is to inform, inspire, solidarize [*sic*] or just to entertain', the same rhetorical forms are in operation.[9] We can note this in the way there was no disjunction, no sense of inappropriateness, in comments on the referendum result being made on the red carpet going into the Fox Studios opening. Rather, it would have been odd if nothing had been said on the subject that day. Entertainment celebrities had been drafted by both sides during the campaign. Nor was there any disjunction in Rupert Murdoch himself parading along, not just because he was the chairman of the company ultimately responsible for the whole affair, but because the red carpet is equally home to businessmen, politicians and entertainment figures even if the photographs of them are not equally numerous and evenly dispersed.

Wernick observes that this homogenisation is balanced by a semiological complexity which enables interest to be maintained despite the flow of sameness. The red carpet may be a cliché, but precisely who treads it, with whom, wearing what, in which company, preceding and following which other habitués and in honour of what precise product, retains allure. For Wernick, this is part of a 'cheapening of our symbolic currency', a devaluation of our social values and cultural myths consequent on the pervasiveness of the market. He accuses promotional culture of 'bad faith':[10]

> From top to bottom, in short, promotional culture is radically deficient in good faith ... Considering the sugar coating which pastes a personal smile, and a patina of conformist values, over

Rupert Murdoch and new wife Wendi Deng, centre of attention at opening of Fox Studios in Sydney, 7 November 1999 (photograph copyright Jon Reid)

> the pervasively self-interested motives which underlie virtually all publicly communicated words and images, the total impression it makes (against which, of course, we screen ourselves through wise inattention) is not merely vacuous, but emetic in its perpetual untruth.

It is difficult not to take his general point seriously, as well as a further suggestion that the ultimate direction of this promotional culture is entropic because of its tendency to become 'depleted of the (existential and cosmological) meaningfulness which those implicated in it, just because it is a culture, seek to derive from its symbolic material'. Meaning runs out, he argues, used up by the commercial construction of cultural meaning around the objects of publicity and promotion. His book concludes by insisting on the importance of 'releasing cultural production from its currently overwhelming commercial imperative', to 'revalorize the public realm itself as a space for disinterested expression and communication'.[11]

Wernick is responding to what he sees as a systemic flaw in the public sphere today, and we have some sympathy with him. Our overall approach, however, is slightly different in its emphases. We have sought to understand the operation of the celebrity industry. For us, it is not merely an ugly growth on a media system, the removal of which will return us to a prior and better state of being, but part of a much deeper transformation of the processes by which information and entertainment are produced, distributed and consumed. We are committed to seeing this transformation clearly, and not simply deploring or denying it, as a means of coming to an understanding of the processes through which the contemporary Australian media actually works. That said, however – and this would apply to a raft of other media processes in Australia today – there are plenty of characteristics which provoke political or ethical concerns. Consequently, there are aspects of the celebrity industry which no amount of understanding would enable us to condone.

One of the most serious is the issue of privacy. The obsessive interest in signs of the 'authentic self' leads to intrusive behaviour on the part of the press,[12] which can readily be disavowed as the activity of paparazzi, as it was when the excesses were deplored after the death of the Princess of Wales, but which is nevertheless systematically encouraged by the decline in staff photographers and the increased dependence by media outlets on freelancers of all kinds. While intrusive activities may be thought defensible to some extent for public figures, they are not in the case of accidental celebrities. Selling one's story exclusively to a chosen outlet should not be the only way to move a media circus off one's doorstep, when they have camped there just because one has survived a criminal act or a natural disaster (or one's child has not). Exposing the private lives of ordinary people to the public gaze for the purpose of attracting greater audiences, and defending it in the name of public interest, should not be tolerated as freely as it is. We are far from alone in taking this view. The draft recommendations in the Productivity Commission's report on broadcasting regulations are based on expert evidence about the inadequacy of current methods of correction and redress for ordinary members of the public and constitute one of the few instances where a stronger regulatory structure is proposed.[13]

Rendering ordinary people as celebrities subjects them to both idolisation and, in Connell's terms, 'oppositional resentment'.[14] Prominence for any reason leads to excessive interest and to suspicion. Thus, our review of the media's discussion of Stuart Diver's decisions following his survival of the Thredbo disaster revealed a number of themes: the continued picking over his handling of the grief over his wife's death; admiration for his decision not to capitalise on his fame outside his realm of expertise; and what seemed petty speculation about what he was *really* like, since he could not be the pleasant unassuming person he appeared to be *and* a celebrity. His being represented by Harry M. Miller fuelled this last suspicion since it could be advanced as signalling his intending to profit from death (for why else would he need representation?).

While gossip is not necessarily a destructive activity, but rather multi-faceted, there is no denying that it does include negative components based on jealousy which assume that all elevation above the ordinary is unjustified, that all those elevated have ugly secrets just waiting to be exposed, and that the media's aggressive attempts to reveal those secrets are usually justified. The intense competition for stories and audiences means that there is often a complete lack of proportion here in media practice. Poor taste in underwear, or infidelity, can be made to seem as reasonably in the public interest as revelations of financial malfeasance, and all three are equally usable as celebrity stories. For a celebrity well located within the industry, their reputation a formal commodity guarded by professionals, this may be a different matter than it is for someone less prepared, someone for whom all publicity most certainly is not good publicity. They do not have a product to sell; rather, they are simply this week's target of attention, used to sell a paper or a magazine.

A key focus for the critique of contemporary celebrity has been through discussion of the perceived decline in news and current affairs which argues that public debate is skewed and undernourished through, among other things, the concentration on personalities. Countervailing views, such as those of Catharine Lumby and John Hartley, hold that tabloidisation may in fact be a development of the mass-mediated public sphere which democratically challenges the past hierarchies of news values in ways that are politically progressive.

Our research, however, qualifies some of the more positive claims that might be made for what Hartley calls 'democratainment' – a more democratically accessible and responsive media.[15] We have shown how the growth of public relations and publicity agencies has transformed the actual process of developing news; and Clara Zawawi's research demonstrated the effect of the expansion of public relations upon traditional journalism over the last twenty years by providing evidence of the print media's increased reliance on press releases for their content. The intensification of competition for exclusive stories has also increased the commercial currency of the sensational, the scandalous or the celebrity story for television, newspapers and magazines, inevitably opening up the ethical minefield of chequebook journalism. And personality management organisations attempt to control the media frenzies which result from this intense competition.

There is no doubt that the trends which give rise to the tag of tabloidisation exist. However, there is still room for genuine debate about what to make of them, because of the generality of so much of the criticism and because there is considerable doubt about how widespread or homogeneous the trends in question might be. That is why we have provided empirical evidence of the trend towards celebrity journalism in the media outlets we surveyed. It is worth adding to this survey a rider which reminds us that, despite the general media shift, celebrity-style coverage varies greatly across outlets, media and occasion. Big news stories can still displace celebrity news almost entirely. The situation in East Timor dominated news outlets and popular concern for several months in 1999 and celebrity stories were relegated to other sites.

East Timor, though, had a geographic closeness and relevance to the Australian population. What occurs more often in news and current affairs is that conflicts, international political and economic events, and natural disasters present sequences of negative stories which, though dominating the bulletin, may seem to be of limited relevance to the audience. Rather than pushing such stories aside, celebrity stories may provide variety and pleasure, if not direct personal connection, to what otherwise could seem (and be) unrelenting gloom.

Kate Langbroek, at the Brisbane Writers Festival, suggested how celebrity news might be regarded as 'a dessert', a treat to make the other material concerning events both unpleasant and distant from viewers more palatable.[16] Intuitively persuasive though this observation might be, it needs some deeper investigation. Is there today a greater need for dessert in our news diet than there was a decade or so ago? Our analysis shows celebrity stories forming a greater proportion of news and current affairs. What did the 'other news', to call again on Langer's term,[17] consist of before the recent rise of the celebrity? Standard filler items about cute animals, improbable inventions and local anniversaries, all still to be found, would probably have constituted a greater proportion of the 'soft' stories. It may be – but we have no evidence to support this at all – that there was not quite such a need for dessert under the greater domination of the modernist doctrine of progress, in contrast to more contemporary pervasive scepticism. Rather than such Zeitgeist-ian explanations, though, the rise of the celebrity dessert is more likely to reflect changes in the structure and operation of the industry. The composition of news bulletins has changed in response to industrial contingencies: radio bulletins have become shorter as staff downsize and regulatory requirements relax; and television bulletins use more national content since the establishment of national networks. In such a context, and where 'soft' items need some kind of relevance to appeal to a wider audience, what may have been of interest to a local audience is of insufficient prominence for a national one. It can be argued that celebrities provide this, in addition to their value in promoting related products.

But there is more to this increase in the significance and frequency of celebrity stories. We are in the throes of a shift from a commercial media which (more or less) attempted to balance information and entertainment, to a commercial media which is unashamedly based on entertainment and which is increasingly implicated in the construction of cultural and personal identity. The emergence of the celebrity industry in Australia as it is connected to changed news values is part of the shift to the concerns of the personal. Whether those who embody this personalisation of news are accidental celebrities or regularly rostered celebrities, the news effect is quite similar: stories become organised around revealing more private emotions, visceral violence, intimate retellings, overt revelation of sexual proclivities, and these forms have moved to centre stage in terms of news value and cultural significance.

It would be easy to claim that what has occurred in Australia in its development of a celebrity industry is just a version of what has already happened in other countries, specifically the United States. There is no question that celebrity culture moves transnationally and that this flow of international stars is a defining feature of globalisation. Globalisation is a process which does not respect local or national cultures, and its effects have been particularly strongly felt in the publicity and entertainment industries. The dominance of the United States is profound, and the chance of systematically challenging that dominance is zero. As film producer David Elphick says:

> I think the thing that gets everybody's backs up, whether they be British, French, Italian, Australian, or any other country, is when the means of distribution and exhibition are so controlled by multinational corporations that bad Warner Bros films get cinema space, when better films from Australia or France don't. Another factor is the publicity machines. The TV shows and magazines will publicise a bad film because it has got Tom Hanks in it, when there might be a really good Australian film without Tom Hanks in it that gets no attention.[18]

There is no question that Elphick's perception is an accurate one, and that, despite the burgeoning of the local industry both in celebrity and in film, Australia is always going to be competing on an unequal basis with the United States.

However, while we might think of the US celebrity as the footsoldier of globalisation, and therefore deplore the industry which supports them, there is a cultural nationalist dimension to the Australian promotions industry. Both despite these global realities and because of them, there are two key points that have developed from this study of the synergy between the Australian media and celebrity. First, in the maintenance of national television, film, popular music and print media, there has been an effort through celebrities to increase the economic and cultural value of productions that have emerged from these various industries. It is not logical to applaud the success of these national industries without accepting the part played in that success by the local production of celebrity. And, second, as a result of the maturing of the Australian publicity apparatus – an apparatus that actively produces a local culture as well as marketing the products of imported cultures – celebrity now operates as a currency of value that moves between media forms. Publicity is at the core of the entertainment industries and is also, now at least, fundamental to the process of public presentation in business, politics and sport, if not in most other institutions/professions. Celebrity, with its connection to the mediatised representation and celebration of the self, has been progressively naturalised and normalised throughout Australian culture, so that it is not possible any longer to discuss it in isolation from that culture.

What do we make of all this?

A number of things, not without their contradictions. On the one hand, dealing directly with industry practitioners as we have done makes it both difficult and implausible to demonise them or their activities in the way, perhaps, that Wernick's arguments would have us do. It is appropriate for us to acknowledge the legitimacy of the practitioners' views of their professional practices. That might look like a classic example of incorporation, or maybe of hostages identifying with their captors, but we would prefer to see it as a result of a research process whereby our previous, more simplistic understandings of the operation of the industry have been revised in favour of better informed, more complicated, though still probably incomplete, ones. There are limits to such protocols, of course, and there are plenty of instances throughout the book where we have articulated points of view – critical, ethical, political, strategic –that are at odds with those sincerely held by our industry informants. The account we have given, after all, is our own. As a result, and given the number of specific instances where one would want to vigorously question the current ethical conduct of the media in Australia, it is difficult to offer unqualified assent to the most positive constructions of current media trends which would see them as, on balance, progressive or implicitly democratic. The normalisation of chequebook journalism across the media, the revelations in the 'cash for comment' inquiry of talkback radio's abuse of its stars' commercial power, and the callous exploitation of unwitting subjects which has become routine in television current affairs encourage a view that the Australian contemporary media is a long way from serving objectives we would recognise as democratic or even socially responsible. That said, however, we also believe that there is little point in bewailing the existence of such trends in order to reclaim some golden time when no such problems seem to have occurred. Langer's criticism of the elite agenda underlying much of the contemporary 'lament' for journalism, in particular, seems to us to be well aimed. Such complaints can get in the way of properly recognising that the media now operates in ways which are fundamentally different from what many of us might remember. In order to develop a critique of the contemporary media, it seems helpful to understand the way in which it now operates as *the current situation to be addressed* – not some aberration that will eventually be redressed.

The attack on tabloidisation is an example of a broad-based and motivated rejection of an extraordinarily extensive range of media behaviours, all of which are somehow seen to be symptomatic. Some critiques of celebrity are similarly broadly based. As a point of principle, and indeed as a result of what this project has taught us about the contemporary operation of the Australian media, we would regard such broad-based critiques as of limited usefulness at present. Media messages serve complicated patterns of interests and are composed within highly varied and contingent contexts. The specific consumption of celebrity, in particular, is highly individualised as each of us constructs our own mix of personalities and attributes in whom we maintain an interest. To see every one of those patterns of consumption as explicable through one set of principles, or as the provocation for either blanket approbation or moral panic, is to misunderstand the cultural processes at play. As has happened elsewhere in cultural studies where the arguments for a progressive strain within popular culture run up against the need to criticise specific and more regressive aspects of that culture, this project has to insist on the specificity of particular instances as well as on the necessity of critique. There is indeed much to criticise, and there is much to be done to improve the regulatory and legal context within which media content is produced in Australia. The comprehensive commercialisation of the public sphere has proved repeatedly that it does not automatically carry benefits to civil society and thus it should be scrutinised, justified and, in some cases, regulated and constrained.

However, it is almost impossible to separate critiques of the prominence of celebrities from assumptions of taste and cultural value. Often, it is a matter of *which* celebrity deserves attention, rather than whether or not celebrities deserve attention at all. Yet the values which can be invested in celebrities by readers, viewers or consumers are not inconsiderable, nor are they irrelevant to the way in which meaning is constructed at this point in our history. The values that individual celebrities carry certainly seem to be important enough to provoke contestation, and members of media audiences continue to choose particular celebrity figures as especially, personally, interesting.

The Australian celebrity industry articulates a changed media landscape, a transformed relationship of audiences to what constitutes cultural significance, and points us to a different focus for our concerns about the practices and regulation of media. With publicity being the new field of endeavour that has proliferated in Australian media, and celebrity being one of the principal commodities to be regularly produced from this industrial growth, we hope we have developed some new territory for media scholarship, journalistic debate and the discussion of cultural value.

Notes

1 Celebrity and the Media

1 Marion Hume, 'Death of a style icon for the people' (in 'Curse of the Kennedys' special report), *Australian*, 20 July 1999, pp. 1, 10.
2 B. Franklin, *Newszak and News Media*, London, Edward Arnold, 1997, p. 4.
3 J. Schultz, *Reviving the Fourth Estate: Democracy, Accountability and the Media*, Cambridge, Cambridge University Press, 1998, pp. 18, 6, 56–7.
4 Ibid, p. 56.
5 C. Zawawi, 'Sources of news: Who feeds the watchdog?', *Australian Journalism Review* 16:1, 1994, pp. 67–71.
6 J. Hartley, *Popular Reality: Journalism, Modernity, Popular Culture*, London, Edward Arnold, 1996, p. 155.
7 J. Habermas, *The Structural Transformation of the Public Sphere* (trs T. Burger and F. Lawrence), Cambridge, Mass., MIT Press, 1989.
8 Hartley, *Popular Reality*, p. 156.
9 For a range of discussions of Habermas' work in this area, see Craig Calhoun (ed.), *Habermas and the Public Sphere*, Cambridge, Mass., MIT Press, 1993.
10 Hartley, *Popular Reality*, p. 156.
11 Ibid, p. 157.
12 C. Lumby, *Gotcha: Life in a Tabloid World*, Sydney, Allen & Unwin, 1999, p. 15.
13 Ibid, p. xiii.
14 RePublica and Helen Grace (eds), *Planet Diana: Cultural Studies and Global Mourning*, University of Western Sydney, Research School in Intercommunal Studies, 1997.
15 Lumby, *Gotcha*, p. 87.
16 Ibid, pp. 90–1.

17 F. Alberoni, 'The powerless elite: Theory and sociological research on the phenomena of the stars', in D. McQuail (ed.), *Sociology of Mass Communications: Selected Readings*, Harmondsworth, Penguin, 1972, p. 5.

18 J. Langer, *Tabloid Television: Popular Journalism and the 'Other' News*, London, Routledge, 1998, p. 45.

19 D. Marshall, *Celebrity and Power: Fame in Contemporary Culture*, Minneapolis and London, University of Minnesota Press, 1997.

20 Langer, *Tabloid Television*, p. 46.

21 Marshall, *Celebrity and Power*, p. 124.

22 Ibid.

23 R. Dyer, *Stars*, London, BFI, 1979, p. 24.

24 Marshall, *Celebrity and Power*, p. x.

25 Langer, *Tabloid Television*, p. 59.

26 Marshall, *Celebrity and Power*, p. ix.

27 Langer, *Tabloid Television*, p. 55.

28 I. Connell, 'Personalities in the popular media', in P. Dahlgren and C. Sparks (eds), *Journalism and Popular Culture*, London, Sage, 1992, pp. 66, 82.

29 Ibid, p. 74.

30 Langer, *Tabloid Television*, p. 51.

31 Marshall, *Celebrity and Power*, p. xi.

32 M. Wark, *The Virtual Republic: Australia's Culture Wars of the 1990s*, Sydney, Allen & Unwin, 1997.

33 M. Wark, *Celebrities, Culture and Cyberspace: The Light on the Hill in a Postmodern World*, Sydney, Pluto, 1999, p. 33.

34 Compare Jennifer Coates and Deborah Cameron (eds), *Women in Their Speech Communities*, New York, Longmans, 1989; Deborah Jones, 'Gossip: Notes on women's oral culture', in Deborah Cameron (ed.), *The Feminist Critique of Language*, London, Routledge, 1990; Neal Gabler, *Gossip, Power and the Culture of Celebrity*, London, Macmillan, 1995; R. Dunbar, *Grooming, Gossip and the Evolution of Language*, London, Faber & Faber, 1996.

35 Dunbar, *Grooming, Gossip*, p. 79.

36 J. Stacey, *Star Gazing: Hollywood Cinema and Female Spectatorship*, London, Routledge, 1994.

37 Ibid, pp. ix, 51.

38 C. Sparks, 'Popular journalism: Theories and practices', in P. Dahlgren and C. Sparks (eds), *Journalism and Popular Culture*, London, Sage, 1992, p. 42.

39 J. Gripsrud, 'The aesthetics and politics of melodrama', in P. Dahlgren and C. Sparks (eds), *Journalism and Popular Culture*, London, Sage, 1992, p. 92.

40 Given the differences in the manner of expressing the results between newspapers, magazines and television, cross-media comparisons from this data would not be appropriate.

41 The highest score in the February survey is from SBS (14.3%), perhaps surprisingly, but this is a consequence of our decision to treat at least some of the coverage of the death of Deng Xiaoping as a celebrity story. If we had not done that, the SBS score for February would have been 9.2%.

42 Philip Bell, Kathe Boehringer and Stephen Crofts, *Programming Politics: A Study of Australian Television*, Sydney, Sable, 1982; Peter Gerdes and Paul Charlier, *TV*

News: That's the Way It Was: A Comparative Analysis of Sydney's Television News, August 1978 and August 1983, Sydney, Australian Film, Television and Radio School, 1983; John Henningham, *Looking at Television News*, Melbourne, Longman Cheshire, 1988. In surveys of television news conducted in 1978 and 1983, Gerdes and Charlier used a 'General Interest' category which, while slightly more extensive, included the kinds of items our survey counted as celebrity stories. According to Gerdes and Charlier, the average proportions of news bulletins devoted to General Interest were 3.2% in 1978 and in 1983, 4.2%. Since this category also included 'animals, kids, babies, health and odd records', the actual number of stories which would have been about celebrities was probably a little lower than the figures suggest (pp. 40–5). They are, however, roughly consistent with the figures generated by Henningham's survey of television news from 1986, where he found that the percentage of stories dealing with his category of 'Famous People' across all channels was 3.7%.

43 Henningham, *Looking at Television News*, p. 165.

44 Bell et al., *Programming Politics*, pp. 74–5.

45 A fuller discussion of this survey can be found in Frances Bonner, Rebecca Farley, David Marshall and Graeme Turner, 'Celebrity and the media', *Australian Journal of Communication* 26:1, 1999, pp. 55–70.

46 P. Schlesinger, *Putting 'Reality' Together: BBC News*, London, Constable, 1978 (rev. edn, London, Methuen, 1987): Henningham, *Looking at Television News*.

47 T. Gitlin, *Inside Prime Time*, New York, Pantheon, 1983 (rev. edn, London, Routledge, 1994).

Epigraph sources: Van Morrison, 'New Biography', *Back on Top*, 1999 used by kind permission of Exile Publishing Ltd.; Walter Isaacson, managing editor, *Time Magazine*, quote unpublished; Nene King on taking over as editor of *Woman's Day*, in Mark Day, 'I was ruthless with other people's lives', *Australian, Media Supplement*, 12–18 August 1999, pp. 6–7.

2 The Rise of Promotional Culture

1 A. Wernick, *Promotional Culture: Advertising, Ideology and Symbolic Expression*, London, Sage, 1991; J. Hartley, *Popular Reality: Journalism, Modernity, Popular Culture*, London, Edward Arnold, 1996, p. 36.

2 B. Franklin, *Newszak and News Media*, London, Edward Arnold, 1997, p. 19.

3 J. Tunstall, *Journalists at Work*, London, Constable, 1971.

4 Franklin, *Newszak and News Media*, p. 19.

5 G. Epaminondas, 'Guerrillas on the list', *Weekend Australian Magazine*, 9–10 May 1998, p. 15.

6 Ibid, p. 17.

7 Candy Tymson and Bill Sherman, *New Australia and New Zealand Public Relations Manual*, 2nd edn, Alexandria, Millennium, 1996, p. 23.

8 Jan Quarles and Bill Rowlings, *Practising Public Relations: A Case Study Approach*, Melbourne, Longman Cheshire, 1993, p. 6.

9 Ibid, p. xii.

10 Ibid.

11 H. Wilson, 'Public relations: Mobilizing consent', in Helen Wilson (ed.), *Australian Communication and the Public Sphere*, Melbourne, Macmillan, 1989, p. 165.

12   Quarles and Rowlings, *Practising Public Relations*, p. 6.
13   Tymson and Sherman, *New Australia and New Zealand Public Relations Manual.*
14   Quarles and Rowling, *Practising Public Relations*, p. 9.
15   Ibid, p. 12.
16   Ibid, p. 4.
17   Michael Batten, 'More sophistication in the public relations industry', *Rydges* 52, March 1979, pp. 76–8.
18   Wilson, 'Public relations', p. 166; Tymson and Sherman, *New Australia and New Zealand Public Relations Manual*, p. 14.
19   R. Tiffen, *News and Power*, Sydney, Allen & Unwin, 1989, p. 73.
20   Wilson, 'Public relations', p. 166; Tymson and Sherman, *New Australia and New Zealand Public Relations Manual*, p. 15.
21   B.-A. Butler, 'Politics, public relations and primetime news: Comparative analyses of the roles and sources of journalists in building television news agendas', PhD dissertation, University of Queensland, 1996.
22   Ibid, pp. 89, 90.
23   Wilson, 'Public relations', p. 169.
24   Tiffen, *News and Power*, p. 74.
25   *Media Report*, Radio National, 15 August 1996.
26   Tiffen, *News and Power*, pp. 39–41.
27   G. Turner, *Making It National*, Sydney, Allen & Unwin, 1994.
28   'Spin-doctoring', *Media Report*, Radio National, 24 September 1998.
29   Ibid.
30   *Media Report*, Radio National, 24 September 1998.
31   Butler, 'Politics, public relations and primetime news', p. 87.
32   Ibid, p. 97.
33   J. Schultz, 'Accuracy in Australian newspapers', Working Paper no. 1, University of Technology Sydney, Australian Centre for Independent Journalism, 1990. Her sources claimed a 30% success rate in generating coverage for their stories in newspapers, and a high percentage had their press releases reproduced without significant alteration.
34   J. Schultz, *Reviving the Fourth Estate: Democracy, Accountability and the Media*, Cambridge, Cambridge University Press, 1998, p. 56.
35   J. McNamara, 'Public relations and the media: A new influence in "agenda-setting" and content', unpublished MA dissertation, Deakin University, 1993.
36   Electoral and Administrative Review Commission (EARC), *Report on the Review of Government Media and Information Services*, Brisbane, EARC, April 1993. Analyses of its findings can be found in Butler, 'Politics, public relations and primetime news', as well as in Turner, *Making It National*, ch. 7.
37   C. Zawawi, 'Sources of news: Who feeds the watchdog?', *Australian Journalism Review* 16:1, 1994, pp. 67–71.
38   Ibid, pp. 70–1.
39   Ibid, p. 71.
40   'Celebrity power grows', *B&T*, 22 July 1982, p. 4.
41   P. Rogers, 'Talent getting too grasping?' *B&T*, 29 July 1982, p. 5.
42   'Case history: *TV Week*', *B&T*, 29 July 1982, p. 55.
43   M. Safe, 'Mr Twenty Per Cent', *Weekend Australian Magazine*, 13–14 May 1995, p. 67.
44   L. Nicklin, 'Stars wanted: Apply anywhere', *Bulletin*, 3 October 1989, p. 34.

45 Byron Smith, 'When stars lose shine', *B&T*, 5 February 1999, p. 14.

46 See Graeme Turner, 'Tabloidisation, journalism and the possibility of critique', *International Journal of Cultural Studies* 2:1, 1999, pp. 59–76.

47 The kind of point Hartley makes in his *Popular Reality*.

48 Denis O'Brien, *The Weekly*, Melbourne, Penguin, 1982, p. 112.

49 M. A. Reid, *Long Shots to Favourites: Australian Cinema in the 90s*, Sydney, Australian Film Commission, 1993, pp. 45–9.

50 One of the locations where this is visible is in the *Australian Women's Weekly* liftout, 'Teenagers' Weekly'.

51 For a discussion of this history, see Sally Stockbridge, 'From *Bandstand* and *Six O'Clock Rock* to *MTV* and *Rage*', in Philip Hayward (ed.), *From Pop to Punk to Postmodernism: Popular Music and Australian Popular Culture from the 1960s to the 1990s*, Sydney, Allen & Unwin, 1992.

52 S. Frith, 'Youth/music/television', in Simon Frith, Andrew Goodwin and Lawrence Grossberg (eds), *Sound and Vision: The Music Video Reader*, Routledge, London and New York, 1993, pp. 67–84.

53 Andy Bizoriek, 'The sale of celebrity', *Australian Professional Marketing*, May 1996, pp. 9–12.

54 Simon Pristel, 'Familiar faces work at being familiar faces', *Courier-Mail*, 15 February 1999, p. 3.

Epigraph source: Public Relations Institute of Australia, cited in Jan Quarles and Bill Rowlings, *Practising Public Relations: A Case Study Approach*, Longman Cheshire, Melbourne, 1993, p. 4.

3 Producing Celebrity

1 10BA was the clause in the tax Act that related to the tax concessions used to encourage investment in the Australian film industry from 1981. It was gradually wound down as its costs increased over the 1980s, leading to the establishment of the Film Finance Corporation in 1988–89.

2 Harry M. Miller and Denis O'Brien, *Harry M. Miller, My Story*, South Melbourne, Macmillan, 1983, pp. 147–54.

3 See Louise Evans, 'Max Markson's ring of confidence', *Sydney Morning Herald Good Weekend*, 14 July 1990, pp. 30–1, 33–4.

4 P. Sheehan, *Among the Barbarians: The Dividing of Australia*, Sydney, Random House, 1998.

5 I. Roberts, *Finding Out*, Sydney, Random House, 1998.

6 That said, it is not all a matter of celebrity promotion, as Thomas reveals: 'We have a very close relationship with the Nine Network [it is in fact a co-production] ... but ... *Water Rats* has sold to 168 countries and Australia is only one of them and what we need to meet their requirements and promotion can be very different from overseas ... Overseas they love the shots of the Harbour Bridge and the Opera House every five minutes.'

4 Managing the Media

1 'Melba' column, *Australian*, 3 February 1999, p. 11.

2 K. Negus, *Producing Pop: Culture and Conflict in the Popular Music Industry*, London, Edward Arnold, 1992, p. 123.

3 Apparently, *TV Week* is frequently associated by visiting celebrities with less reputable overseas magazines of the same name, despite being one of the most innocuous outlets for celebrity stories in Australia.

4 M. Colman, 'A sticky wicket', *Courier-Mail*, 10 December 1998, p. 15.

5 B. Ellis, *Goodbye Jerusalem: Night Thoughts of a Labor Outsider*, Vintage, Milsons Point, 1997.

6 Solomon Haumono temporarily retired from professional rugby league in January, 2000, reportedly to devote his life to his family and Islam.

7 M. Safe, 'Mr Twenty Per Cent', *Australian Magazine*, 13–14 May 1995, p. 64.

8 The subject of Schultz's *Reviving the Fourth Estate*, Cambridge, Cambridge University Press, 1998.

9 J. Robertson, Letters page, *Courier-Mail*, 5 August 1997. Robertson remains on the list of Miller's clients.

10 Karen Middleton, 'Publicist engaged to marshal media bids', *Age*, 5 August 1997.

11 Darren Lovell, 'Hayley's wedding frenzy', *Sunday Mail*, 14 September 1997, p. 11.

5 Core Territory: Celebrities and the Women's Magazines

1 G. Greer, *The Whole Woman*, London, Doubleday, 1999, p. 312.

2 Elizabeth Wynhausen, 'The crisis in women's magazines or do Dannii's breasts really matter?' *Australian Magazine*, 8–9 June 1996, p. 26.

3 Jennifer Craik, 'The gloss wears off', *Australian Left Review*, no. 130, July 1991, p. 16.

4 Jill Dupleix, 'Gastrotomes', *Sydney Morning Herald: Good Living*, 15 September 1998, p. 1.

5 Andrew Hornery, 'Newsagents drowning in paper', *Sydney Morning Herald*, 18 May 1998, p. 37.

6 Audit Bureau of Circulation data, from Paula Bombara, 'Diana's death cuts sales', *B&T*, 7 August 1998, p. 45.

7 M. Ferguson, *Forever Feminine: Women's Magazines and the Cult of Femininity*, London, Heinemann, 1983, p. 167.

8 Quoted in Humphrey McQueen, *Gone Tomorrow: Australia in the 80s*, Sydney, Angus & Robertson, 1982, p. 137.

9 See Denis O'Brien, *The Weekly*, Ringwood, Penguin, 1982, pp. 8–14; and Beatrice Faust, 'What the *Weekly* women are reading now', in Bruce Elder (ed.), *International Forum: Contemporary Essays*, South Melbourne, Macmillan, 1978, p. 79.

10 O'Brien, *The Weekly*, pp. 79–93.

11 Faust, 'What the *Weekly* women are reading now', p. 80.

12 Beatrice Faust, *Women, Sex and Pornography*, Ringwood, Penguin, 1981, p. 140.

13 Frances Bonner, Susan McKay and Kathryn Goldie, 'Caring for the family: Fifty years of health in the *Australian Women's Weekly*', *Journal of Australian Studies* 59, 1998, p. 158.

14 For example, Sian Powell, 'The last word on sex, scandal and sleaze', *Weekend Australian* 29–30 October 1994, pp. 3–4; Wynhausen, 'The crisis in women's magazines'; Keith Windschuttle, *The Media: A New Analysis of the Press, Television, Radio and Advertising in Australia*, 2nd edn, Ringwood, Penguin, 1988.

15 Her most exorbitant celebrity-style personal revelation involved her facelift, which was not only reported in the pages of her own magazine but also screened nationally on the television program *Good Medicine*.

16 H. Frizell, 'Singer climbs mountains to be alone', *Australian Women's Weekly*, 6 August 1949, p. 21.

17 S. L. Bolon, 'The happy sequel to a tragic love story', *Australian Women's Weekly*, 2 May 1956, pp. 12–13.

18 D. Drain, 'It seems to me', *Australian Women's Weekly*, 3 October 1951, p. 16.

19 Powell, 'The last word on sex, scandal and sleaze', p. 3.

20 It is also very useful as a defensive strategy for celebrities under investigation by reporters suspecting a scandal might be in the offing. Even if an actual exclusive deal is not organised, mere publication in a rival magazine may be enough to buy time and remove media packs.

21 Kate Halfpenny and Louise Talbot, 'Panel man', *Who Weekly*, 5 October 1998, pp. 67–8.

22 Tommy Lee as told to Todd Gold, 'Home alone', *Who Weekly*, 5 October 1998, pp. 24–30.

23 Halfpenny and Talbot, 'Panel man'.

24 Warren Gibbs, 'Black widow's jail baby', *Woman's Day*, 30 December 1996, pp. 10–11.

25 Johan Galtung and Mari Ruge, 'Structuring and selecting news', in Stanley Cohen and Jock Young (eds), *The Manufacture of News: Social Problems, Deviance and the Mass Media*, rev. edn, London, Constable, 1981, pp. 56–9.

26 'Shock baby for Sam', *New Weekly*, 28 July 1997, pp. 8–9.

27 John Langer, *Tabloid Television: Popular Journalism and the 'Other' News*, London, Routledge, 1998. Langer's category of 'other' news (effectively, anything that is not political or economic news) is developed to discuss television news, but his acknowledgement of the implicit hierarchies within the category of news is informative for other media too (p. 28). His 'other' news category includes 'fires, accidents, beauty contests, celebrities, popular occupations and hobbies' (p. 32), all classic instances of human interest stories and fillers – novelty items conventionally used to conclude bulletins (p. 33). These kinds of stories are far more prominent in mass-market women's magazines than in television news bulletins, too, but in their inversion of the system of news values Langer describes the magazine editors may turn out to be just as restricted as the journalists and the academics he criticises. For them, celebrity gossip is the only news fit to print.

28 Gold, 'Home alone'.

29 Wark, *Celebrities, Culture and Cyberspace*, p. 67.

30 Michael Sheather, 'Pain, passion and politics', *Australian Women's Weekly*, April 1998, pp. 2–5.

31 Shelley Gare, 'Political covergirls find if the dress fits ...', *Australian*, 25 March 1998, p. 2.

32 P. Cole-Adams, 'Beazley gallant while Kernot's critics see red', *Courier-Mail*, 25 March 1998, p. 2.

33 Darren Delvyn, 'I've lost my rock', *Woman's Day*, 30 November 1998, pp. 6–7.

34 J. Hermes, *Reading Women's Magazines: An Analysis of Everyday Media Use*, Cambridge, Polity Press, 1995, p. 124.

35 S. Hall, 'The rediscovery of "ideology": Return of the repressed in media studies', in M. Gurevitch, T. Bennett, J. Curran and J. Woollacott (eds), *Culture, Society and the Media*, London, Methuen, 1982, pp. 56–91.

36 A. Wernick, *Promotional Culture: Advertising, Ideology, and Symbolic Expression*, London, Sage Publications, 1991.

37 Steve Kelly, 'The camera never lies ... or does it?' *New Weekly*, 26 July 1997, pp. 42–4.

38 Annette Alison, 'Kerri-Anne shapes up', *Australian Women's Weekly*, June 1997, pp. 10–13.

39 Sally Jackson, 'Making a splash', *Australian*, 2 October 1998, p. 36.

40 Powell, 'The last word on sex, scandal and sleaze', p. 3.

41 Wynhausen, 'The crisis in women's magazines', pp. 22, 26.

42 See, for example, Myra MacDonald, *Representing Women: Myths of Femininity in the Popular Media*, London, Edward Arnold, 1995.

43 P. Edgar and H. McPhee, *Media She*, Melbourne, Heinemann, 1974.

44 J. Winship, *Inside Women's Magazines*, London, Pandora, 1987; E. McCracken, *Decoding Women's Magazines: From Mademoiselle to Ms*, New York, St Martin's Press, 1993.

45 N. Wolf, *The Beauty Myth: How Images of Beauty Are Used against Women*, New York, Morrow, 1991.

46 R. Denfield, *The New Victorians: A Young Woman's Challenge to the Old Feminist Order*, New York, Warner, 1995.

47 C. Lumby, *Bad Girls: The Media, Sex and Feminism in the 90s*, Sydney, Allen & Unwin, 1997; S. Faludi, *Backlash: The Undeclared War against Women*, London, Chatto and Windus, 1992.

48 C. Lumby, *Gotcha: Life in a Tabloid World*, Sydney, Allen & Unwin, 1999.

49 Ferguson, *Forever Feminine*, pp. 49–50.

50 Winship, *Inside Women's Magazines*, p. 82.

51 McCracken, *Decoding Women's Magazines*, p. 167.

52 Edgar and McPhee, *Media She*, p. 21.

53 B. Bonney and H. Wilson, *Australia's Commercial Media*, Melbourne and Sydney, Macmillan, 1983, p. 241.

54 Windschuttle, *The Media*, pp. 250, 247–8.

55 S. Sampson, 'The *Australian Women's Weekly* today: Education and the aspirations of girls', *Refractory Girl* 3, 1973, p. 16.

56 McQueen, *Gone Tomorrow*, p. 141.

57 Ferguson, *Forever Feminine*, p. 167.

58 Ros Ballaster, Margaret Beetham, Elizabeth Frazer and Sandra Heron, *Women's Worlds: Ideology, Femininity and the Woman's Magazine*, London, Macmillan, 1991.

59 Hermes, *Reading Women's Magazines*.

60 Ibid, p. 122.

61 Ibid, p. 124.

62 Ibid, pp. 118, 121, 131.

63 Ibid, p. 128.

64 Joan Barrell and Brian Braithwaite, *The Business of Women's Magazines*, 2nd edn, London, Kogan Page, 1988, p. 3.

65 C. White, *Women's Magazines 1693–1968*, London, Michael Joseph, 1970, p. 26.

66 Deborah Jones, 'Gossip: Notes on women's oral culture', in Deborah Cameron (ed.), *The Feminist Critique of Language*, London, Routledge, 1990, pp. 242–53.

67 'Bad news for entertainment', *Adnews: ABC Audit Results Year to July 1999*, 13 September 1999, pp. A8–9.

68 C. Kershaw, 'Youth mags set for spice-up', *B&T*, 30 January 1998, p. 17.

69 'Bad news', p. A13.

70 L. Johnson, *The Modern Girl: Girlhood and Growing Up*, Sydney, Allen & Unwin, 1993, p. 119.

71 Hermes, *Reading Women's Magazines*, p. 121.

72 For example, Lisa L. Duke and Peggy J. Kreshel, 'Negotiating femininity: Girls in early adolescence read teen magazines', *Journal of Communication Inquiry*, 22 January 1998, pp. 48–71.

73 T. M. Willemsen, 'Widening the gender gap: Teenage magazines for boys and girls', *Sex Roles: A Journal of Research* 38, 9–10 May 1998, pp. 851–61.

74 A. McRobbie, *Feminism and Youth Culture: From Jackie to Just Seventeen*, London, Macmillan, 1991, pp. 144, 169, 168.

Epigraph sources: McKenzie Wark, *Celebrities, Culture and Cyberspace: The Light on the Hill in a Postmodern World*, Sydney, Pluto, 1999, p. 49; Don Walker (Cold Chisel), 'Ita', *East*, WEA, 1980.

6 Changes in the Media Landscape

1 Sarah Bryden-Brown, 'Costing a code of practice', *Australian Media Supplement*, 4–10 November 1999, p. 9.

2 Anthony Dennis and Garry Maddox, 'Celebrities carpeted over Fox extravaganza', *Sydney Morning Herald*, 8 November 1999, p. 3.

3 D. Boorstin, *The Image: A Guide to Pseudo Events in America*, New York, Atheneum, 1961.

4 K. Brisbane, 'The arts and the pre-emptive buckle', *Weekend Australian Review*, 30–31 October 1999, p. 18.

5 R. Dyer, *Stars*, London, BFI, 1979, p. 111.

6 Ibid, p. 48.

7 K. Langbroek, 'The plague of the gorgeous', panel presentation at Brisbane Writers Festival, 16 October 1999.

8 The weakest case in this list of celebrities is the politician. While there has been considerable homogenisation into a single type of celebrity figure, as just argued, there still are distinctions between the activities that promote politicians, on the one hand, and those that promote celebrities, on the other. The formal requirements of being a serving politician – election and re-election, party membership, parliamentary sessions and electorate duties, being in government or opposition – all constrain the extent to which politicians can be quite the same as other celebrities. We have minimised the examination of political celebrities in this book because the industry that produces them operates in different ways from the one tied to entertainment. We have chosen to concentrate on the entertainment industry because it is more clearly focused on promotion. Yet the personnel and the practices are not separate: party spin doctors change employers and work for

media companies; politicians leave politics and join the celebrity speakers circuit. That politicians are not quite celebrities can probably be most clearly seen in the way formal politics calls on 'real' celebrities to promote its concerns and courts celebrity endorsements as enthusiastically as charities, health promotions and issue-based campaigning do.

9 A. Wernick, *Promotional Culture*, p. 187.
10 Ibid, pp. 188, 189, 194.
11 Ibid, pp. 196, 197.
12 Dyer, *Stars*, pp. 23–4.
13 Productivity Commission, *Broadcasting*, draft report, Ausinfo, Canberra, 1999.
14 Ian Connell, 'Personalities in the popular media', in P. Dahlgren and C. Sparks (eds), *Journalism and Popular Culture*, London, Sage, 1992, p. 66.
15 John Hartley, *Uses of Television*, London, Routledge, 1999, chs 12 and 14.
16 Langbroek, 'The plague of the gorgeous'.
17 J. Langer, *Tabloid Television: Popular Journalism and the 'Other' News*, London, Routledge, 1998.
18 Quoted in Scott McQuire, *Crossing the Digital Threshold*, Brisbane, Australian Key Centre for Cultural and Media Policy, 1997, p. 45.

Epigraph source: Pat Hackett (ed.), *The Andy Warhol Diaries*, New York, Warner Books, 1989.

Index